Macroeconomic Theory:
Diversity and Convergence

To our mothers

Macroeconomic Theory: Diversity and Convergence

Edited by

Gary Mongiovi

St John's University
New York, US

and

Christof Rühl

Universität Hohenheim
Stuttgart, Federal Republic of Germany

Edward Elgar

Published by
Edward Elgar Publishing Limited
Gower House
Croft Road
Aldershot
Hants GU11 3HR
England

Edward Elgar Publishing Company
Old Post Road
Brookfield
Vermont 05036
USA

A CIP catalogue record for this book is available from the British Library.

Library of Congress Cataloging-in-Publication Data
Macroeconomic theory: diversity and convergence/edited by Gary
　　Mongiovi and Christof Rühl.
　　　　p.　cm.
　　　1. Macroeconomics.　I. Mongiovi, Gary.　II. Rühl, Christof.
　　HB172.5.M333　1992
　　339–dc20　　　　　　　　　　　　　　　　　　　92–15812
　　　　　　　　　　　　　　　　　　　　　　　　　　　　CIP

ISBN 978-1-8527-8368-6

Printed and bound by CPI Group (UK) Ltd, Croydon, CR0 4YY

Contents

Figures

Tables

Contributors

Arie Arnon: Ben-Gurion University of the Negev, Beer Sheva, Israel, and Research Department, The Bank of Israel.

Avi J. Cohen: York University, Toronto, Canada.

Christian Gehrke: Universität Graz, Austria.

Chidem Kurdas, Pennsylvania State University, York Campus, USA.

Marc Lavoie: University of Ottawa, Canada.

Fiona C. Maclachlan: Manhattan College, New York, USA.

Gary Mongiovi: St. John's University, New York, USA.

Juan Carlos Moreno Brid: Universidad de las Américas and Centro de Economía y Política, Mexico City, Mexico.

Marco Musella: Università di Napoli, Italy.

Carlo Panico: Università di Catania, Italy.

Fabio Petri: Università di Siena, Italy.

Christof Rühl: Universität Hohenheim, Stuttgart, Germany.

Malcolm C. Sawyer: University of Leeds, Great Britain.

Peter Skott: Aarhus University, Denmark.

Hans-Michael Trautwein: Universität Lüneburg, Germany.

Preface

Maffeo Pantaleoni believed that economists ought not to speak of different schools of thought within their discipline. When alternative points of view solidify into competing schools, reasoned discourse is often replaced by divisive polemics. In the end, Pantaleoni argued (1897, p. 51), there are only two schools: the first is comprised of those who understand economic reasoning; to the second belong those who do not understand it.

Reality has not conformed to Pantaleoni's statement. Over the last decades several heterodox theoretical perspectives have emerged outside what might be called the neoclassical mainstream: the classical surplus approach, post-Keynesian theory, the modern Austrian tradition, Kaleckian economics. All these alternative traditions have subjected mainstream macroeconomic analysis to steady critical scrutiny and have attempted to cast new light on old problems, that is to advance economics in a constructive manner.

Yet despite overlapping concerns, and in particular the shared view of mainstream theory as unable to adequately deal with a large set of issues relevant to the world we live in, there has been a conspicuous lack of dialogue *across* the different heterodox approaches. Debate between alternative traditions too often fails to rise above the level of a squabble about what issues ought to be the focus of analysis. Some authors have made the roles of money and uncertainty the centre of discussion; some have focused on the static theory of value and distribution; still others trace social interaction and political institutions. But, unlike economists working on the same problems under the umbrella of neoclassical theory, they have split into schools. These schools, moreover, exhibit a strong tendency towards complacency; increasingly, dialogue faded from the agenda. It is perhaps more usual that legitimate points of contention are simply left undiscussed; in consequence, little or no progress has been made towards the resolution of key theoretical problems. There is a lack of co-operation beyond the criticism of neoclassical theory.

This book originated as a response to the situation we have just described. The papers collected here were written for a conference on *Alternative Traditions in Macroeconomics: Diversity and Convergence*, which took place at the University of Hohenheim in Stuttgart, Germany, in July 1990.

Our aim in organizing the conference was to stimulate discussion across the various heterodox traditions. To this end we invited a group of economists (all of whom can be said to be working outside the mainstream) and asked each of them to address a specific topic of our choosing. The intention was to set up a forum in which no author could avoid confronting issues which had been raised (often with critical intent) by a paradigm other than his own. The selected topics would force the participants to assess different analytical perspectives, and to respond to criticism levelled against their own.

The issues discussed at the conference fell into three main categories. The first set of topics dealt with monetary theory and pricing; the second block of contributions was concerned with macroeconomic fluctuations and business cycles; the last group of papers addressed topics in growth theory, investment and technological change. This order has been preserved in this book.

In the opening piece, Marc Lavoie investigates the possibility of integrating post-Keynesian monetary economics with the Cambridge view of distribution. Malcolm Sawyer follows with a discussion of heterodox perspectives on pricing and distribution in a growing economy, with particular emphasis on the work of Kalecki. Marco Musella and Carlo Panico then buttress the case for Kaldor's approach to monetary policy. Hans-Michael Trautwein confronts the arguments and draws out the practical implications of two competing schools of thought, namely post-Keynesian monetary theory and the New Monetary Economics. Next, the relation between the classical surplus approach and modern monetary theory is taken up by Gary Mongiovi and Christof Rühl. Rounding out the section on monetary issues, Arie Arnon and Juan Carlos Moreno undertake in their respective papers to sort out the policy implications of heterodox approaches to money.

The explanation of macroeconomic fluctuations is the focal point of the next section. Christian Gehrke argues that while neo-Austrian traverse analysis and the Austrian theory of business cycles have some elements in common, the former is in principle incompatible with the latter. Then Fiona Maclachlan investigates the consequences of some unexpected parallels between post-Keynesian and Austrian theories of the rate of interest.

Finally, accumulation becomes the central concern. Chidem Kurdas opens this section by constructing a model of Research and Development spending along the product cycle, discussing its macroeconomic implications and drawing conclusions for investment policy. Fabio Petri evaluates Kalecki's theory of investment from the standpoint of the Cambridge critique of capital theory. Peter Skott integrates neo-Marxian and post-Keynesian concepts in order to elucidate the importance of a link between class conflict and accumulation. The volume concludes with a methodological essay by Avi Cohen, who raises the question whether equilibrium analysis can be reconciled with analytical perspectives stressing disequilibrium, uncertainty and historical time.

This project was not aimed at achieving a consensus; its guiding principle has been that diversity of perspective is essential to the vitality of economic science. The diversity necessary to fruitful discussion, however, can only flourish in the absence of unnecessary barriers to discourse. This is the precondition for a productive convergence of opinions on important points of dispute. It is our hope that this book may make a small contribution toward the removal of the mentality which gives rise to doctrinal schools – the mentality, that is, against which Pantaleoni issued his warning.

Neither the book nor the conference would have been possible without generous financial and organizational support from various sources. We thank the University of Hohenheim for providing all the facilities necessary for organizing a successful conference in an exceedingly pleasant atmosphere. We also acknowledge, with much gratitude, the financial support extended to us by the Daimler–Benz Corporation, Stuttgart; and by the Business Research Institute at St. John's University, New York.

Special thanks are due to Harald Hagemann and Helmut Walter for encouragement and administrative support. We are grateful to Norbert Schley, not only for helping us finish our last bottle of good whisky, but also for his co-ordination of the conference logistics and for his impressive transformation of chaos into order. Thanks also to Silvia Straub for performing the tedious task of compiling, checking and editing the references.

All of the contributions to this volume were blind-refereed prior to publication. We appreciate the efforts of our referees, whose efficient and enthusiastic participation enhanced the final product: Giovanni Caravale, Harvey Gram, Augusto Graziani, Harald Hagemann, Omar Hamouda, Heinz Kurz, David Laibman, Neri Salvadori, Willi Semmler and Peter Spahn.

Gary Mongiovi
Christof Rühl

REFERENCES

Pantaleoni, M. (1897) [1964] *Erotemi di Economia* (vol. 1), Padova: A. Miliani.

PART I

Monetary theory and pricing

1. A Post-Classical View of Money, Interest, Growth and Distribution

Marc Lavoie[1]

Money has been noticeably neglected in the Cambridge alternatives to neoclassical theory, or in what one might wish to call *post-classical* theory (Henry 1982). This neglect is quite obvious of course in the neo-Ricardian models of prices of production, but it is also evident in the Cambridge models of growth and distribution derived from the work of Robinson, Kaldor and Pasinetti, a fact which Kregel (1973, p. 161) underlined, and later tried to explain (Kregel 1985). The omission of money is still a characteristic of the newer Cambridge models of growth and distribution, those based on Kaleckian foundations.

In partial reaction to those moneyless growth models, post-Keynesians in the United States have emphasized the importance of money and monetary institutions in explaining short-run variations in output, the instability of capitalism and the inability of the latter to sustain full-employment growth (Davidson 1972; Minsky 1975). In Europe, similar reactions to the Cambridge alternatives to neoclassical theory have emerged. In France and in Italy the so-called monetary circuit approach has been the main response to moneyless Cambridge growth models (Graziani 1989).

Although real analysis seems to have been the prevalent concern of opponents of neoclassical theory, money has slowly been brought back to the forefront. In part, the formidable impact of monetarism has forced alternative schools to explicitly abandon standard IS/LM analysis. Post-Keynesians have been induced to revise their monetary theories by increasing their non-orthodox content. Neo-Ricardians have started to establish links between their theories of distribution and the monetary economy, while the consequences of the Cambridge controversies have been extended to monetary theory (Rogers 1989).

We shall see that there are common traits to all these non-orthodox versions of the monetary sector. Of course, there are disagreements on the finer details, for instance the role of liquidity preference. However, all of these approaches have a common vision of the monetary economy. Their foundations are identical. Having identified those, we shall attempt to analyse the relationship between the rate of interest and the rate of profit, as well as the impact of the former on accumulation.

COMMON ELEMENTS OF POST-CLASSICAL MONETARY THEORY

From a research tradition point of view *à la* Laudan, one can say that post-classical monetary theory is an outgrowth of the Banking School. The standard causal interpretation of the Quantity equation is emphatically denied. Three propositions stand out: first, money is endogenous, that is, it is demand-determined, arising from credit requirements; second the rate of interest is exogenous, that is, it is not a market-determined endogenous variable; third, there are no natural financial constraints to expansion. Other propositions could be put forth, such as the belief that excess demand rarely explains inflation. We shall however focus on the above three propositions.

Endogenous Money

Lawson (1989) has argued that realism characterized Kaldor's approach to economic theorizing and that realism should characterize an alternative approach to neoclassical theory. Endogenous money is a case in point. When an endogenous theory of money was originally proposed (Le Bourva 1962), it was partly as a reaction against models which assumed the existence of reserves in countries where such reserves did not exist. It turns out that very few countries function or have functioned according to the high powered money fantasy. Indeed, when economists have attempted to describe precisely how central banks act, or could act, they invariably abandoned the excess reserves fable and told an endogenous money story. Post-classical monetary theory is an exercise in realist economics.

It is well-known that Kaldor (1970, 1982) and Moore (1988) have been long-standing advocates of an endogenous theory of money. They have argued in favour of reversed causation, where demand for credit arises out of expected increases in the demand for goods, with this inducing a demand for credit-money and ultimately a demand for high powered money. In that sense, money is demand determined, that is to say, credit driven. This is a typical post-Keynesian proposition (Lavoie 1985b; Arestis and Eichner 1988), although some post-Keynesians add some degree of eclecticism to this endogenous view of money (Rousseas 1986; Davidson 1988).[2]

Neo-Ricardians also have adopted an endogenous money approach. Whereas at one time one had to refer to Sraffa's critique of Hayek to support the idea that money contracts or monetary values were of some significance to the neo-Ricardians, there now exists more direct evidence for such a claim. Not surprisingly, French neo-Ricardians, probably influenced by the strong currents of anti-Quantity Theory that were always present within their country, led the attempt to integrate a classical theory of production within the Banking School view of money. In fact, as can be seen from Arena and Graziani (1985), the search for non-orthodox foundations of a monetary theory has paralleled that of the Naples group in Italy, the latter being also closely associated with the French circuit approach.[3] There is thus some irony in noting that those French neo-Ricardians interested in money have ended up resurrecting the same classical authors and the same analyses as those researchers working within the circuit approach, a school which, along with American post-Keynesianism, emerged as a reaction against what was felt to be an exclusively real analysis.

On the transalpine front, neo-Ricardians have also attempted to integrate a monetary analysis into their Sraffian models. This can be seen in models of prices of production incorporating debt, interest costs and asset interest revenues (Panico 1985).[4] The main neo-Ricardian monetary exposition however is that of Pivetti, who explicitly refers to an endogenous view of money (Pivetti 1985, p. 96). Pivetti relies on Tooke's contention 'that the prices of the commodity do not depend upon the quantity of money . . . but that on the contrary the amount of circulating medium is the consequence of prices'. For Pivetti then, 'the money supply accommodates itself to the needs of trade', so that the quantity of money is an effect, rather than a cause, of the level of monetary expenditures. One must thus conclude that there is a large consensus among post-classicals on the notion of endogenous credit-money.

Conventional Interest Rates

This consensus is most evident in the work of Rogers (1989) whose main objective is to demonstrate that the Cambridge controversies have undermined any claims to legitimacy for all real theories of the rate of interest. Rogers (1989, p. 253) also argues that 'the interest rate reflects psychological, institutional, and other historical factors which cannot be specified *a priori*'; it is, in other words, an exogenous variable. This treatment is precisely what Kaldor (1982, p. 24) advocates, and it also reflects Pasinetti's (1974, p. 44) view of how to interpret Keynes's liquidity preference theory. The economic model becomes recursive with the rate of interest being exogenous, that is, influenced by the decisions of the monetary authorities and the sentiments of the public about liquidity.

The most vigorous exponent of such an exogenous theory of the rate of interest is of course Moore (1988), who has described how the central bank could fix the short-term interest rate within a narrow range and how commercial banks would follow suit. It has been argued against Moore's theory of endogenous money that it eliminates Keynes's liquidity preference and that this represents a setback for a proper monetary theory incorporating expectations and uncertainty (Dow and Dow 1989). Rogers' analysis is quite illuminating in that respect. He makes not only the usual distinction between short-term and long-term interest rates, but also a second distinction between transitory and permanent interest rate changes (Rogers 1989, p. 252). Now, if a generalization of the liquidity preference for money is added, then the exogeneity of interest rates, the endogeneity of credit-money and a form of Keynes's liquidity preference can all be retained.

Such a generalization has been proposed by Le Héron (1986), who argues that in the *General Theory* Keynes erroneously restricted the concept of liquidity preference to households. Le Héron believes that all agents in the economy exhibit some form of liquidity preference. Firms express their liquidity preference by refusing to invest or to borrow. Banks express their liquidity preference by setting short-term interest rates (the money rates) at levels that are different from those offered by the central bank, and by resisting changes in interest rates initiated by the central bank (Kregel 1984–85). The liquidity preference of households and non-banking financial institutions, those that we shall call rentiers (the owners of financial capital), is mainly reflected in the long-term rates of interest, or more precisely in the spread between the long-term and the short-term rates of interest (Wells 1983, p. 533). Liquidity preference sets the conventional rate of interest around that determined by the central bank. This means that liquidity preference, as usually understood, sets the term structure of interest rates (Mott 1985–86, p. 224). The discount rate, upon which all the other rates of interest depend, is set by the central bank, according to its assessment of the monetary and economic situation (that is, according to its own liquidity preference).[5]

What the generalized liquidity preference theory tells us is that any change in interest rates orchestrated by the monetary authorities will be considered transitory as long as banks and rentiers have not adjusted to it. The rate of interest set by the monetary authorities becomes permanent when the liquidity preference of the public stops playing a role. Then, imperfections excluded, the central bank discount rate, the money market rate and the long-term rate of interest will all be equal.[6]

This, in my view, is how the lack of importance attached to the liquidity preference theory of money by the neo-Ricardians (Eatwell and Milgate 1983, p. 7) can be reconciled with the post-Keynesian emphasis on that theory. Since neo-Ricardians are generally concerned with the so-called permanent effects, rather than transitory ones, the above analysis shows that in long period analysis, liquidity preference indeed has no particular role. What is of importance is the exogenous rate of interest, that is the permanent rate, which acts through channels that shall be discussed later. In the short period, one might wish to attribute a causal influence to liquidity preference. This in fact is precisely how Kregel (1976, p. 219) recommends that the real world should be 'tamed' when dealing with models of growth and capital accumulation. While some variables (such as capacity) become endogenous, others have to become given; Kregel regards liquidity preference and propensities to save as examples of the latter.

This view of liquidity preference corresponds broadly to that of Panico (1988), who placed great emphasis on the exogenous and conventional nature of the interest rate. Following Keynes, Panico argues that the main role of liquidity preference is to force market interest rates to converge towards the normal rate of interest. The latter is mainly determined by monetary authorities, provided they are sufficiently persistent and consistent. As Robinson observed, 'If [the authorities] persist resolutely, a moment will come when the bears are convinced that the new low rate has come to stay' (1952, p. 30). Of course, at any moment of time, the behaviour of the monetary authorities may be influenced by what the most powerful groups in society, presumably the rentiers, think the normal rate of interest should be. But ultimately, the decision to determine the normal rate of interest rests on the shoulders of the monetary authorities. The central point of Panico's analysis is thus that the rate of interest is of a conventional character. Any level of the interest rate, within a fairly wide range, can be the durable level.[7]

Pivetti (1985) also emphasizes this distinction between transitory and permanent changes in interest rates. Like Panico, he relies on Keynes's idea of a conventional interest rate. His main argument is that in long-period analysis, one should deal with lasting, rather than temporary changes in interest rates. The money rate of interest must be considered a causal element in a theory of distribution and growth because it is an exogenous variable. The rate of interest is under the direct control of the monetary authorities, whereas the money supply is not. Pivetti (1988, p. 282) is thus of the opinion that 'interest rate determination is not subject to any general law ... The level of interest rates prevailing in any given situation appears clearly to be determined by the monetary authorities on the basis of policy objectives and constraints ...' We now consider this role of the monetary authorities in more detail.

The Causal Role of Investment

A theory of endogenous money with conventional money rates of interest has many implications. As noted above, the standard theories of inflation, based upon an excess supply of money or excessive growth rates of the money supply, lose their validity in such a setting. The same could be said of Pigou effects or other Patinkin related effects. In this section, however, I focus upon the consequences of a theory of endogenous money for the causal role of investment in contrast to savings, a theme that has recently attracted some attention.

As we all know, various post-Keynesians have asserted that the causal link from investment to saving is a crucial distinguishing feature of post-classical economics.

> The fundamental difference between neoclassical economics and Keynesian economics thus remains the same, whatever the context of analysis – a short period model of fluctuations, or a long period growth model, an under-employment or a full employment model. In each case are implied suppositions concerning the chain of causation which are 'behind the equations' so to speak – in the neoclassical where the rate of interest is the main regulator, and where savings *govern* investment, and the Keynesian where investment governs savings, and where the share of profits in output is the main regulator. (Kaldor 1962, p. 249)

Thus the chain of causation 'behind the equations', in the long period as well as in the short period, relies upon the ability of the economic system 'to create monetary claims in advance of actual output' (Kregel 1973, p. 159). This is the important role played by credit-money. As a consequence, the neo-Ricardians also perceive this crucial link between money and Keynesian causality: 'Money does play an essential role for effective demand in that ... it allows the circle production–income–demand–production to break in the savings–investment link' (Garegnani 1983, p. 78). In neoclassical economics, money, like all other commodities, must be scarce to be of some value and hence its supply is usually considered to be a stock, that is a given endowment. In post-classical economics, money is not scarce as such; the rate of interest is not so much its price as an income distribution variable; credit-money does not depend on a pre-existing stock of gold or high-powered money. 'Credit-money does not exist as some fixed stock "out there" in the economy' (Moore 1988, p. 296). An analogy can be made between this non-scarcity view of money and the refusal to consider prices of production as scarcity indices.

The link between production and credit-money has been aptly described by the monetary circuit school.[8] Production cannot be conceived without credit-money and any process of production must start with the acquisition of credit. Either firms borrow or they make use of their circulating capital, Keynes's 1937 revolving fund, which in any case comes from as yet unrepaid loans; this is Graziani's initial financement (1984). At the *final* financement stage, the circuitistes argue in cash-flow terms that the necessary finance must be identical to the amount required; this is Keynes's much discussed identity (rather than equilibrium condition) between savings and investment. Circuitistes thus argue that, whether the economy is in equilibrium or disequilibrium, long-term fund finance will always be forthcoming. Variations in interest rates are not needed to equalize savings to investment. The belief that all production requires credit-money and that a lack of savings cannot financially restrain investment now prevails among post-Keynesians (Moore 1988, ch. 12; Eichner 1987, sec. 12.1.5; Nell 1986, p. 30).

This helps to explain why scarcity analysis, so dear to neoclassical economists, cannot even enter financial markets. To claim that a growing economy will eventually trigger rising (real) interest rates, presumably as a consequence of excess credit demand or lack of savings, or that the supply of money has a rising schedule in the income–interest rate plane (as in any ordinary demand and supply analysis), is to reintroduce scarcity analysis through the back door. Of course, no one will deny that in output accelerating situations central banks are tempted to raise nominal interest rates, because of balance of payments constraints for instance. The truth of the matter is that disregarding inflationary forces which may encourage the central bank to respond to the lobbying of those rentiers without indexation clauses, there are no natural forces which inescapably force up interest rates (nominal or real). As Robinson (1952, p. 128) points out, 'when the boom is spread evenly over the world . . . it is hard to see why finance should check the upswing.' If interest rates do rise, it is because central banks have consciously taken the political decision to increase them. When liquidity preference forces are brought into the picture, one could argue that interest rate increases brought about by a fall in confidence could only be of a temporary nature. Monetary authorities have the power to enforce a permanent rate of interest, provided they show some consistency of purpose.

Some post-Keynesians, in the Minsky (1975) or Rousseas (1986; 1989) tradition, still believe that rising activity necessarily leads to increased (real) rates of interest. Their arguments usually rely on some form of generalized theory of liquidity preference, whereby rising activity should induce less liquid balance sheets for both firms and banks (Wray 1989, p. 1188). Kalecki's principle of increasing risk is also usually invoked. However, the macroeconomics of this principle are such that they may lead to lower interest rates and easier borrowing, a fact underlined by Robinson (1952, p. 23; 1956, p. 51).

To argue that the money supply is horizontal, as do Moore (1988) and Kaldor (1982), is not to argue that there are no constraints on credit. On the contrary, post-Keynesians know that price alone is not a valid exclusion mechanism. Banks generally meet the loan requests of firms, 'provided that the latter meet the banks' minimum collateral and risk requirements' (Moore 1988, p. 58). Modifications to those requirements, as pointed out above, may vary in paradoxical directions. They are better interpreted as shifts of the 'effective' demand curve for credit (Lavoie 1985b).

Recessions induced by financial or monetary causes are not a necessary and unassailable evil. They are orchestrated by the monetary authorities. As noted by Eichner (1987, p. 860), 'the basic interest rate is a politically determined distributional variable rather than a market-determined price.' Those who keep arguing that investment is the causal factor must recognize that money is endogenous and that interest rates are conventional. Otherwise the proposed causality could not hold, and scarcity analysis would prevail.

MODELS OF GROWTH AND DISTRIBUTION

On the Absence of Money and Interest Rates

As noted in the introduction to this chapter, one of the surprising aspects of the evolution of Cambridge theory is that, starting from Keynes's *General Theory* which described a monetary production economy, the Cambridge post-Keynesians have failed to incorporate money within their models of growth and distribution. For instance, although Robinson (1956; 1962) devotes several pages to rentiers, interest rates and finance constraints, she ends up adopting assumptions 'intended to reduce the importance of monetary policy in the operation of the model to a minimum, except as a stopper to inflation' (1962, p. 44). In her famous double-edged relationship between the rate of profit and the rate of growth, she indicates (1962, p. 43) that the finance constraints appear among the general animal spirits of the entrepreneurs, symbolized by the expected rate of profit necessary to induce a given rate of accumulation. But monetary factors do not enter, even implicitly, the second curve, described by the famous $r = g/s_c$ formula.

It is also well known that one of Davidson's major objections to Cambridge growth models is that they lack explicit monetary variables. Davidson (1972, ch. 12) has in particular been critical of Pasinetti (1962) and Kaldor (1966) on those grounds.[9] With respect to the so-called neo-Pasinetti theorem, Davidson was appalled at Kaldor's use (1966) of an implicit rate of interest (the valuation ratio) for what he understood to be a return to the classical mechanism allowing full employment (Samuelson's Jean-Baptiste Kaldor). He also noted that no money was present in Kaldor's model, since any income not spent was assumed to be invested directly into the stock market. Kaldor himself has never publicly commented on the drawbacks of his 1966 model. However he recognized that he 'did not realize that the valuation ratio indicates an implicit rate of return on shares'.[10] Kaldor referred to his 1939 article on 'speculation and economic activity' to defend the idea that implicit rates of interest did not need to be closely related to the money rate of interest. He insisted that the expected rate of profit and the money rate of interest were the pertinent rates of return considered by firms making investment decisions, while implicit rates of return (the valuation ratio), except in exceptional circumstances, were totally irrelevant.

If Kaldor had been forced to answer Davidson's objection that households use their savings only partly to buy shares, the other part being held as banking deposits, he might have answered along the lines of Robinson's interpretation of the neo-Pasinetti theorem, that is, 'the banking system is assumed to be generating a sufficient increase in the quantity of money to offset liquidity preference' (Robinson 1971, p. 123). It comes down to assuming that bankers, who pocket the difference between the implicit rate of return on shares and the money rate of interest, behave precisely as the rentiers would, had they not chosen to keep their wealth in safe banking deposits. Robinson (1956, p. 249) herself associated the income of financial institutions with that of rentiers and thought it appropriate to include the expenditures of the former with those of the latter.

Some authors have attempted to explicitly model money interest rates within growth models of the Cambridge type. For instance, Taylor (1985) and Franke (1988) take into account the rate of interest on borrowed capital. However, they do not seem to realize that the propensity to save on gross profits (s_p) is dependent upon the distribution of these profits between the shareowners of the firm (retained earnings and dividends) and the creditors of the firms (interest on bonds and loans). When money or money interest rates are taken into account, they must surely have some impact on distribution and therefore on the savings function.

Indeed, this is precisely what can be found in Skott's revamped version of Kaldor's neo-Pasinetti theorem. Skott (1989) adds to the equity market, where returns are variable, a money market with a fixed rate of interest. There, the higher the (real) rate of interest, the smaller the overall propensity to save and also the higher the share of profits and the rate of growth of output (Skott 1989, pp. 58, 64, 68). These surprising results, of which Skott does not seem to be aware or which he does not believe to be worthy of mention, are due to effective demand. Higher interest rates redistribute income from firms to households, whose propensity to save is lower. Money and interest rates thus do have a role to play in a theory of growth and distribution, even when the valuation ratios are considered endogenous, as is done by Kaldor and Skott.[11]

Rates of Interest and Rates of Profit

A controversy has arisen among post-classical authors with regard to the causal link between the rates of interest and profit. Cambridge post-Keynesians, as is well known, claim that the determination of the rate of profit rests on the realized rate of growth modulated by the saving propensities on profits. The rate of interest is left hanging in the air, independent of the rate of profit. 'The level of interest is . . . not closely tethered to the level of profits and enjoys, so to say, a life of its own' (Robinson 1956, p. 242). It has even been asserted recently that 'the normal rate of profit determines the long-term rate of interest' (Nell 1988, p. 267). On the other hand, neo-Ricardians, acting on suggestions by Garegnani (1979), have claimed that the rate of interest set by the monetary authorities determines the rate of profit.[12] The causality proposed by the neo-Ricardians has generally irritated post-Keynesians who have called it an 'inexplicable suggestion' (Bhaduri and Robinson 1980, p. 103), which is 'excessively fanciful' (Robinson 1979, p. 180). Nonetheless, as we have seen, some causal relationship leading from interest rates to profit rates (or shares) can be established within Kaldorian models. Furthermore, Kaldor himself has granted that 'interest costs are passed on in higher prices in much the same way as wage costs' (1982, p. 63).[13]

The explanation proposed by Pivetti (1985; 1988), and endorsed by Roncaglia (1988), appears quite reasonable. It explicitly relies on a form of full-cost theory of prices, the same kind of price theory proposed by post-Keynesians, but where the determinant of profit margins are the overhead costs due to interest payments on borrowed capital and the opportunity costs on the firms' own capital. Pivetti's analysis, as he himself recognized (Pivetti 1985, p. 91), can be linked to the exogenous profit margin assumed by the Kaleckians. For the latter and for the neo-Ricardians, a considerable degree of autonomy is granted to profit margins. For those two groups of economists, effective demand has little effect on profit margins, whereas post-Keynesians assume that profit margins and profit rates are determined by growth rates. For Kaleckians, class struggle or the degree of monopoly is the determinant of profit margins; for neo-Ricardians, the level of the interest rate is the crucial factor: 'My analysis carries the view that the interest rate determines the mark-up over nominal wages' (Pivetti 1988, p. 282).

In the end, we thus have three views of pricing which rely on some form of the full-cost or mark-up model of the firm. In the Kaleckian view, the profit margin is basically exogenous, influenced by neither the interest rate nor the growth rate. This corresponds to recent Kaleckian growth models (Rowthorn 1981; Amadeo 1986; Dutt 1990; Kurz 1991). In the post-Keynesian view, the margin of profit is largely influenced by the financing needs of accumulation of firms (Eichner 1976). To this second view correspond the post-Keynesian models of growth of the late 1950s and early 1960s.[14] Finally, there is the neo-Ricardian view, where the profit margin depends on the rate of interest.

Each of these three views has elements of plausibility; but there are also drawbacks. The neo-Ricardian view assumes that in the long period, at the standard rate of utilization of capacity, the rate of profit is the sum of two *independent* elements: the rate of money interest, and the normal profit of the entrepreneur (Pivetti 1985, p. 87). As pointed out by Wray (1988, p. 272, fn. 7), this presumes that there are no conflicts between rentiers and entrepreneurs; it could well be that higher interest costs lead to cuts in retained earnings, a possibility that we shall now examine.

A Post-Classical Model of Growth
We are now in a position to incorporate within a simple model of growth and distribution some of the ideas that have been put forth in the previous sections. The role of credit-money, and that of the money rate of interest, should explicitly appear in that model. The foundations of our model are the recent Kaleckian models of growth, where the rate of utilization can be different from its normal value, even in long-run equilibrium.[15] Assuming linear forms, we can write the following system of five equations:

$$g^s = (r-i) + s_h i \tag{1.1}$$

$$g^d = j + \sigma u + \phi(r-i) + \rho m_o \tag{1.2}$$

$$m = m_o + \alpha g + \beta i \tag{1.3}$$

$$r = mu/v \tag{1.4}$$

$$g^s = g^d \qquad\qquad (1.5)$$

Equation (1.1), the savings function in growth terms (g^s), assumes that the rate of interest i on loans or bonds is exogenous, and also equal to the rate of distributed dividends on shares. As a consequence, $r - i$ are the retained earnings per unit of capital. It is also assumed, for simplification, that there are no savings out of wages, and therefore the only savings by households, $s_h i$, are those arising from interest or dividend payments. Note that a higher interest rate leads to lower savings.

Equation (1.2) is the investment function, which depends on variables that have frequently been considered in the more recent Kaleckian growth literature. Growth would be enhanced by higher animal spirits j; a higher degree of utilization of capacity u; a more favourable class context for entrepreneurs m_o, as underlined recently by Radicals and other authors (Kurz 1991; Marglin and Bhaduri 1990); and a higher gross retention ratio $[= (r - i)/r]$ (cf. Steindl 1952, p. 114). With respect to the last of these influences on investment, it could be said more simply that growth is induced by a larger spread between the rate of profit and the rate of interest, giving some role to Kalecki's principle of increasing risk and its possible paradoxical behaviour, as underlined earlier.

Equation (1.3) depicts the margin of profit, m, and hence implicitly the pricing model. This margin would depend positively on three parameters: the strength of entrepreneurs with regard to class conflicts, m_o: this would be the Kaleckian (Marxian) part of the foundations; the rate of growth g: this would be the Kaldorian (Eichnerian) foundations; the permanent rate of interest cost i: this is the neo-Ricardian contribution.

Equations (1.4) and (1.5) are standard definitional and equilibrium relations. Taking the total derivatives, and solving the system by computing the inverse matrix yields Table 1.1:[16]

In our model, while it is clear that higher household savings induce slower growth, the relations between accumulation, interest rates and profit margins are somewhat ambiguous. In the standard under-consumptionist models, or Kaleckian models, an increase in the profit margin redistributes income towards profits, the recipients of which have a lower propensity to consume than do wage earners. As a result, the rate of utilization of capacity and hence the rate of accumulation are lower. In Radical or similar models, investment is a positive function of the profit margin. This effect may overcome the distribution effect and therefore a higher profit margin may induce a higher rate of accumulation.

In the present model, when interest rates are changed, various effects come into play. A higher interest rate initially leads to a redistribution from the firm towards the household rentiers, which creates an increase in

Table 1.1   Post-classical growth model

	dg	dr	du	dm
dj	+	+	+	+
ds$_h$	−	−	−	−
dm$_o$	?	?	?	+
di	?	?	?	?

$$\left.\begin{array}{l} dg/dm_o \\ dr/dm_o \end{array}\right\} < 0 \text{ if } u/m > \rho/\sigma$$

$dg/di \qquad < 0 \text{ if } s_h \phi u/v > (1 - \sigma s_h - \beta u/v)$

$dr/di \qquad < 0 \text{ if } \phi m/v + \sigma \beta u/v > (m/v + \alpha \sigma u/v)(1 - s_h)$

$du/dm_o \qquad < 0 \text{ if } u/v > \rho/(1 + \rho \alpha - \phi)$

More complex conditions for du/di, dm/di.

consumption.[17] Higher interest costs, however, are partially passed on to consumers, through higher markups, which implies lower real wages and hence less consumption. This secondary effect is further reinforced by the investment function, a smaller spread between profit and interest rates leading to less confident bankers and entrepreneurs, and hence a lower rate of accumulation. It may be that the rate of profit and the rate of interest move in sympathy, leaving the rate of growth relatively unchanged. But it may also turn out that the hike in interest rates will bring down the rates of profit and growth, a result more akin to Keynesian theory. We can thus concur with Pivetti's presumptions when he says that:

> Changes in interest rates *will* tend to be associated with changes in aggregate demand, but by a different route from the one traditionally envisaged ... The direction of such influence, however, cannot be predicted ... The point, of course, is the significance of income distribution for effective demand: if money plays an important role in determining income distribution, it will also play an important role in the determination of the level and composition of output. (1985, pp. 99–100)

CONCLUSION

This chapter has attempted to show that most post-Keynesian and neo-Ricardian authors hold a similar vision of a monetary production economy. In most strands of the post-classical research tradition, economists contend that interest rates are exogenous variables, under the authority of the decisions of the central bank; that money is an endogenous credit-led and demand-determined variable; that as a consequence, in monetary economies, causality runs from investment to saving, rather than the reverse; and that the rate of accumulation is constrained by effective demand rather than by insufficient saving.

There are no natural forces operating to raise the money rate of interest when accumulation steps up. Monetary authorities must always take a stance, deciding which level of interest rate is the most appropriate for their purpose. The central bank takes decisions that have an impact on the distribution of income between entrepreneurs, rentiers and wage-earners, through changes in the margin of profit and through the feedback effect of those changes on aggregate demand. No definite relationship between the rate of profit and the money rate of interest could be established in a model where higher interest costs are integrated to a higher margin of profit, and where the feedback effects on effective demand are taken into account.

The analysis conducted above illustrates that there is room for monetary theory within the neo-Ricardian research programme.[18] Furthermore, neo-Ricardians have brought to our attention the impact of changes of monetary interest rates on income distribution and on effective demand, a consideration that had generally been omitted in mark-up models or saving functions by those who claimed to be concerned with monetary production. Interaction between neo-Ricardian and post-Keynesian viewpoints can be fruitful; what appears to be required is a post-classical synthesis integrating these two traditions.[19]

NOTES

1. I have benefited from comments made by participants at the conference, and also those of the referee and A.K. Dutt. Numerous stylistic improvements were also suggested by the editors. I wish to thank W. Ma and E. Yalcin for their assistance, made possible by a grant from the Social Sciences and Humanities Research Council of Canada.
2. Different strands of non-neoclassical theories all borrow from this endogenous post-Keynesian view of money: European radicals (Lipietz 1982) or American ones (Devine 1987, 26), and Institutionalists (Parker Foster 1987).
3. Incidentally, the views of Arena (1987) on a possible post-classical (or 'classical–Keynesian') synthesis are close to those of the author.
4. For another attempt to explicitly integrate the banking sector within multi-sector production models, see Franke (1988).
5. Wray (1992) presents a formalized representation of a variant of this generalized liquidity preference, based on the work of Boulding. Portfolio effects might explain the structure of interest rates, but they cannot explain the base rate.
6. In actual time, these imperfections will always exist, and hence, unless by luck, these rates will never be equal.

7. While in the short run, there may be no upper or lower limit to the rate of interest set, this is not true in the long run. For instance, we all know now that past accumulated debts may become unsustainable if interest rates are too high.
8. D'Autume (1989), a neoclassical economist, in his short survey of macroeconomic theory in France, notes that besides disequilibrium theory, the original contributions of the French economists concern the theory of endogenous money and the circuit school. See Lavoie (1985a) and Graziani (1989) for introductory syntheses and bibliographies of the French circuit school.
9. Davidson's critique of Pasinetti's model, and the various attempts to introduce money into it, are discussed in Lavoie (1987, ch. 6).
10. From a letter of N. Kaldor to the author, November 1983.
11. Skott's presentation contains a drawback that is also present in my own previous work (Lavoie 1987, ch. 7). Skott (1989, p. 55 and p. 77) assumes that firms have control over the retention rate on gross profits, that is, profits before interest payments are made. Skott (p. 127) himself seems to realize the awkwardness of this assumption, borrowed from Wood (1975). If any behavioural hypothesis may be put forth regarding the retention rate, it should be related to net profits – profits once the fixed interest rate payments have been made – as done by Pettenatti (1967) and now by Taylor (1991, p. 130).
12. 'Keynes's suggestion that the average level of interest on long-term loans will be determined by conventional factors, ultimately subject to the policy of the monetary authorities . . . would suffice to constitute a theory of distribution . . . If, then, the rate of interest depends on the policy of the monetary authorities, both the long-term movement of the rate of profit . . . and that of the real wages are explained by that policy.' (Garegnani 1979, p. 81)
13. Furthermore, when governments have large debts and run deficits, rising interest payments could easily sustain rising profit margins through their effect on aggregate demand. Taylor (1985, p. 395) links this causality to the Latin American structural inflation literature (cf. Moreno's contribution in this volume).
14. As pointed out by Agliardi (1988), there is some inconsistency between these two views since the first implies an inverse relationship between margins and growth, while the second has margins and growth rates moving together. See also Sawyer (1990).
15. Some authors, from various quarters, are critical of such a possibility. See Committeri (1986), Auerbach and Skott (1987) and Duménil and Lévy (1989).
16. We have the standard stability condition:

$$dg^s/du > dg^d/du$$

i.e., $$m/v > \sigma + \phi m/v$$

17. The consequent symmetrical positive effect of lower interest rates on effective demand was also noted by Robinson (1956, p. 253): 'A permanent fall in the level of interest rates relatively to the rate of profit has reduced the rentiers' share in profits (assuming that dividends have not been raised correspondingly), and this is likely to have a more important effect in reducing the proportion of consumption to profits than any effect there may be of lower interest in increasing the ratio of consumption to rentier income.'
18. A claim also made recently by Dutt and Amadeo (1990, p. 80).
19. Needless to say that a full synthesis would also incorporate the insights of the Radical School. See Epstein (1990) for a recent macroeconomic model with three classes (entrepreneurs, rentiers, labour), which takes into account Keynesian, Kaleckian and neo-Marxian elements.

REFERENCES

Agliardi, E. (1988) 'Microeconomic Foundations of Macroeconomics in the Post-Keynesian Approach', *Metroeconomica*, **39**, 275–97.

Amadeo, E. J. (1986) 'The Role of Capacity Utilization in Long-Period Analysis', *Political Economy*, **2**, 147–60.

Arena, R. (1987) 'L'école internationale d'été de Trieste (1981–85): vers une synthèse classico-keynésienne?', *Économies et Sociétés*, **21**, 205–38.

Arena, R. and Graziani, A. (eds) (1985) *Production, circulation et monnaie*, Paris: Presses Universitaires de France.

Arestis, P. and Eichner, A.S. (1988) 'The Post-Keynesian and Institutionalist Theory of Money and Credit', *Journal of Economic Issues*, **22**, 1003–22.

Auerbach, P. and Skott, P. (1987) 'Concentration, Competition and Distribution – A Critique of Monopoly Capital', *International Review of Applied Economics*, **2**, 42–61.

Bhaduri, A. and Robinson, J. (1980) 'Accumulation and Exploitation: An Analysis in the Tradition of Marx, Sraffa and Kalecki', *Cambridge Journal of Economics*, **4**, 103–15.

Committeri, M. (1986) 'Some Comments on Recent Contributions on Capital Accumulation, Income Distribution and Capacity Utilization', *Political Economy*, **2**, 161–86.

D'Autume, A. (1989) 'La macroéconomie contemporaine', in *La science économique en France*, Paris: La Découverte.

Davidson, Paul (1972) *Money and the Real World*, London: Macmillan.

Davidson, Paul (1988) 'Endogenous Money', the Production Process and Inflation Analysis', *Economie Appliquée*, **41**, 151–69.

Devine, James A. (1987) 'An Introduction to Radical Theories of Economic Crises', *The Imperiled Economy*, vol 1, New York: Union for Radical Political Economics.

Dow, A.C. and Dow, S. (1989) 'Endogenous Money Creation and Idle Balances', in J. Pheby (ed.), *New Directions in Post Keynesian Economics*, Aldershot: Edward Elgar.

Duménil, G. and Lévy, D. (1989) 'Les régulationnistes pouvaient-ils apprendre davantage des classiques?', Working paper, CEPREMAP.

Dutt, A.K. (1990) *Growth, Distribution and Uneven Development*, Cambridge: Cambridge University Press.

Dutt, A.K. and Amadeo, E.J. (1990) *Keynes's Third Alternative. The Neo-Ricardian Keynesians and the Post Keynesians*, Aldershot: Edward Elgar.

Eatwell, J. and Milgate, M. (eds) (1983) *Keynes's Economics and the Theory of Value and Distribution*, Oxford: Oxford University Press.

Eichner, A.S. (1976) *The Megacorp & Oligopoly/Micro Foundations of Macro Dynamics*, Cambridge: Cambridge University Press.

Eichner, A.S. (1987) *The Macrodynamics of Advanced Market Economics*, Armonk, NY: M.E. Sharpe.

Epstein, G. (1990) 'A Political Economy Model of Comparative Central Banking', Working Paper 1990–93, Department of Economics, University of Massachussets in Amherst.

Franke, R. (1988) 'Integrating the Financing of Production and a Rate of Interest into Production Price Models', *Cambridge Journal of Economics*, **12**, 257–72.

Garegnani, P. (1979) 'Notes on Consumption, Investment and Effective Demand: II', *Cambridge Journal of Economics*, **3**, 63–82.

Garegnani, P. (1983) 'Two Routes to Effective Demand', in J.A. Kregel (ed.), *Distribution, Effective Demand and International Economic Relations*, London: Macmillan, 69–80.

Graziani, A. (1984) 'The Debate on Keynes' Finance Motive', *Economic Notes*, 5–32.

Graziani, A. (1989) 'The Theory of the Monetary Circuit', *Thames Papers in Political Economy*, Spring.

Henry, J. (1982) 'Les méthodes post-keynésiennes et l'approche post-classique', *L'Actualité économique*, **58**, 17–61.

Kaldor, N. (1962) 'Comment', *Review of Economic Studies*, **29**, 246–50.

Kaldor, N. (1966) 'Marginal Productivity and the Macro-Economic Theories of Distribution', *Review of Economic Studies*, **33**, 309–19.

Kaldor, N. (1970) 'The New Monetarism', *Lloyds Bank Review*, 1–17.

Kaldor, N. (1982) *The Scourge of Monetarism*, Oxford: Oxford University Press.

Kregel, J.A. (1973) *The Reconstruction of Political Economy: An Introduction to Post-Keynesian Economics*, London: Macmillan.

Kregel, J.A. (1976) 'Economic Methodology in the Face of Uncertainty: The Modelling Method of Keynes and the Post-Keynesians', *Economic Journal*, **86**, 209–225.

Kregel, J.A. (1984–85) 'Constraints on the Expansion of Output and Employment: Real or Monetary?', *Journal of Post Keynesian Economics*, 7, 139–52.

Kregel, J.A. (1985) 'Hamlet without the Prince: Cambridge Macroeconomics without Money', *American Economic Review*, **75**, 133–9.

Kurz, H. (1991) 'Technical Change, Growth and Distribution: A Steady State Approach to Unsteady Growth on Kaldorian Lines', in E.J. Nell and W. Semmler (eds), *Nicholas Kaldor and Mainstream Economics: Confrontation or Convergence*, London: Macmillan.

Lavoie, M. (1985a) 'The Dynamic Circuit, Overdraft Economies, and Post-Keynesian Economics', in M. Jarsulic (ed.), *Money and Macro Policy*, Boston: Kluwer–Nijhoff.

Lavoie, M. (1985b) 'The Post Keynesian Theory of Endogenous Money: A Reply', *Journal of Economic Issues*, **19**, 843–8.

Lavoie, M. (1987) *Macroéconomie: Théorie et controverses post-keynésiennes*, Paris: Dunod.

Lawson, T. (1989) 'Abstraction, Tendencies and Stylised Facts: A Realist Approach to Economic Analysis', *Cambridge Journal of Economics*, **13**, 59–70.

Le Bourva, J. (1962) 'Création de la monnaie et multiplicateur du crédit', *Revue économique*, **13**, 29–56.

Le Héron, E. (1986) 'Généralisation de la préférence pour la liquidité et financement de l'investissement', *Économies et Sociétés*, **20**, 67–93.

Lipietz, A. (1982) 'Credit Money', *Review of Radical Political Economics*, **14**, 49–57.

Marglin, S.A. and Bhaduri, A. (1990) 'Profit Squeeze and Keynesian Theory', in S.A. Marglin and J.B. Schor (eds), *The Golden Age of Capitalism*, Oxford: Oxford University Press.

Minsky, H.P. (1975) *John Maynard Keynes*, New York: Columbia University Press.

Moore, B.J. (1988) *Horizontalists and Verticalists: The Macroeconomics of Credit Money*, Cambridge: Cambridge University Press.

Mott, T. (1985–86) 'Towards a Post-Keynesian Formulation of Liquidity Preference', *Journal of Post Keynesian Economics*, **8**, 222–32.

Nell, E.J. (1986) 'On Monetary Circulation and the Rate of Exploitation', *Thames Papers in Political Economy*, Summer.

Nell, E.J. (1988) 'Does the Rate of Interest Determine the Rate of Profit', *Political Economy*, **4**, 263–7.

Panico, C. (1985) 'Market Forces and the Relation between the Rates of Interest and Profits', *Contribution to Political Economy*, **4**, 37–60.

Panico, C. (1988) *Interest and Profit in Theories of Value and Distribution*, London: Macmillan.

Parker, Foster, G. (1987) 'Financing Investment', *Journal of Economic Issues*, **21**, 101–12.

Pasinetti, L.L. (1962) 'Rate of Profit and Income Distribution in Relation to the Rate of Economic Growth', *Review of Economic Studies*, **29**, 267–79.

Pasinetti, L.L. (1974) *Growth and Income Distribution: Essays in Economic Theory*, Cambridge: Cambridge University Press.

Pettenati, P. (1967) 'Il teorema di Pasinetti in un diverso quadro di riferimento', *Studi Economici*, **22**, 581–8.

Pivetti, M. (1985) 'On the Monetary Explanation of Distribution', *Political Economy*, **1**, 73–103.

Pivetti, M. (1988) 'On the Monetary Explanation of Distribution: A Rejoinder to Nell and Wray', *Political Economy*, **4**, 275–83.

Robinson, J. (1952) *The Rate of Interest and Other Essays*, London: Macmillan.

Robinson, J. (1956) *The Accumulation of Capital*, London: Macmillan.

Robinson, J. (1962) *Essays in the Theory of Economic Growth*, London: Macmillan.

Robinson, J. (1971) *Economic Heresies*, London: Macmillan.

Robinson, J. (1979) 'Garegnani on Effective Demand', *Cambridge Journal of Economics*, **3**, 179–80.

Rogers, C. (1989) *Money, Interest and Capital: A Study in the Foundations of Monetary Theory*, Cambridge: Cambridge University Press.

Roncaglia, A. (1988) 'The Neo-Ricardian Approach and the Distribution of Income', in A. Asimakopulos (ed.), *Theories of Income Distribution*, Boston: Kluwer Academic.

Rousseas, S. (1986) *Post Keynesian Monetary Economics*, Armonk, NY: M.E. Sharpe.

Rousseas, S. (1989) 'On the Endogeneity of Money Once More', *Journal of Post Keynesian Economics*, **11**, 474–8.

Rowthorn, B. (1981) 'Demand, Real Wages and Economic Growth', *Thames Papers in Political Economy*, Autumn.

Sawyer, M.C. (1990) 'On the Post-Keynesian Tradition and Industrial Economics', *Review of Political Economy*, **2**, 43–68.

Skott, P. (1989) *Conflict and Effective Demand in Economic Growth*, Cambridge: Cambridge University Press.

Steindl, J. (1952) *Maturity and Stagnation in American Capitalism*, Oxford: Blackwell.

Taylor, L. (1985) 'A Stagnationist Model of Economic Growth', *Cambridge Journal of Economics*, **9**, 383–403.

Taylor, L. (1991) *Income Distribution, Inflation and Growth*, Cambridge, MA: MIT Press.

Wells, P. (1983) 'A Post-Keynesian View of Liquidity Preference and the Demand for Money', *Journal of Post Keynesian Economics*, **5**, 515–22.

Wood, A. (1975) *A Theory of Profits*, Cambridge: Cambridge University Press.

Wray, L.R. (1988) 'The Monetary Explanation of Distribution: A Critique of Pivetti', *Political Economy*, **4**, 269–73.

Wray, L.R. (1989) 'Two Reviews of Basil Moore', *Journal of Economic Issues*, **23**, 1185–9.

Wray, L.R. (1992) 'Alternative Theories of the Rate of Interest', *Cambridge Journal of Economics*, **16**, 69–91.

2. Prices and Pricing in the Post-Keynesian and Kaleckian Traditions in the Short Run and in the Long Run

Malcolm C. Sawyer[1]

INTRODUCTION

Whilst there has been a variety of approaches to price setting within the post-Keynesian and Kaleckian traditions, two approaches have come to the fore. One has stressed the links between prices and investment (specifically that prices are set so as to generate profits to help finance investment). The other has focused on price as a mark-up over costs where the mark-up is set in an effort to fulfil short-run objectives: in particular to maximize short-run profits. It would then appear that the former stresses the long-term influences on price whilst the latter stresses the short-term influences. This chapter discusses these approaches to price setting with particular emphasis on the relationship between the short term and the long term. In comparing these different approaches to price setting, each has to be presented in a simplified way with the obvious dangers of misrepresentation.

Theories of price operate on a number of different levels. It is useful to draw on the distinction made by Eichner (1987) between theories of pricing and theories of price determination. Theories of pricing are seen as concerned with the setting of prices at the level of the firm, whilst theories of price determination are concerned with an overall equilibrium configuration of prices. The main concern in the post-Keynesian and Kaleckian literature on price (and even more so in the mainstream industrial economics literature, which has interesting overlaps with the Kaleckian literature) has been with pricing, with the price-setting firm considered largely in isolation (though there is some recognition of the impact of competitors' behaviour). Whilst many post-Keynesian authors have been fully aware of the macroeconomic implications of and impact on pricing, this has not always been fully apparent in the formal modelling. Further, there has been very little recognition of the interrelationships between prices which are required for a configuration of prices to satisfy some type of steady-state conditions operating at the level of the economy. Theories of price determination (for example, those of Sraffa) are not concerned with the process of price formation at the micro level, but rather with an equilibrium configuration of prices. In that dichotomy, the Walrasian general equilibrium analysis provides a theory of price determination but not of pricing, since there are no mechanisms of price setting (unless the auctioneer is so considered). The approaches to pricing considered below are capable of being both theories of pricing and of price determination. They are based on views as to how prices are set but can be placed within an overall framework such that equilibrium configurations can be investigated.[2]

Post-Keynesian authors frequently emphasize the problems surrounding the notion of optimization that arise from a lack of relevant information or from limited computational abilities. Yet, as Reynolds (1989) has argued, many post-Keynesian models of pricing do not incorporate uncertainty in any fundamental way, and that is reflected here. The use of algebraic formulation to explore the interrelationships leads inevitably to a downgrading of the emphasis on uncertainty.

There is a sense in which decisions on price, investment, output and so on can be treated independently in neoclassical economics. The elementary treatment does indeed do that: for example, the demand for labour is based on the marginal product of labour and equated with the real wage. There are, of course, more sophisticated treatments in which a variety of decisions are integrated. But it is still the case that a firm's operations in one market are not severely restricted by its operations in other markets. In post-Keynesian and Kaleckian approaches, firms have to acquire finance for the purchase of factors of production (especially of capital equipment) and finance may come from internal or external sources. External finance is often viewed as more expensive than internal finance, and a preference for internal finance leads to a link between profits and investment. But finance can come from borrowing from banks which would lead to some initial increase in the stock of money, with the eventual impact on the stock of money, depending on the reactions of those to whom the money is paid. Although it may well be the case that banks are willing to extend further loans when the demand for loans is forthcoming, nevertheless some individual firms may be constrained from further borrowing when banks regard them as bad risks.

The coverage of this chapter is limited to the Kaleckian approach to pricing and to the post-Keynesian investment requirements approach. There are a number of approaches to price which could be regarded as post-Keynesian but which are ignored here, the major examples being full-cost pricing (for example, Hall and Hitch 1939) and administered pricing (for example, Means 1936). The contribution of Hall and Hitch (1939) is important for, *inter alia*, casting doubt on the applicability of profit maximization and for suggesting an evolutionary approach to pricing behaviour. However they can be seen as viewing price as a short-term decision without any direct reference to financing requirements. Further, their treatment of price as a mark-up over costs is, in our simplification, indistinguishable from the equation representing the other approaches. The administered pricing approach says little about the relationship between price and costs, or between profits and investment. Further, the emphasis on price rigidity does not fit with the other approaches considered here since they are not inherently concerned with price rigidity.[3] It has not been possible, in the space available here, to discuss the Sraffian approach to price determination. To consider arguments based on the equilization of the rate of profit would be an important extension of the model presented below.

Most post-Keynesian and Kaleckian theories of pricing in effect assume the expectations of firms regarding price and output are largely fulfilled. In so far as producers miscalculate the demand which they face, the effect will be felt on sales (at the prices set by firms), and differences between actual demand and expected demand will largely be absorbed by unintended stock changes. Whilst the particular course of a business cycle will be influenced by these expectational mistakes, there is a sense in which enterprises are assumed to be well informed about demand conditions. In the analysis of investment expenditure, there has been a post-Keynesian emphasis (arising from Keynes 1937) on the role of 'animal spirits' and the essential uncertainty of the future, in which case it is impossible to formulate investment decisions with any precision; investment expenditure is thus viewed as being subject to sharp changes and conditioned by waves of optimism and pessimism. Nevertheless, investment expenditure has sometimes been modelled in the post-Keynesian approach as though expectations about the future were firmly based. Eichner (1987, p. 375), for example, argued that 'the megacorp-price leader and other firms in the industry must be able to discern what the industry's rate of expansion is likely to be and then translate that perceived secular growth rate into plans for adding to their productive capacity'. In contrast, the approaches of Kalecki and Steindl involve firms with *imprecise* expectations on the future. Kalecki and Steindl are concerned with the broad influences on investment, and they do not incorporate expectations explicitly into their models; views on future profitability are simply assumed to be strongly influenced by current levels.

KALECKIAN APPROACH TO PRICING

Kalecki's views on pricing, and on investment, went through a number of versions (Kriesler 1987). We deal here only with those prices which are, in Kalecki's terminology, cost determined and leave out of consideration prices which are demand determined.

A notable feature of Kalecki's approach is the separation between pricing and investment decisions in the sense that prices are set without any direct regard to the financing of investment expenditure. Investment decisions are not implemented immediately and the time gap between decision and implementation means that current profitability influences future investment expenditure. Decisions on investment expenditure are influenced by pricing decisions in the sense that the profits and output (and changes in output) which arise as a consequence of the chosen price set are important influences on future investment expenditure. But the price decision is not modelled as influenced by any thoughts of the finance requirements for investment.

A second, and related, feature is the short-term orientation of pricing decisions. In some formulations of Kalecki's approach (for example, Cowling and Waterson, 1976) the objective of enterprises is assumed to be short-term profit maximization, even though 'in view of the uncertainties faced in the process of price fixing it will not be assumed that the firm attempts to maximise its profits in any precise sort of manner' (Kalecki 1971, p. 44), which is interpreted from the context to mean that firms do pursue profit maximization, albeit imperfectly. A convenient expression of this approach is given by Baran and Sweezy (1966), when they argue that

> [t]he firm ... always finds itself in a given historical situation, with limited knowledge of changing conditions. In this context it can never do more than improve its profit position. In practice, the search for 'maximum' profits can only be the search for the greatest *increase* in profits which is possible in the given situation, subject of course to the elementary proviso that the exploitation of today's profit opportunities must not ruin tomorrow's. This is all there is to the profit maximization principle, ... (Baran and Sweezy, 1966)

In his later formulations, Kalecki did not make explicit reference to the objectives of firms, and focused on the relationship connecting a firm's price and its costs to the prices of other firms. This led him to a formulation which does not explicitly require profit maximization, but does incorporate the view that price is set as a mark-up over average direct costs, with the size of the mark-up influenced by the 'degree of monopoly', but not directly by the investment requirements of the firm. Below, we discuss further problems surrounding the use of the concept of short-run profit maximization.

THEORIES OF PRICING BASED ON INVESTMENT REQUIREMENTS

The second approach to pricing considered here is represented by the work of authors such as Eichner (1973, 1987), Wood (1975), and Harcourt and Kenyon (1976), who emphasize the role in the pricing decisions of profit margins required to meet growth targets. Large corporations are generally treated as manager-controlled and concerned with growth. The level of profit is viewed as a means to growth rather than as an end in itself.

The approach of Eichner is illustrative of those approaches which suggest that profit margins are to some degree adjusted in the light of the financing requirements for investment. It is important to note that the adjustment of profit margins is undertaken at the level of the enterprise to achieve the required amount of internal finance. An apparently similar conclusion was drawn by Steindl (1952, p. 48): 'the rate of internal accumulation is determined largely by the rate of expansion of the industry'. For Steindl, however, this result was brought about by competitive pressures and holds only in equilibrium and at the level of the industry.

Eichner's approach centres on the enterprise bringing its demand for investment finance into equality with its supply of investment finance. The demand for finance depends inversely on its cost, presumably for the usual reasons associated with the ranking of investment projects in order of their expected profitability. The supply of finance is drawn from internal and external sources. The effective price-setter in an industry is the price-leader; it is assumed that the leader's price permits the follower firms to finance their investment. Internal finance can always be augmented by raising price, since the demand curve facing a typical industry is taken to be inelastic, and the elasticity facing the price leader is also perceived to be less than unity. In contrast, Kalecki and others (cf. Cowling and Waterson 1976) have assumed that the perceived elasticity of demand facing an individual enterprise is greater than unity, and is higher at the firm level than at the industry level. In Eichner's approach, higher profit margins would encourage entry by other enterprises and substitution by consumers, and thus higher profits can only be achieved at some long-term cost. These future costs are expressed as an implicit rate of interest on internal finance.

There are three possible outcomes in connection with the intersection of the demand for and the supply of investment finance, as compared with the initial position. The first would mean a reduction in the profit margin and therefore in the use of internal finance as compared with the previous period. This case would involve a clear departure from profit maximization (whether interpreted as short-term or long-term), and arises when the enterprise has limited profitable investment outlets. This case could be ruled out if non-financial enterprises acted as financial institutions lending out funds. The firm could acquire finance at a negative (implicit) rate of interest, and lend it out at a positive rate. The second possible outcome would involve internal finance only, whilst the third outcome would be that the enterprise made use of both external and internal finance.

The interaction between microeconomic and macroeconomic phenomena raises certain difficulties for theories of pricing based on investment requirements. The first difficulty is that firms are often portrayed as deciding upon price and investment expenditure on the basis of expectations of future growth and a target rate of capacity utilization. In general, the rate of growth, which comes about as a result of the price (and thereby real wage) and investment decisions of firms, will not be equal to the firms' expected growth rate, nor the rates of capacity utilization to their target rates.

The second difficulty relates to the equality between the demand for and supply of investment funds at the level of the firm. The price set by the price leader to secure adequate finance (possibly including some external finance) may not generate sufficient finance for the other firms. A more important issue concerns the equilibrium requirement of *ex ante* equality between savings and investment. If all enterprises are able to finance investment out of their own savings, and there is no saving by households, then the equality between saving and investment would hold at the micro-level, and this equality would also hold (by summation) at the macro-level. On the other hand, if enterprises resort to external finance, rentiers and/or workers must generate sufficient saving in order to match that demand for external finance, a point to which we shall return.

In so far as price leadership is successful, Eichner's approach implies a high 'degree of monopoly'. The number of enterprises in the industry is not directly relevant here, though it could well be argued that price leadership is easier to achieve when the number of enterprises is small. Price leadership also means that the industry elasticity of demand is relevant for calculations of joint profit maximization, thus reinforcing the assumption of low elasticity of demand. However if the price set by the price leader is not exactly matched by all other firms in the industry the profit margin–profits function would have a more substantial curvature. Alternatively, as suggested by Reynolds (1989), 'the additional risk that other firms may not follow [the price leader] will provide an additional constraint on the mark-up. Analytically, . . . it may be . . . converted to an implicit interest rate.' Similarly, a higher degree of monopoly may arise from a lower risk of entry: in that sense a higher degree of monopoly would lead to a lower implicit cost of raising profit margins. Thus, the degree of monopoly might influence the mark-up, in Eichner's approach as well as in Kalecki's, and this is taken into account below.

The two assumptions of inelastic demand and interdependence between periods raise difficulties for the postulate of short-term profit maximization. The former assumption could lead to an infinite price in the short term, whilst the latter would indicate that short-term profit maximization may harm long-term profitability. Shapiro (1981), drawing on Steindl (1952), postulates the dependence of the growth rate of sales on the (current) profit margin. A strong interdependence of demand between periods would then arise. In contrast, Kaleckian and similar formulations do not take explicit account of interdependence between periods. This lack of interdependence requires two assumptions. The first is that the firm approaches profit maximization by considering the long-run elasticity of demand, rather than the short-run elasticity (or equivalently that the elasticity of demand does not change with the length of the time period of adjustment). The second assumption arises from taking barriers to entry into account. It could be assumed, following Cowling (1982) and others, that entry is effectively blocked or alternatively that firms follow a pricing limit strategy to prevent entry.

Shapiro (1981) notes that 'if the price of a commodity is to promote the growth of the firm, pricing has to be based on the principles of the maintenance and augmentation of (1) profit margins and (2) markets' (cf. also Levine 1981, Steindl 1952). If, for convenience, investment and profits are expressed net of depreciation, the argument can be stated as follows. The finance available for investment is derived from internal finance of $t.(p-c).q$ (where t is the proportion of profits saved, p is price, c is unit costs and q is output); and external finance which is taken to be a proportion z of internal finance. Growth of capital stock, g, is then given by:

$$g = (1+z).t.(p-c).q/p_K.K = (1+z).t.((p-c)/p).(q/q^*).(q^*/K). \quad (2.1)$$
$$(p/p_K) = (1+z).t.(m/1+m).u/v.(p/p_K).$$

where p_K is the price of capital goods and q^* is full capacity output. This provides a relationship between the growth of capital and the profit margin (g,m) given: the dividend policy (reflected in t); the debt–equity policy (reflected in z); the level of capacity utilization (u); and the capital–output ratio (v). Decisions by the enterprise concerning, for example, dividend policy (t) and debt-equity policy (z) are likely to be interdependent.

The variables g, m and u in equation (1) can be regarded as unknowns, and we will leave t, z and v to one side for the moment. The focus is on the determination of the first group of variables. The growth performance of any single firm will be heavily constrained by the growth prospects of the industry to which it belongs. Faster growth is possible by price reductions and appropriation of market shares of other firms. Following Shapiro (1981), the growth rate and the profit margin are set by the interaction of equation (2.1) with the dependence of the growth of sales on price, assuming that firms aim for and achieve a normal level of capacity utilization.

Equation (2.1) is capable of a number of interpretations. The work of Eichner would suggest that enterprises have expectations about growth and targets for the rate of capacity utilization, so that equation (1) determines the mark-up when the enterprises have calculated the desired mix between internal and external finance (that is, the value of z). Steindl (1952) distinguishes between the cases of competition and oligopoly. Under strong competition, capacity utilization will be pushed towards full capacity and the profit margin will be driven towards that which would yield a 'normal' rate of profit. However, under conditions of oligopoly, this pressure on capacity utilization is not present; Steindl and others have elaborated on the reasons why enterprises will accept spare capacity (for example, to inhibit new entry, or to be able to meet upsurges in demand). When the profit margin is set by the 'degree of monopoly', equation (2.1) serves to determine the degree of capacity utilization for a given growth rate.

DIFFICULTIES WITH THE PROFIT MAXIMIZATION APPROACH

There are at least two significant shortcomings in the neoclassical approach to pricing based on short-term profit maximization. Similar problems, moreover, are faced by the Kaleckian approach. The first is that there is no allowance for the impact of the short term on the long term or vice versa. The second is that the theory is vacuous unless the nature of the short term is defined; unless, for example, the theory specifies which costs can be varied in the short term. It has become conventional to identify short-term variable costs with labour and material costs, though it is clear that some capital inputs can be more easily varied than some labour inputs. The difficulties of pinning down marginal cost have been discussed in connection with some economists' advocacy of marginal cost pricing for public enterprises. Many of these difficulties would also arise if attempts were made to test the prediction of price as a mark-up over marginal cost. Kalecki also faced the problem of deciding which labour costs should be included in direct costs for the purposes of price formation

(Sawyer 1985, pp. 271–7). He appears to have distinguished between wages (paid to manual workers) and salaries (non-manual workers) on the basis of the variable nature of the former and the fixed nature of the latter.

The Kaleckian approach will now be modified by formalizing the Baran and Sweezy proposition quoted above in order to avoid the first of these difficulties. The starting point is a notion of the maximization of sustainable profits. An enterprise which contemplates long-term operation will not wish to charge a high price in the short run if by doing so it adversely affects profits in the longer run. But it may be postulated that an enterprise aims to set a price that would yield the highest level of profits which could be maintained over time (provided that all other factors were held constant). This would mean, for example, that an enterprise that was not threatened by entry would use long-run elasticity of demand rather than short-run elasticity in its calculations. This does not mean, of course, that an enterprise would ever face an unchanging situation from period to period.

The maximization of sustainable profits is an artificial construction. Consider a firm with a given stock of capital equipment (which it will augment through investment), which is facing given demand conditions. It would then be possible to calculate for this situation the price and the level of output, as well as the size of the labour force, which the firm would choose, under the assumption that the initial conditions will continue indefinitely. This would mean, for example, that the firm uses a long-term elasticity of demand in its calculations. The variety of ways in which demand in different periods of time can be related would also be taken into account. The use of inputs other than the capital stock would be adjusted so as to generate maximum profits. This does not imply that all types of labour, for example, are variable inputs: in practice it may be easier for a firm to vary its use of some capital equipment (such as vehicles) than to vary the use of some types of labour (for example, skilled labour with long-term contracts).

For any set of demand conditions, there would be a sustainable profit maximizing price, output and input usage. The firm could set that price and output, though in general the actual use of inputs would differ from the sustainable profit maximizing levels. Employment of inputs will be heavily conditioned by past employment of inputs and by expectations of future employment since there are hiring and firing costs and so on. The price and the output derived from sustainable profit maximization does not necessarily lie on the short-run demand curve facing the firm. In such circumstances, the firm may maintain price at its long-term level and allow output to deviate from the chosen level in the short run. This has strong similarities with the normal cost pricing view of Coutts, Godley and

Nordhaus (1978). The use of inputs will be varied somewhat, but in general not to the same extent as output.

When the notion of sustainable profit maximization is adopted, enterprises would base their pricing decisions on non-capital costs, and would seek to adjust prices in response to changes in those costs. A long-term perspective on pricing suggests that the appropriate costs should be more broadly defined than is usually signified by the expression variable costs. Indeed, the possibility of variation in the use of inputs is not relevant to whether the cost of that input is also included in the cost calculations of the enterprise. Furthermore, growth and investment requirements influence prices even if firms do not explicitly take such requirements into account when setting price. The long-term viability of a firm will require that it is able to finance most of its investment out of profits.

The notion of sustainable profit maximization is an attempt to overcome the clearly myopic nature of short-run profit maximization. It suggests that pricing can be viewed as a decision with long-term implications without making it dependent on the growth prospects of the enterprise. However, it retains the separation of the price decision from the investment decision.

A ONE-SECTOR MODEL

A one-sector model can be constructed to illustrate some of the points made above. It is inevitable that in such a model a number of important ideas are suppressed. In particular, there is no role for relative output prices and the tendency towards the equalization of the rate of profit. Labour and capital equipment are the only inputs, and hence complications arising from the use of produced means of production do not arise.

The output of the single product is labelled X, the capital stock (composed of the same product) K, and the employment/output ratio is a; employment is then $a.X$. The money wage is w, the product price is p and the rate of profit is r.[4] The demand for the single output is the sum of workers' consumer expenditure (which is given by $(1-s).w.a.X$), capitalists' consumer expenditure (which is $(1-t).r.p.K$) plus investment expenditure $(g.K)$, where s is the propensity to save out of wages, t the propensity to save out of profits and g is the growth rate. For simplicity, depreciation is ignored. With output adjusting to demand (which in effect assumes correct expectations on the part of producers) we have:

$$p.X = (1-s).w.a.X + (1-t).r.p.K + g.K \qquad (2.2)$$

The rate of profit and the real wage are linked via the accounting identity:

$$p = p.K.r/X + w.a \qquad (2.3)$$

These equations can be expressed in a scale-free form which also brings in the rate of capacity utilization as follows:

$$u/v = (1-s).(w/p).a.(u/v) + (1-t).r + g \qquad (2.2')$$

$$(w/p).a = (1 - v.r/u) \qquad (2.3')$$

The investment equation is put in growth form with investment influenced by the expected rate of growth, the rate of profit and the rate of capacity utilization relative to some target level u*, that is:

$$g = f(g^e, r, u/u^*) \qquad (2.4)$$

Equation (2.4) combines the influence of expected growth and capacity utilization (Eichner) with that of the rate of profit and capacity utilization (Kalecki and Steindl).

Taking account of the financing of investment expenditure yields:

$$g.p.K = t.r.p.K + E, \qquad (2.5)$$

where E is external finance. This equation can be rewritten as:

$$g = t.r + e \qquad (2.5')$$

where $e = E/p.K$. The price is set by firms according to:

$$p = (1+m).w.a \qquad (2.6)$$

with the mark-up (m) influenced by the degree of monopoly (d), the rate of capacity utilization and the growth rate. Thus:

$$m = m(d,u,g) \qquad (2.7)$$

Implicit in these equations are the requirements for the equality of savings and investment and of workers' savings with external finance. There are six equations in six unknowns: $e,g,m,r,u,w/p$.

We can use this model for three distinct purposes. First, the model incorporates, albeit in a very simple form, a theory of pricing and a theory of price determination. Equations (2.6) and (2.7) reflect the way in which prices are set. But prices also have to conform to the equilibrium requirements of the overall economic system. In effect, variables such as the level of capacity utilization and the growth rate vary until the mark-up established by firms in the light of the prevailing circumstances produces prices which conform to the system requirements. In particular, finance must be available to meet the investment requirements. The model is Kaleckian in spirit in that the level of capacity utilization is not constrained to be that of full capacity or some target level (a point to which we briefly return below).

Second, we are in a position to explore the predicted impact of the degree of monopoly and other exogenous factors on the endogenous variables. It is not possible to establish unambiguously the sign of the effects of a variation in the degree of monopoly, though the impact on capacity utilization, the growth rate and the rate of profit would be negative unless the partial derivative of the growth function with respect to capacity utilization is, in some sense, large. The inclusion of the effect of growth on the mark-up reinforces the likely negative effects. A positive relationship between capacity utilization and the mark-up operates in the same manner.

Third, the model can be used to illustrate some problems which arise in the post-Keynesian approaches to pricing and growth. There is no particular reason to think that the expected rate of growth and the target rate of capacity utilization will be achieved. This however does not seem to raise any particular difficulties in a Kaleckian approach. In the short run, expectations and intentions may well be frustrated. (In this model expectations over price and output are fulfilled, though output may not yield the target rate of capacity utilization.) For Kalecki, the long run is a sequence of short runs and over the course of time firms find that their long-run expectations and objectives are disappointed.

The investment requirements approach to pricing implies that expectations regarding growth and capacity utilization targets would, at least on average, be realized. There remains the question of how expectations about the growth rate are formed; and it may be reasonable to postulate that expectations are based on experience, so that expected growth rates converge on actual growth rates. However, the target rate of capacity utilization is based on considerations of cost and strategic advantage.

When the long-run is characterized by the fulfilment of growth expectations and the achievement of the target rate of capacity utilization, then the investment equation would simplify to $g = f(g,r,1)$ where the relationship between growth rate and the rate of profit is positive (provided that the derivative of f with respect to its first argument is less than unity). With expectations and targets achieved, there emerges a set of six equations which can in principle be solved for the six endogenous variables, although there is no guarantee that meaningful values for the variables would be obtained (for example, capacity utilization may be greater than full capacity). This set of equations could be viewed as indicating the value of real wages, rate of profit, and so on, required to sustain steady growth.

In this formulation, growth arises from the investment decisions of the enterprises, and there is no requirement that this growth rate coincides with any 'natural' rate of growth based on labour force growth and the pace of technical progress. The possibility of divergence between the growth rate established in this model and the 'natural' rate of growth clearly does not arise from an inflexibility of the real wage (which is an endogenous variable within the model). It would be possible to replace the investment equation (equation (2.4)) by the requirement that the growth rate equal the 'natural' rate (that is, $g = n$), and thereby to compute the real wage, the rate of profit, and so on compatible with growth at the 'natural' rate. Alternatively, we could build into the investment function the requirement that the growth of capital equipment is such as to ensure conformity with the 'natural' rate of growth, with enterprises ensuring that capacity utilization does not deviate (on average) from the target rate.

A second problem area arises from the implied equality between workers' savings and external finance, which has been achieved by treating the level of external finance as an endogenous variable. But in the investment requirements approach, external finance was a choice variable of the firms. It is, of course, the case that when workers save there must be external finance (unless the government operates a budget deficit to absorb workers' savings). One extension of the model sketched above would be to allow for the influence of interest rates on the external finance decision (and perhaps on workers' savings decisions); another, following Steindl, would be to take account of the influence of external finance and the gearing ratio on investment decisions.

CONCLUSION

In this chapter we have compared two approaches to pricing, and have pointed to some of the problems within each approach. The simple model constructed above reveals that these theories of pricing can be turned into theories of price determination, within which prices set by enterprises nevertheless conform to an overall equilibrium configuration of prices.

NOTES

1. I have benefited greatly from comments on an early draft by Philip Arestis, Amitava Dutt, Geoff Harcourt, Marc Lavoie, Fred Lee, Peter Reynolds, Nina Shapiro, Peter

Skott, Jan Toporowski and the editors. They have saved me from a number of errors of formulation and interpretation, though they will not all agree with the thrust of this paper.
2. Dutt (1988) presents such an approach; this has been extended in Sawyer (1990a, b) to encompass a variety of approaches to price setting.
3. The relationships between post-Keynesian theories of pricing including full-cost pricing and administered pricing are further discussed in Sawyer (1992).
4. Since there is only one product in this model, its price need not be explicitly mentioned in which case w would be treated as real product wage (rather than money wage). We retain p as product price to emphasize that firms set product price (as in equation (2.6)).

REFERENCES

Arestis, P. and Kitromilides, Y. (eds) (1989) *Theory and Policy in Political Economy*, Aldershot: Edward Elgar.

Baran, P. and Sweezy, P. (1966) *Monopoly Capital*, New York: Monthly Review Press.

Coutts, K., Godley, W. and Nordhaus, W. (1978) *Industrial Pricing in the United Kingdom*, Cambridge: Cambridge University Press.

Cowling, K. (1982) *Monopoly Capitalism*, London: Macmillan.

Cowling, K. and Waterson, M. (1976) 'Price Cost Margins and Market Structure', *Economica*, **43**, 267–74.

Dutt, A.K. (1988) 'Competition, Monopoly Power and the Prices of Production', *Thames Papers in Political Economy*, Autumn (reprinted in Arestis and Kitromilides, 1989).

Eichner, A.S. (1973) 'A Theory of the Determination of the Mark-up under Oligopoly', *Economic Journal*, **83**, 1184–1200 (reprinted in Sawyer 1988).

Eichner, A.S. (1987) *The Macrodynamics of Advanced Market Economies*, Armonk, NY: M.E. Sharpe.

Hall, R. and Hitch, C. (1939) 'Price Theory and Business Behaviour', *Oxford Economic Papers*, (2), 12–33 (reprinted in Sawyer 1988).

Harcourt, G.C. and Kenyon, P. (1976) 'Pricing and the Investment Decision', *Kyklos*, **29**, 49–77 (reprinted in Sawyer 1988).

Kalecki, M. (1971) *Selected Essays on the Dynamics of the Capitalist Economy*, Cambridge: Cambridge University Press.

Keynes, J.M. (1937) 'The General Theory of Employment, *Quarterly Journal of Economics*, **51**, 209–23.

Keynes, J.M. (1973) *The General Theory and After: Part II Defence and Development*, Collected works, vol. 14, London: Macmillan.

Keynes, J.M. (1983) *Economic Articles and Correspondence: Investment and Editorial*, Collected works, vol. 12, London: Macmillan.

Kriesler, P. (1987) *Kalecki's Microanalysis: The Development of Kalecki's Analysis of Pricing and Distribution*, Cambridge: Cambridge University Press.

Levine, D. (1981) *Economic Theory, vol II*, London: Routledge and Kegan Paul.

Means, G.C. (1936) 'Notes on Inflexible Prices', *American Economic Review*, **26**, Supplement, 23–35.

Reynolds, P. (1989) 'Kaleckian and Post-Keynesian Theories of Pricing: Some Extensions and Implications', in Arestis and Kitromilides (1989).

Sawyer, M. (1985) *The Economics of Michal Kalecki*, London: Macmillan.

Sawyer, M. (ed.) (1988) *Post Keynesian Economics*, Aldershot: Edward Elgar.

Sawyer, M. (1990a) 'On the Post Keynesian Tradition and Industrial Economics', *Review of Political Economy*, **2**, 43–68.

Sawyer, M. (1990b) 'Pricing, Prices and Growth: An Attempted Synthesis' mimeo, University of York.

Sawyer, M. (1992) 'On the Relationship between the Origins of Post Keynesian Pricing Theory and Macroeconomics' in P. Arestis and V. Chick (eds), *Recent Developments in Post Keynesian Economics* Aldershot: Edward Elgar.

Shapiro, N. (1981) 'Pricing and the Growth of the Firm', *Journal of Post Keynesian Economics*, **4**, 85–100.

Steindl, J. (1952) *Maturity and Stagnation in American Capitalism*, Oxford: Blackwell.

Wood, A. (1975) *A Theory of Profits*, Cambridge: Cambridge University Press.

3. Kaldor on Endogenous Money and Interest Rates

Marco Musella and Carlo Panico

This chapter deals with two related aspects of Kaldor's writings on endogenous money and interest rates. The first concerns the links between his work in the 1930s and 1950s and the subsequent polemic against monetarism. The second concerns the role of the horizontal money supply function in his analyses.

According to Desai (1989, p. 171), Kaldor's writings on monetarism contain no reference to his previous work. This view is held by other authors,[1] who claim that the notion of endogenous money was introduced by Kaldor in 1970 when he attributed a horizontal slope to the money supply curve. This horizontal money supply curve is widely considered to be *the* crucial feature of his position on endogeneity.[2] For Kaldor, it is claimed, the horizontal slope of the money supply is a necessary consequence of the way the monetary authorities and the banking system operate in a credit money economy, rather than a simplifying analytical device.

There is evidence, however, which raises doubts about this interpretation. In his later writings Kaldor stated (1986, p. 73) that he had introduced the notion of endogenous money as early as 1939. In addition, he claimed in his rejoinder to Friedman in 1970 that

> all the points I made in my paper in criticism of the 'Chicago School' were put forward by me in a succession of meetings at the Merrill Center in Southampton, Long Island, in 1958. These views were also implicit . . . in both my oral and written evidence to the Radcliffe Committee in 1958. (1970, p. 26, fn. 1)

This chapter reconsiders Kaldor's writings, denies the absence of links between his earlier and later work, challenges the usual interpretation of the role of the horizontal money supply, and claims that his analyses do not attribute a passive role to the monetary authorities and to the banking sector. The post-Keynesian literature is reviewed briefly, outlining two main positions on endogenous money. The first[3] does *not* consider the supply of money necessarily to be horizontal. The second[4] claims, instead, that in a credit money economy the monetary authorities and the banking sector are bound to accommodate *fully* the supply of money to the demand for it, thereby making the money supply *necessarily* horizontal. This is followed by a chronological analysis of Kaldor's monetary writings which underlines the elements of continuity between his earlier work in the 1930s and his better known contributions of the 1970s and 1980s. The concluding section draws some implications for the development of a 'conventional' theory of the interest rate, similar to the one proposed by Keynes in the *General Theory*, and for the analytical treatment of the money supply.

THE POST-KEYNESIAN LITERATURE

In the post-Keynesian literature there is considerable agreement on how the notion of an exogenous money supply should be criticized. According to Lavoie, this critique is based on four points. First of all, he observed,

> the existence of a credit multiplier, as a result of some exogenous control by the monetary authorities, does not necessarily imply a causality running from high powered money to money stock ... Secondly, post Keynesians argue that central banks generally prefer to accommodate the needs of commercial banks. Thirdly, even if central banks attempt to control the stock of money, they can do so only through the level of interest rates. Finally, post Keynesian theory claims that it can be done only at the cost of disrupting financial markets. (Lavoie, 1984, p. 776–7).

While this critique is largely accepted, there are amongst post-Keynesian authors different views on how endogenous money ought to be characterized. In what follows, for a convenient comparison with Kaldor's analyses, these views will be grouped, at the risk of severe simplification, into two main positions.

The first is characterized by the fact that money, defined in the broad or broadest sense,[5] is 'credit driven'; that is, increases in its supply are the consequence of banks' decisions to extend their loans beyond the limits previously set by their reserves.[6] The supply of money becomes endogenous when the financial system reaches the stage of institutional development at which banks can accommodate safely the demand for their loans, owing to the role of lender of last resort played by the central bank (cf. Chick, 1986).

Those who accept this position reject both the orthodox thesis that considers the supply of money to be *fully controlled* by the central bank, and the extreme position that the supply of money is *fully determined* by the demand for it. According to these authors, the monetary authorities can control monetary aggregates to some extent. However, to fulfil their institutional tasks, they tend to accommodate the supply of monetary base to the demand for it, avoiding large fluctuations of the interest rates.[7] Such fluctuations would increase financial instability, disrupt the efficiency of the markets, cause dramatic falls in production and employment (cf. Davidson and Weintraub, 1973; Weintraub, 1978a and 1978b), and induce financial innovation, which might imperil the authorities' control over these markets (cf. Minsky, 1957, pp. 182–4 and S.C. Dow, 1988, pp. 29–32).

The use of moderate interest rates fluctuations for policy purposes is recognized by these authors[8], and the supply of money is thus conceived as an increasing function of the interest rate, the elasticity of which is high, but not necessarily infinite:

> The money supply is endogenous to a marked degree without being perfectly so. Demand does create, to a greater or lesser extent, but never entirely so its own supply! The degree to which the supply of money is positively sloped depends on the discretionary policy of the Federal Reserve. (Rousseas, 1989, p. 478)[9]

For some of these authors (cf. Chick, 1986, p. 116) a horizontal money supply can be accepted as a polarized description of the working of the financial system or as a simplifying analytical device to be opposed to the similarly simplified notion of a vertical money supply. The horizontal slope of the money supply curve, in any case, does not characterize its endogeneity.

According to the second position,[10] the supply of money, again in the broad or broadest sense, is not only 'credit driven' but also *fully* determined by the demand for it. This is due to the assumption that for the individual banks the supply of loans is a 'non-discretionary variable' (Moore, 1988a, p. 373), while the monetary authorities are bound to accommodate fully the supply of monetary base to the demand for it. In modern financial systems banks cannot modify, on their own initiative, the volume of outstanding loans. The latter is varied unilaterally by the borrowers, owing to the existence of overdraft facilities.[11] It does not depend on a discretionary choice of the banking sector, which is seen as 'price setter' and 'quantity taker'.

Central banks, on the other hand, have no ability to reduce the monetary base. They can only increase it to support an expansion of bank intermediation (cf. Moore, 1988b, p. 17; 1988c, p. 87). This asymmetry is explained by the fact that in periods of expansion, when the central bank may wish to constrain the monetary base, 'commercial banks . . . have allocated most of their earning asset portfolios to customer loans' (Moore,

1988c, p. 16) and can consequently find it difficult to reduce their reserves. The sale of securities by the central bank will thus drive the banks to the discount window. As a consequence, a policy aimed at constraining deposits through the reduction of reserves cannot succeed (cf. Moore, 1988c, pp. 94–5; Arestis, 1988, p. 43).

According to this position, then, the endogeneity of the money supply depends on the 'non-discretionary' character of the bank loans as well as on the ability of the central banks to control the interest rate rather than the monetary base. Analytically, this means that the supply of money either coincides with the demand for it or is infinitely elastic with respect to the interest rate.[12] Indeed, the horizontal trend of the money supply characterizes endogeneity. In an analysis of a credit money economy, this trend of the money supply is a 'logical necessity' rather than an approximate description of the behaviour of central banks and of the banking sector (cf. Moore, 1988b, p. xi). This characterization of the endogeneity of the money supply, however, is not a correct account of Kaldor's position.

KALDOR IN THE 1930s

When Kaldor first presented his analysis of the money supply in 1939, in a paper on the term-structure of interest rates, his aim was to generalize the theory of interest and money presented by Keynes in the *General Theory*, by taking account of the existence of financial assets and interest rates of different maturity. In the *General Theory*, Keynes assumed away the existence of financial assets of different maturity and thereby 'invented some short-cuts through the maze of complications of a multi-market analysis and . . . reduced the essential aspects of the problem to manageable dimensions. [This invention] was the short-cut of a genius' (Kaldor, 1960, pp. 3–4). These short cuts, however, exposed Keynes's theory to Robertson's 'bootstraps' critique and led to the false conclusion that the long-term interest rate is equal to the risk premium associated with the changes of value of these assets in terms of money. Kaldor tried to present, instead, an explanation of the short-term interest rate that, by being independent of the expectations of future interest rates, was not subject to Robertson's critique. In his analysis, moreover, the risk premium associated with changes in the value of financial assets in terms of money influences only the difference between the long- and the short-term rates.

The analysis began from the evaluation of the total benefit enjoyed by the holder of these assets. This benefit[13] is composed of an interest rate, $r \geq 0$, and a 'convenience yield', $q \geq 0$, expressed in percentage terms and reflecting the non-monetary advantages associated with the transferability of that asset. The expected value, $E(a)$, of the gain or loss that can be made on changes in the market value of the asset is also part of the total benefit. It can be greater, equal to or less than zero, and is calculated on the basis of a probability distribution of the future values of a, the gain or loss being expressed in percentage terms. Finally, to compensate for the risk of financial loss incurred by holding that asset, a risk premium, $s \geq 0$, calculated in percentage terms, must be considered as part of the total benefit. In calculating $E(a)$ and s, Kaldor anticipated some elements of the analysis of Markowitz (1952) and Tobin (1958). He claimed (Kaldor, 1939, p. 5) that the risk premium varies directly with the size of commitments and with the standard deviation of the probability distribution of the future market values of the asset, adding subsequently that it also depends upon 'the individual psychological propensities to bear risks' (Kaldor, 1960, p. 28).

The total benefit given by each asset to its holder is thus equal to $[r + q + E(a) - s]$, the sum maximized by financial operators when they decide upon the composition of their portfolio. Its role in the determination of the term structure of interest rates can be described by supposing a simplified monetary system in which the non-banking public can hold positive amounts of three financial assets: money, short-term and long-term financial investments of perfect security.

Money, defined as central bank money held by the non-banking public plus current deposits with clearing banks, yields no interest. It has, however, a positive 'convenience yield', q_1, since it is accepted as a proper medium for discharging debts.[14] For the money holder, this yield is directly related to the amount of transactions that he has to carry out and is inversely related to the amount of money available to him, owing to the fact that this asset is only demanded for transaction purposes. The expected gain or loss, $E(a_1)$, and the risk premium, s_1, are both equal to zero, as there can be no uncertainty about the future value of this asset in terms of itself.

Short-term financial investments of perfect security include saving deposits and short-term paper of all kinds. Kaldor grouped together these close substitutes for money, and made the simplifying assumptions that they all yield the same interest rate, r_2, and that $E(a_2) = 0$ since it is always possible to convert these assets in money at the same value by paying a fee.[15] Yet, although these assets give nearly the same advantages that money does as means of payment and store of value, their convenience yield, q_2, is smaller than q_1, while, owing to the risk of having to pay a fee, their risk premium, s_2, is positive. For the sake of simplicity, however, he assumed that q_2 is equal to zero and that given the short maturity of these

Table 3.1   Benefits of financial assets

	r	q	$E(a)$	s	Total benefit
Money	0	q_1	0	0	q_1
Short-term assets	r_2	0	0	0	r_2
Long-term assets	r_3	0	$E(a_3)$	s_3	$r_3 + E(a_3) - s_3$

assets and the small amount of the fee s_2 is so small as to make it insignificant.[16]

Long-term financial assets pay a positive interest rate, r_3, and a convenience yield, q_3, which Kaldor assumed to be zero. The holder of these assets must furthermore take into account the possibility of an expected gain or loss, $E(a_3)$, and of a compensating risk premium, s_3. Table 3.1 sums up the benefits of the three assets.

The preference for the asset with the highest total benefit, together with the inverse relationships between q_1 and the amount of money held, and between s_3 and the amount of long-term financial paper held, generates a tendency toward the equilibrium of all benefits. The maximization of these benefits furthermore, leads each agent to extend the holding of money up to the point where $r_2 = q_1$. As a consequence, according to Kaldor, the demand for money for each agent and for the whole economy does not depend on the future value of interest rates. It is related directly to the level of income in nominal terms, Y, and inversely to the short-term interest rate.

According to Kaldor the supply of money on the other hand, is related only to the short-term interest rate. The former is an increasing and highly elastic function of the latter. The high elasticity assumption makes the money supply endogenous. It implies that the monetary authorities are able to fix a specific level for the short-term interest rate, allowing it limited variations. In dealing with the supply of money, Kaldor made use of the deposit multiplier identity[17] and described the behaviour of the monetary authorities by referring to their 'power ... to determine the [short-term] rate (by varying the quantity of money)' (Kaldor, 1939, p. 26; cf. also pp. 14 and 15, n. 4).

He finally made clear that the validity of the high elasticity assumption depends on the way the monetary authorities define their priorities among conflicting policy objectives. However, there may be a tension between the two policy objectives identified by Kaldor in 1939:

> The monetary authorities are not free to vary the short-term rate as they like; if they want to maintain activity at a satisfactory level, they must keep the mean

level of the short-term rate sufficiently low so as to secure a long-term rate which permits a sufficient amount of long-term investment. Alternatively, if they want to secure stability by means of monetary policy, they must allow the average level of employment to fall to a low enough level to permit the mean level of the short-term rate to be sufficiently high. Thus the two main aims of monetary policy, to secure a satisfactory level of incomes, and to secure stability of incomes, may prove incompatible: the one may only be achieved by sacrificing the other. (Kaldor, 1939, p. 27)

The endogeneity of the money supply thus depended on the way the monetary authorities solve the conflicts between alternative policy objectives. In 1939, Kaldor considered the high elasticity assumption to be appropriate since, in his opinion, the monetary authorities would choose to stabilize the interest rate at low levels. Hence the bank rate mechanism as an instrument of economic policy was expected 'to become increasingly ineffectual' (Kaldor, 1939, p. 27).

On the basis of these assumptions, Kaldor (1939, p. 14) presented an explanation of the short-term interest rate, which depended on the nominal level of income. This was accomplished by means of a diagram describing, for a given level of the money income, the supply of and demand for money as functions of this rate (see Figure 3.1). This analysis showed that Keynes's liquidity preference analysis holds 'if under "rate of interest" is meant the short rate of interest, and under "money" . . . bank notes and current deposits' (Kaldor, 1939, p. 15).

The same explanation can be presented with a set of simultaneous equations in which it is assumed, to avoid unnecessary complications, that the non-banking public uses only deposits for their transactions. The deposit multiplier is consequently expressed in a simplified form which does not include the notes–deposits ratio.

$$M^s = M^d \tag{3.1}$$

$$M^d = M^d(Y, r_2) \tag{3.2}$$

$$M^s = BM\frac{1}{b} \tag{3.3}$$

$$BM = BM(r_2) \tag{3.4}$$

$$b = b(r_2) \tag{3.5}$$

where M^s is the supply of money, M^d is the demand for money, Y is the level of income in monetary terms (assumed to be given), BM is the monetary base, and b is the reserve ratio of the banks. In equations 3.1–

Figure 3.1   Money supply and demand as a function of the interest rate

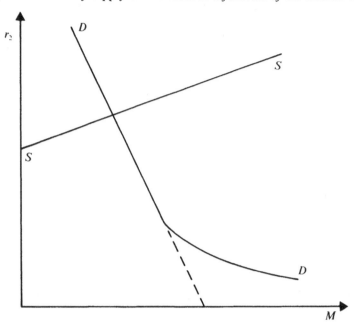

3.5, the supply of money is a function only of the short-term rate, which in turn is determined independently of expectations of the future values of interest rates.[18] The validity of these equations is limited, however, by their failure to point out that the rate of interest on bank loans, r_c, also influences the decisions made by banks regarding their reserve ratio, and thus the supply of money.

To take into account the influence of r_c on the reserve ratio of the banks and on the supply of money, equations 3.1–3.5 are reformulated below. To remain as close as possible[19] to Kaldor's conclusion that the determination of the short-term interest rate is independent of expectations of future values of interest rates, it is assumed that banks do not invest in bonds,[20] that bonds are only issued by the government and that non-banking private agents can only be financed through bank loans of the same maturity.

$$M^s = M^d \qquad (3.6)$$

$$M^d = M^d(Y, r_2) \qquad (3.7)$$

$$M^s = BM\frac{1}{b} \qquad (3.8)$$

$$BM = BM(r_2) \tag{3.9}$$

$$b = b(r_2, r_c, Y) \tag{3.10}$$

$$(1 - b)M^s = L^d(Y, r_c) \tag{3.11}$$

Here equation 3.10 models the banking system reserve ratio (b) as a function not only of r_2, but also of r_c and Y, on the supposition that individual banks set their reserve ratio on the basis of a profit maximization rule.[21] In equation 3.11, $L^d(Y, r_c)$ is the demand for bank loans as a function of Y and r_c. Equations 3.6–3.11 allow the determination of six unknowns: M^s, M^d, r_2, r_c, BM, b. As a matter of fact, they define a relationship between Y and r_2, similar to the LM curve of the Keynesian tradition. In equations 3.6–3.11, the assumption of an endogenous money supply does not imply a horizontal supply curve. Endogeneity is thus compatible with non-fully accommodating behaviour of the monetary authorities and with a profit-maximizing banking sector, which, under certain conditions, tends to adjust the supply of loans to the demand for them,[22] by varying the reserve ratio during the trade cycle. The latter thus turns out to be unstable with respect to the interest rates.

The fact that the supplies of money and of monetary base are non-horizontal did not prevent Kaldor from stating that the level of the short-term interest rate is set by the monetary authorities. A horizontal money supply curve *can* be introduced in his analysis by assuming either that the supply of monetary base is horizontal (that is, equation 3.9 is replaced by one stating that r_2 is given) or that the supply of bank loans is a non-discretionary variable for the banking firm (that is, equation 3.10 is replaced by one stating that r_2 is given). Simultaneous adoption of a horizontal supply of monetary base and of a non-discretionary supply of banks loans cannot however, be allowed, since this would make both models 3.1–3.5 and 3.6–3.11 indeterminate. The introduction of a horizontal money supply does not modify the substance of Kaldor's conclusion on the determination of the short-term interest rate. It does not modify his analysis of the behaviour of the monetary authorities nor of the banking sector, if it is presented as a simplifying device that gives an approximate description of the way these agents operate.

It will be noticed that in equations 3.6–3.11 the narrow definition of money used in 1939 can be replaced by a broad one,[23] if this is considered convenient for the high degree of substitution among financial assets brought about by the institutional development of the financial system. In this case, however, it would be even more difficult to disregard the influence of the whole structure of interest rates on the demand for and the supply of money, as Kaldor proposed.

KALDOR IN THE 1950s

Twenty years later, Kaldor returned to monetary issues in a group of papers related to the Radcliffe Report (Kaldor, 1964) and in a collection of essays on growth and stability (1960). In these papers he did not to any significant degree change his view either on the money supply or on interest rates. His previous analysis was presented again with some modifications in the description of the behaviour of the monetary authorities and in the treatment of the demand function for money.

> The main point on which I have modified my views since 1939 concerns the demand function for cash balances . . . I would not now regard the desire to hold cash balances as a single-valued function of the level of money income . . . and of the short-rate of interest . . . but would say that, in addition, the desire to hold cash will vary with the amount of 'money substitutes' available (e.g. bills, savings deposits of all kinds, and other forms of short-term paper). (Kaldor, 1960, p. 5)

This change in the treatment of the demand function for money was induced by his observation of the stimulative effects of the restrictive monetary policy of the mid 1950s on financial innovation.[24] The effects of this policy on the velocity of circulation of money, defined again in a narrow sense (cf. 1960, pp. 62–3), were recalled to criticize the views of the quantity theorists.

> In the U.K. there has been a spectacular rise in the velocity of circulation, particularly since 1955, which fully compensated for the failure of the money supply to expand *pari passu* with the rise in prices and in money incomes . . . It could not be seriously maintained that this change in the velocity of circulation was in any sense an *independent* phenomenon which happened to coincide in time with the change in monetary policy. It was simply a reflection of this policy: if the supply of money had not been restricted the increase in the velocity of circulation would not have taken place . . . Those who maintain the opposite view (the adherents of the quantity theory of money) argue that the social and institutional factors which determine the frequency of recurring payments of various kinds . . . together with the uncertainty concerning the exact timing of these payments leads to individuals and businesses having a certain 'desired' cash balance in relation to turnover which is independent of the supply of money. (1964, pp. 129–30)

The modification in the analysis of the demand for money implied no change in that of the money supply, whose endogeneity was still related to its high elasticity with respect to the short-term interest rate:

> In a modern community it is best to regard the short rate of interest . . . (rather than the quantity of money) as being fixed by the policy of the monetary

authorities (as was implied by the [upward] slope of the [money] supply curve in [Figure 3.1] above) and the quantity of currency in circulation as being determined by the demand for cash balances by the public. (1960, p. 64)

This passage confirms that for Kaldor the high elasticity assumption implied that the short-term interest rate is determined by the monetary authorities. The quantity of money in circulation is determined, instead, by the demand for it.

Kaldor presented a more extensive treatment of the high elasticity assumption in his Memorandum to the Radcliffe Committee. Although his analysis was still developed in terms of conflicting policy objectives, stressing that the bank rate mechanism requires 'sufficient elbow room' (Kaldor, 1958, p. 135), that is high interest rates, in order to be effective, the efficacy of this mechanism was considered in greater detail, adding new arguments to show that its full adoption was not convenient for the authorities.

Changes in the short-term rate, Kaldor argued, prove very effective when disequilibria in the balance of payments are to be corrected. In the majority of cases variations in this rate promptly eliminate these imbalances. It is thus convenient for the monetary authorities to allow some variability of this rate to favour the external stability of the currency (cf. Kaldor, 1964, p. 135). The bank rate mechanism proves less effective, however, as far as domestic objectives are concerned. It can be used to influence the holding of stocks of materials and finished goods. Variations in inventories, that for Kaldor depend mainly on the expectations of price changes in the international markets, are likely to be little influenced however, by changes in interest rates.[25] From the point of view of policy instruments, the best that the monetary authorities can do is to develop 'an international buffer stock scheme . . . Failing this, monetary policy can and should be used to moderate these fluctuations though one cannot feel entirely confident of the promptness and efficacy with which it can be made to operate' (Kaldor, 1964, p. 151).

The effects on investment in fixed capital are not favourable either. Kaldor did not deny that increases in interest rates are ultimately effective in curbing capital expenditure. Yet, he contended that *small* variations in the short rate cannot significantly influence the long-term rate, which is the one that is relevant for investment decisions in fixed capital. Furthermore, he argued, moderate changes in the long-term rate may have no appreciable effect on investment decisions (cf. Kaldor 1964, pp. 132–5).

At the time of the Radcliffe Report, Kaldor thus confirmed his 1939 view that the use of monetary policy to stabilize demand requires large variations in interest rates. These, however, are not convenient because they make it difficult for the monetary authorities to achieve three other 'highly desirable' policy objectives: smooth funding of the government debt; smooth working of financial markets; and high and stable long-run rates of economic growth. The problems caused by drastic changes in interest rates for the funding of the government debt were one major motive advanced for the reluctance of the authorities to allow large variations in these rates (cf. Kaldor, 1964, pp. 135–6). Drastic and rapid changes in interest rates would also result in a high degree of instability in bond prices and in the capital market. This weakens those financial institutions whose reserves are usually held in 'large blocks of bonds of reasonably stable value' (Kaldor, 1964, p. 159), and makes more speculative and less efficient the working of the capital market (cf. Kaldor, 1958, p. 136). Other undesirable consequences for the long-period development of the economy were described by Kaldor in two steps. First, he pointed out that vast and rapid fluctuations in bond prices increase the risk premia associated with the holding of these assets, widening the average differential between the long- and the short-term interest rates (cf. Kaldor, 1960, p. 66).

> The speculative risk involved in long-term loans of any kind would be very much greater than they are now, and the average price that the investors would demand for parting with liquidity would be considerably higher . . . Those who argue in favour of credit policy as the main economic stabiliser frequently overlook the fact that the increased instability of interest rates which is a necessary precondition for the effective use of monetary policy as an economic regulator can be bought at the cost of making the *average* level of long-term interest rates higher than it would be if the interest rates were relatively stable. (Kaldor, 1964, pp. 136–7)

Second, Kaldor noted the effects of higher *average* interest rates on the rate of profit, whose level is also related, in the post-Keynesian theory of growth and distribution, to the ratio between the rate of growth and the proportion of profit saved.

> Since average rates of interest are bound to be considerably higher, the rate of profit required to make investment attractive in the long run would also have to be higher; to achieve this effect Government policies would have to aim at stimulating consumption at the same time as they restrain investment. By the force of circumstances rather than by design, a government relying on credit control for combating inflationary tendencies would be bound to stimulate consumption rather than investment in times of inadequate demand . . . and would thus gradually transform the economy into one of high consumption and low investment – with all the undesirable consequences on long-run rates of economic growth. (Kaldor, 1964, pp. 136–7)

According to Kaldor then, previous experience and economic considerations *should* lead the monetary authorities to avoid drastic changes in interest rates. On the basis of his previous analysis, this is presented as the only choice that the authorities can make if they want to avoid violent financial instability and the other 'undesirable consequences' described above. If they follow this line, the assumption of a high elasticity of the money supply, which makes it endogenous without eliminating the possibility of using moderate fluctuations of the interest rate for policy purposes, becomes adequate to describe their behaviour.

This examination of Kaldor's early writings on money thus throws some new light on his conception of the money supply by underlining the important role played by the analysis of the behaviour of the monetary authorities. This analysis, together with that relative to the behaviour of the banking sector, was intended to justify the view that the short-term interest rate can undergo limited variations around a level decided by the monetary authorities, while 'the quantity of currency in circulation [is] determined by the demand for cash balances by the public' (Kaldor, 1960, p. 64).

KALDOR'S WORK IN THE 1970s

In 1970, Kaldor published his first paper against monetarism. His aim was to undermine the growing popularity of this school by weakening Friedman's assertion, based on empirical findings, that the demand function for money and the velocity of circulation are stable. To facilitate the discussion of Friedman's position, Kaldor introduced some new analytical elements and dealt only briefly with the problems analysed in his previous work. These new elements, however, did not change in any important way his view that endogeneity is related to the decision of the monetary authorities to avoid large fluctuations in the interest rates.

To challenge Friedman's arguments, Kaldor adopted his broad definition of money which includes 'cash plus clearing bank deposits (both current and deposit accounts) in the hands of the public' (Kaldor, 1970, p. 11, fn. 1), though he did not fully appreciate the problems introduced by this definition. By adopting a narrow definition of money Kaldor had been able, in previous work, to draw a clear-cut distinction between this asset, operating as a means of payment, and the other financial assets, performing the function of store of value. This distinction could not easily be drawn with the new definition, a problem that was mentioned only in subsequent work. In addition, he assumed that the demand for broad money was a decreasing function of the short-term interest rate, as had been the demand for narrow money in previous work, without realizing that unlike the latter, the demand function for broad money is increasing with respect to this rate. Finally, to show that 'international comparisons throw the strongest possible doubt on the Friedman postulate of a stable demand function for money' (Kaldor, 1970, p. 27), he recalled the statistics presented in the memorandum submitted to the Radcliffe Committee, which referred to the velocity of circulation of money, defined in the narrow sense.

No doubts on the stability of the demand function for money were emphasized in 1970. On the contrary, the possibility of a stable function was admitted as a normal occurrence (cf. 1970, p. 8). As long as the monetary authorities provide 'enough money of the accustomed kind to discourage the growth of new kinds' (1970, p. 10), the velocity of circulation and the demand for money function are likely to remain stable. The existence of an accommodating policy and of an endogenous money supply stabilizes financial markets as well as the demand for money.

> Friedman's main contention is that the velocity of circulation, in terms of conventional money, has been relatively stable. That may well be, but only because, in the historical periods observed, the supply of money was unstable. In other words, in one way or another, an increased demand for money evoked an increase in supply. (Kaldor, 1970, p. 11)

The reasons proposed to justify the existence of a supply of money which accommodates itself to changes in the demand represent the major element of continuity with his previous writings. The central point again was the fact that it is not convenient for the authorities to allow large fluctuations of the interest rates, which create 'violent instability in the financial markets' (1970, p. 11, fn. 2) and prevent the achievement of the aforementioned 'highly desirable' policy objectives (cf. 1970, pp. 11 and 16).

With respect to his previous writings, Kaldor presented one new argument to explain the reluctance of the monetary authorities to accept large fluctuations of the interest rates. This was related to the fact that in a credit money economy new means of payment can be easily created by providing loans of any kind to creditworthy people. If the monetary authorities do not provide enough money of the most accepted kind, 'a complete surrogate money-system and payment-system would be established, which would exist side by side with the official money' (Kaldor, 1970, p. 10). This occurrence is regarded as highly undesirable by the monetary authorities, since it would endanger the centrality of their position in the financial system, which depends on their ability to act *with effectiveness* on account of the whole community.[26]

> More fundamentally (and semi-consciously rather than in full awareness) it may have sprung from the realisation of the monetary authorities, be it the Federal Reserve or the Bank of England, that they are in the position of a

constitutional monarch: with very wide reserve power on paper, the maintenance and continuance of which are greatly dependent on the degree of restraint and moderation shown in their exercise. The Bank of England, by virtue of successive Acts of Parliament, has a monopoly of the note issue, at least in England and Wales. But the real power conferred by these Acts depended, and still depends, on maintaining the central role of the note issue in the general monetary and credit system; and this, in turn, was not a matter of legal powers, but of the avoidance of policies which would have led to the erosion of this role. (Kaldor, 1970, p. 12)

As in previous work, then, the authorities' decision to avoid drastic changes in the interest rates was at the basis of the existence of an endogenous money supply, though the possibility of using modest variations in the interest rate as a policy instrument were not denied (cf. Kaldor, 1970, pp. 10–11). Besides, in 1970 the supply of money was dealt with by referring to the deposit multiplier identity.[27] Kaldor denied the monetarist view that banks, being always 'loaned up', are not able to extend their loans beyond the limits previously set by their reserves, and he pointed out that Friedman's data indicate some stability of the deposit multiplier. Yet they do not allow one to regard changes in the monetary base and in the money supply as equivalent. 'While the correlation between the "monetary base" . . . and the "supply of money" was good in general, it was not sufficiently good to be able to regard changes in the one as being the equivalent of changes in the other' (Kaldor 1970, p. 15). To explain these results, Kaldor pointed out that the limited variability of the banks' reserve ratio can be due to the authorities' decision to make the monetary base endogenous.[28] 'If variations in the money supply were closely related to changes in the "monetary base", this is mainly because the latter has also been endogenous, as well as the former' (Kaldor, 1970, p. 16).

In 1970 Kaldor also made reference to some features of the money creation process often recalled in his subsequent work. Dealing with the links between financial innovations and restrictive policies, he noted that in a credit-money economy the creation of new means of payment can only be limited by the availability of creditworthy people. In criticizing the monetarist assertion that an excess supply of money would result in higher inflation, he pointed out that 'those who hold that an "excess supply" of money under these circumstances would *directly* increase spending forget that, barring helicopters, etc., the "excess supply" could never materialise' (1970, pp. 11–12, fn. 2). He thus referred to the fact, noticed already in previous work,[29] that the quantity of money *actually* in circulation is determined by the demand for it. This reference does not deny the validity of his previous determination of the short-term interest rate, but emphasizes the fact that movements along the supply curve can occur only if the demand curve shifts too and that the *actual* amount of money in circulation at a given interest rate can differ from the amount *desired* by the monetary authorities, but not from the amount *desired* by the public for transaction or other purposes.

KALDOR'S WRITINGS IN THE 1980s

Ten years later, Kaldor returned to the critique of monetarism with a group of papers in which he tried to refute the view that an excess supply of money, which is always due to a choice by the monetary authorities,[30] is the cause of larger spending and price inflation. It was in these writings that he introduced a horizontal money supply curve, referring to it so frequently as to lead some authors to consider it *the* crucial feature of his position on endogenous money. This interpretation, which finds apparent support in Kaldor's presentation of the working of a credit money economy, largely disregards however, the content of his earlier writings. It thus fails to notice the existence of evidence suggesting some continuity with his previous work and the possibility of interpreting the horizontal trend of the money supply as a simplification. This evidence shows that, in Kaldor's post-1980 writings also, the authorities' decision to avoid large fluctuations in interest rates is relevant for the endogeneity of the money supply. It also shows that Kaldor never stated that the supply of bank loans is a non-discretionary variable for the individual bank. Furthermore it is possible to argue that his reference to the working of a credit money economy does not imply the non-discretionary character of this variable, but underscores the ability of the banks to vary their reserve ratio during the trade cycle and the weakness of the monetarist policy based on the control of the money supply.

The links with previous work can be found in different parts of Kaldor's papers. His treatment of the definition of money can be considered, as he himself seems to suggest, to be a further development of the analysis he initiated at the time of the Radcliffe Report.[31] It further specifies how financial innovation increases the arbitrariness of the distinction between changes in the quantity of money and changes in the velocity of circulation[32] and reduces the possibility of using the control of the money supply as an anti-inflationary measure. The development of the financial system, Kaldor noted, increases the degree of substitution between current deposits and other financial assets. Saving deposits with clearing banks and with other deposit-taking institutions can be more easily converted into legal tender, while it is possible to observe a large growth of financial assets, called by Kaldor 'potential' or 'hidden money', which are not reflected in the statistics and can be transformed easily into cash at any time.

Under these conditions, he concluded, 'any *broad* definition of the money supply is ... arbitrary since it is invariably surrounded by a spectrum of liquid assets which are not comprised in it but which are close substitutes to it' (Kaldor 1980, pp. 295–6). On the other hand, a narrow definition, which excludes saving deposits of any kind and other financial assets easily convertible into legal tender, 'is not an appropriate control variable for the monetary authorities' (Kaldor and Trevithick, 1981, p. 12), and 'is pretty meaningless for policy purposes' (Kaldor, 1980, p. 295). Yet, it can be appropriate in theoretical work, since some aspects of monetary analysis can be 'best seen if the concept of money is restricted to its original meaning of media of payments or circulating media' (Kaldor 1981a, p. 20, fn. 1).

Kaldor showed (1980, pp. 297–8; 1982, pp. 15, 50 and 75–6) that the demand function for narrow money, unlike that for broad money, is inversely related to the short-term interest rate. He further pointed out, giving a sign that his previous work was still in the background of his analysis, that the elasticity of this function is relevant to the determination of the extent to which the authorities are bound to modify this rate if they want to constrain the money supply.[33] Finally, he stated that Keynes's 'liquidity-preference theory only applied to non-interest bearing deposits' (Kaldor, 1980, p. 296). This conclusion, already reached in 1939, also indicates without ambiguity the existence of close links with his previous writings.

A similar conclusion can be drawn from his treatment of the supply of money, which is based on the deposit–multiplier identity[34] and attributes a central role to an analysis of the behaviour of the monetary authorities which resembles that of previous years. The power of the monetary authorities to control the supply of money 'is severely circumscribed' by the desire to ensure the working of the financial system:

'A monetary system based on credit money can function only so long as the central bank is willing to ensure that the credit pyramid remains in being; i.e., that the major financial institutions which provide the bulk of bank deposits are not exposed to the risk of being unable to pay cash to depositors owing to their illiquidity'. (Kaldor and Trevithick, 1981, p. 7)

Although they rarely admit it publicly, as Kaldor (1985, p. 10) observed, monetary authorities attribute to the stability of financial institutions the highest priority among their policy objectives. They tend to privilege this objective if it happens to be in conflict with others. The performance of this function, however, does not imply *fully* accommodating behaviour on the part of the central bank. It only 'sets ceilings to the extent to which short-term interest can be allowed to rise' (1981a, p. 18) and to the ability of the central bank to refuse to re-discount eligible bills.

> The Central Bank's function of lender of last resort . . . makes it impossible for the Central Bank to *set rigid limits* to the amount of cash which it is willing to put at the disposal of commercial banks through re-discount. The discount window cannot be closed. (Kaldor, 1981b, p. 456; italics added)

Indeed, the possibility of using *moderate* fluctuations of the interest rate as a policy instrument was explicitly recognized and recommended. As he had done in 1958, Kaldor stated that moderate fluctuations of this rate prove effective in maintaining the equilibrium of the balance of payments and have represented, until the monetarist experiment, the core of monetary policy (Kaldor 1985, pp. 10–12).[35] The use of moderate fluctuations of interest rates to achieve domestic objectives was also recognized (cf. 1982, p. 24). This measure, traditionally applied by the central banks, has been supplemented on several occasions by quantitative controls (cf. 1982, p. 6).

A policy aiming at controlling bank credit was considered 'necessary to prevent an undue expansion of credit to the private sector, particularly for speculative purposes or for consumer credit' (Kaldor, 1980, p. 315; and 1982, pp. 106–7).[36] Yet it is difficult to implement since, as he had noticed at the time of the Radcliffe Report, moderate fluctuations of the interest rate have little effect and quantitative controls can cause undesired forms of innovation and 'diffuse difficulty of borrowing' (Kaldor, 1980, p. 313 and 1982, p. 104). These imperfect instruments are nevertheless preferable to the monetarist attempt to regulate monetary aggregates through large fluctuations of the interest rate,[37] an attempt which, as Kaldor noted, 'has not been a happy one . . . [It] has been a foolish and unimaginative innovation which is bound to be abandoned sooner or later' (Kaldor, 1980, p. 315, and 1982, p. 106). The authorities, he concluded, must rely on these imperfect instruments if they want to avoid situations similar to that which occurred in England in the early 1970s when the 'inflation of bank credit . . . led to a rapid expansion of interest bearing liabilities of the banks, and of credit extended to customers for speculative purposes, which created a rapid and unhealthy boom in the property market' (Kaldor, 1980, p. 314; and 1982, p. 105).[38]

Thus, in the 1980s too, Kaldor presented an analysis of the behaviour of the monetary authorities which identifies the desire to avoid large fluctuations of the interest rate as the main reason for their 'inability' to control the money supply and the main determinant of their decision to stabilize the interest rates around a specific level, making the money supply endogenous. As in previous work, he recommended the use of moderate fluctuations of the interest rate for external and domestic purposes, claiming that 'this policy is perfectly compatible with the money supply being a passive element varying automatically with the demand for credit (or with the availability of credit-worthy borrowers)' (Kaldor, 1981b, p. 456; cf. also 1984, p. 13).

In his analysis of the behaviour of the banking sector, on the other hand, Kaldor never stated that the supply of bank loans is non-discretionary for the individual bank. This analysis, which is scattered sparsely throughout his writings, is less clear cut than that relating to the behaviour of the monetary authorities and has therefore led to different interpretations. In spite of that, its content suggests that banks determine the composition of their balance-sheets on the basis of a criterion grounded in the evaluation of the risk of lending. It also suggests that the variability of the bank reserve ratio depends on the application of this criterion.

In line with his statements of previous years, Kaldor maintained that the bank reserve ratio, although varying, is not highly unstable in the face of an accommodating monetary policy.

> The monetarist school point[s] to empirical investigations which show that over a given period the rates of growth of the various forms of money tend to be highly similar . . . All this may be true when no attempt is made to control the supply of money. (Kaldor and Trevithick, 1981, p. 12)

Nonetheless, a modern banking system 'is prepared to accommodate the public's changing demand between different types of financial assets' (Kaldor, 1982, p. 14) and therefore exhibits a remarkable flexibility to changes in financial markets. This flexibility is due to the institutional arrangements that allow the banks easily to adjust their reserves, either through the re-discount of eligible bills with the central bank or through operations in the secondary money market. The possibility of adjusting the reserves influences the behaviour of banks in several ways. It permits them to keep prudential reserves at a low level (cf. 1980, pp. 296 and fn. and 315 fn.; and 1982, pp. 47, 73 and fn., and 106 fn.) and to grant overdraft facilities to their customers. It also allows the banks to respond in changing market conditions by altering their balance-sheets. During periods of expansion, banks can extend their loans beyond the limits previously set by reserves if they see an improvement in the creditworthiness of potential borrowers; and they can move rapidly to a defensive position if trade prospects deteriorate.

The reference to variations in the creditworthiness of potential borrowers clarifies the existence of a criterion upon which banks decide to vary the supply of loans. It also shows that the creditworthiness of a potential borrower depends on the bank's evaluation of the expected cost of his insolvency, which is influenced, in turn, by the level of money income of the economy. The reserve ratios thus tend to vary over the trade cycle and to be unstable with respect to the interest rate.

> When trade prospects are good or when the money value of the borrowers' assets (their collateral) rises as a result of a rise in prices, the demand for bank credit rises but by the same token, the credit worthiness of potential borrowers also improves, so that both the demand and the supply of credit move simultaneously in the same direction. (Kaldor 1981a, p. 15; and 1981b, p. 455)

The existence of a criterion upon which banks' decisions are made contradicts the interpretation that for Kaldor the supply of bank loans is a nondiscretionary variable. This criterion also makes it possible to explain his reference to Wicksell's analysis[39] and to banks' ability to create new credit, if creditworthy people are available, on the basis of a profit-maximizing choice on the part of the banking system rather than on the existence of an institutional element (overdraft facilities) which forces banks to play a passive role in the process of adjustment of the supply of loans to the demand. Kaldor's actual reference to overdraft facilities does not deny that banks decide in a profit-maximizing way the composition of their balance-sheets and the maintenance of positive levels of prudential reserves.[40] Together with references to other forms of 'potential' or 'hidden' money and to the ability of the banks to evade the rules on mandatory reserves,[41] it underscores the limited power of the authorities to use rigid controls of the money supply as an anti-inflationary measure.[42]

To sum up, the content of Kaldor's later writings makes it difficult to argue that for him the supply of loans is a *non-discretionary* variable for the individual bank. His analyses of the behaviour of the monetary authorities and of the banking sector allow one to consider the introduction of a horizontal money supply curve as a simplifying analytical device, which gives an approximate description of the way these institutions operate and avoids complex problems relative to the specification of an increasing money supply in a context of changing money incomes. Moreover, it is analytically useful for a critique of the monetarist findings with respect to the stability of the demand function for money[43] and for the argument that 'the outstanding money stock can never be in excess of the amount which the individuals wish to hold' (Kaldor and Trevithick, 1981, p. 7).[44]

CONCLUSION

Kaldor's writings on monetary issues over a fifty-year period thus show closer links than are at present recognized. The neglect of these links contributes to a misinterpretation of his view of the role played by the monetary authorities and the banking sector in the financial system, and by the horizontal money supply in his analyses. Such neglect also prevents one from appreciating the implications of his work for the theory of the interest rate and for the treatment of the money supply. Some of these implications will be recalled in this concluding section, where the problems that they open to future investigation are pointed out.

The analysis of the behaviour of the monetary authorities presented in the 1958 memorandum to the Radcliffe Committee, together with that presented in 1970 on the pivotal position of central banks in modern financial systems, has important implications for a *monetary* theory of the interest rate, like that proposed by Keynes in the *General Theory* (1936, pp. 202–4).[45] By describing how the authorities set their priorities among policy objectives and decide whether and at which level the interest rate is to be stabilized, Kaldor's analysis can strengthen this theory by providing a developed study, missing in Keynes's work, that shows the historical character of the authorities' decisions. This does not imply, however, that Kaldor himself held a *monetary* theory of the interest rate. Nothing has been said in the previous pages on this point, the treatment of which requires an investigation of his position on the relationship between the long-run theory of growth and distribution and that of the interest rate. This analysis has not been carried out above, nor does it seem to have been presented in the literature. It has thus to be considered one issue in Kaldor's writings deserving future work.

Further work is also required to deal with another problem related to Kaldor's view that an accommodating monetary policy is a necessary condition for the establishment of a smoothly working financial system and for the suppression of instability in bank reserve ratios and in the demand functions for financial assets. Such a study could show when it is possible to develop a macroeconomic short-run model of the interrelation between financial and other markets, directly comparable with those of the dominant traditions. This chapter has recalled some evidence from the writings of Kaldor himself in the 1930s with hints in this direction. Future investigation may further clarify the issue and lead to attempts to endow a short-run Kaldorian model with an appropriate treatment of the money supply. In this respect, a horizontal money supply represents, as Kaldor pointed out, the simplest (and probably the most convenient) hypothesis. More complex solutions can, however, be worked out.[46] One proposal can be made here, following the suggestions of Desai (1989, pp. 176 and 180–81) and S.C. Dow (1988), in terms of a linear supply function which takes into account the fact that the monetary authorities do not apply a fully accommodating policy and may fix some desired levels both for the interest rates and for some monetary aggregates.

$$M^s = BM\frac{1}{b}$$

(3.12)

$$r_2 = r_2^* \{1 + \gamma[\frac{M^s}{M^{s*}} - 1]\}$$

(3.13)

$$b = b(r_2, r, Y)$$

(3.14)

Here, M^{s*} and r_2^* represent the desired levels of money in circulation and of the short-term interest rate (cf. equations 3.8–3.10 above); r is the vector of other relevant interest rates; γ is a parameter[47] measuring the will and the power of the monetary authorities to stabilize[48] the interest rate at the level r_2^*. The usefulness of such proposals represents one more issue in Kaldor's writings upon which future work can be performed.

NOTES

1. Cf. Moore (1987, pp. 14–18; and 1989b, p. 11). A similar position is implied by the outstanding contributions of Thirwall (1987); Targetti (1988, pp. 344 and 356–71) and Lavoie (1988, pp. 6 and 7).
2. Cf. Rousseas (1986, pp. 78–81; and 1989, pp. 475–6); Jarsulic (1989, p. 37); Lavoie (1984, p. 776); Moore (1987; 1989b, p. 11) and Laidler (1989, p. 1150).
3. This view is held by Chick, Davidson, Desai, A.C. Dow, J.C.R. Dow, S.C. Dow, Minsky, Rousseas, Weintraub.
4. This position is mainly associated with B. Moore.
5. The definitions include central bank money plus all kinds of deposits with clearing banks ('broad' definition) plus those with other financial institutions ('broadest' definition).
6. For some authors these decisions are based on portfolio analyses. Cf. S.C. Dow and Earl (1982, pp. 71–74); Goodhart (1984, pp. 193–199); S.C. Dow (1985, p. 188); and Chick (1986, p. 116).
7. Cf. Davidson (1972; 1988; 1989); Davidson and Weintraub (1973); Weintraub (1978a, b; 1981). With respect to these contributions, S.C. Dow and Earl (1982); Goodhart (1984); J.C.R. Dow (1988); and S.C. Dow (1988) seem to argue for a lower degree of control on the monetary base.
8. Cf. Goodhart (1989b, p. 31). The use of mild fluctuations of the interest rates as a policy instrument is recognized by S.C. Dow and Earl (1982, pp. 231–45), Rousseas (1986, pp. 91–6) and J.C.R. Dow (1988, pp. 444–8). According to Gedeon (1985–86, pp. 210–11) and Targetti (1988, pp. 368–71), there must be a limit to the possibility of an accommodating behaviour of the monetary authorities.
9. For a fuller treatment of this point, cf. Rousseas (1986, pp. 73–98). A similar view is

also held by A.C. Dow and S.C. Dow (1989, pp. 149–50). Goodhart's recent analysis of the behaviour of the monetary authorities in different countries from 1970 and 1989 supports Rousseas's position (cf. Goodhart, 1989a, and Meulkendyke, 1989).

10. This position is principally developed by Moore (1979, 1983, 1988a, 1988b, 1988c, 1988d, 1989a and 1989b).

11. Cf. Moore (1988c, pp. 24–5; 1989a, p. 485; Lavoie, 1988, pp. 5–12). For a critical evaluation of this position, cf. Niggle (1989, p. 1185) and Wray (1989, p. 1188).

12. 'In its extreme form, however, post-Keynesian theory of endogeneity further stipulates that $\Delta Ms = \Delta Md$ . . . This, of course, must mean that demand and supply schedules of money are identical as the economy moves from one identical Kaldorian equilibrium position to another' (Rousseas, 1989, p. 474). This is confirmed by Moore (1988b, p. 399) in a reply to a comment by Fand (1988).

13. For the sake of exposition, we will not use Kaldor's notation.

14. A definition of money in the sense here used, underlining the benefits of this asset, can be found in Kaldor's subsequent work.

   The meaning of money in everyday parlance comprises everything which is widely used as an instrument for paying for goods and services bought, or for hire of labour or other factors of production, which is accepted by courts as a proper medium for discharging a debt, and by the Government for the payment of taxes. On this definition 'checking accounts' (or current accounts) with any of the clearing banks form part of the 'money supply' of the non-banking public as well as the notes and coins in circulation outside the banking system. The common feature of all these forms of money is that they do not yield interest; they are held purely for convenience. This, roughly, is the definition of £M1. (Kaldor, 1980, pp. 294–5)

15. Cf. Kaldor (1939, p. 13, fn. 2). This assumption makes these assets more similar to savings deposits than to other short-term financial paper.

16. For the short maturity of the asset, the probability of having to convert it unexpectedly into money is small. If the fee is small too – as, according to Kaldor, is the case – the expected value of the financial loss associated with this asset may be so small as to make it insignificant. For an explicit statement of this point, cf. Kaldor (1960, p. 63).

17. Kaldor assumed that the central bank regulates the monetary base by reacting to variations in its demand, due to changes in the reserve ratio of the commercial banks and in the current to savings deposits ratio. The high elasticity of the supply function of money was explained as follows:

   The elasticity of the supply of money in a modern banking system is ensured partly by the open market operations of the central bank, partly by the commercial banks not holding to a strict reserve ratio in the face of fluctuation in the demand for loans, and partly it is a consequence of the fact that under present banking practices a switch-over from current deposits to savings deposits automatically reduces the amount of deposit money in existence and vice versa. (Kaldor, 1939, p. 14, fn. 1)

18. The lack of inter-relations between r_2 and other interest rates stimulated at the time several critical comments by Tsiang (1943), Kennedy (1949–50) J. Robinson (1951), Robertson (1952) and Kahn (1954). Kaldor answered these criticisms by restating his point with some qualifications (1960, pp. 4–5, fn. 2). In the face of more recent developments, his attempt to isolate the determination of the short rate from that of other rates is scarcely convincing.

19. Kaldor's conclusions are not fully guaranteed by the assumptions introduced in the following lines. For instance, as long as agents can invest in both short and long-term financial securities, it is difficult to maintain that the demand for money is not a function of r_3 too.

20. A similar hypothesis was made by Kaldor himself in his answer to the criticisms raised by Kennedy (1949–50) and Robertson (1952). Kaldor admitted that variations in all rates of interest affecting the structure of revenues and costs of the bank can influence their portfolio decisions, like those between bonds and bills (cf. Kaldor, 1960, p. 5, fn.).

21. In a microeconomic description of banks' decisions, the level of reserves of the individual bank, R, can be determined by maximizing with respect to this variable the bank's

expected profit, $E(\pi)$. This can be taken as equal, in a simplified case, to the revenues on their loans, Lr_c, minus the interest paid to their depositors, I, the expected cost of the insolvency of their customers, S, and the expected cost of their own insolvency, C, which may occur if the outflows of deposits are too large for their reserves. By assumption, $I = hDr_2$, where h is the percentage of savings over total deposits, D. For each bank, besides, $D = L + R$ and D, r_c and r_2 are given. Moreover, the customers' expected insolvency cost is a function of the outstanding loans and depends on the bank's confidence in the future prospects of the borrowers, whose changes may be related to those of the level of money income in the economy. The bank's expected insolvency cost, on the other hand, is a function of its reserves and of r_2. These two expected costs of insolvency can be formalized as follows:

$$S = S(L,Y) = \int_0^1 zL\phi(z,L,Y)dz \qquad (3.\text{i})$$

$$C = C(R,r_2) = \int_{\alpha R}^{\infty} r_2(1+v)(X-\alpha R)f(X)dX \qquad (3.\text{ii})$$

where z is the percentage of unrecovered loans; $\phi(z,L,Y)$ is the probability distribution of z, which depends on the outstanding loans and on the bank's confidence in the future prospects of its customers, represented by Y; v is a non-negative parameter calculated in percentage terms, representing the penalty on the emergency acquisition of reserves; X is the expected outflow of deposits; $f(X)$ its probability distribution; and αR (with α taken as given and $0 < \alpha \leq 1$) is the level of reserves below which emergency acquisitions start.

22. This tendency is realized if the following assumptions can be made:
  (i) $\dfrac{\delta S}{\delta Y} < 0$ [i.e. a rise in Y, by influencing positively banks' confidence, reduces the expected cost of insolvency of its customers];
  (ii) $\int_0^1 z\dfrac{\delta\phi(z,L,Y)}{\delta L}dz > 0$ [i.e., banks extend their loans by accepting the applications of customers who are considered less credit-worthy]; and
  (iii) $\int_0^1 z\dfrac{\delta^2\phi(z,L,Y)}{\delta^2 L}dz > 0$ [i.e., for the banks the risk assumed to extend their loans increases more than proportionally].
23. This would imply some other changes, such as in the definition of the banks' reserve ratio.
24. A similar point can be found in Minsky (1957) and Rousseas (1960).
25. Kaldor claimed that 'the changes in interest rates required to compensate for the changing inducements to hold stocks may have to be pretty severe' (1964, p. 150; cf. also p. 131).
26. A similar view can be found in S.C. Dow (1988, pp. 30–31).
27. Cf. Kaldor (1970, p. 15).
28. In his rejoinder to Friedman, Kaldor referred the reader to the writings of Cramp which provide 'a more extensive and carefully-reasoned analysis of why central banks in a credit money economy *cannot* behave in the manner Friedman and his followers assert they do' (Kaldor, 1970, p. 27, fn. 1; italics in the original). In those writings, Cramp's critique of monetarism assumed a limited variability of the banks' reserve ratio and argued that the authorities are bound to make the monetary base endogenous (cf. Cramp, 1970).
29. Cf. Kaldor, (1960 , p. 64).
30. 'Professor Milton Friedman . . . concluded that . . . even if the initiating factor in the changes in expenditure lies in decisions by the public bodies, business firms or indivi-duals, it *cannot* result in increased total spending unless the monetary authorities follow a passive policy of accommodating the money supply to any change in the demand for loans' (Kaldor and Trevithick, 1981, p. 6).

31. Cf. Kaldor (1980, p. 296; 1982, p. 72) and Kaldor and Trevithick (1981, p. 12).
32. Kaldor stated: 'Indeed the very distinction between changes in the quantity of money and changes in the velocity of circulation comprises an arbitrary element of definition – what appears as a rise in the velocity of circulation under a narrow definition, may appear as a change in the quantity of money, on a broader definition. (This is linked to the arbitrary element in the definition of money)' (Kaldor, 1981b, p. 454).
33. This point, stated already in 1970 (cf. Kaldor, 1970, p. 11, fn. 2), recalls the determination of the short-term rate presented in 1939. In the 1980s it was frequently restated. Cf. Kaldor (1980, p. 297; 1981a, pp. 21–2; 1982, p. 28 and 74); and Kaldor and Trevithick (1981, pp. 7–8).
34. Cf. Kaldor (1980, p. 296; 1981a, pp. 17–19 and p. 18 fn. 1; 1981b, pp. 455–6; 1982, pp. 47 and 73; 1985, p. 11); and Kaldor and Trevithick (1981, p. 7).
35. Cf. also Kaldor (1981a, pp. 16–17; 1981b, p. 456; 1984, pp. 12–13).
36. For a similar view, cf. S.C. Dow (1988, pp. 31–2).
37. In a speech in the House of Lords on June 13, 1979, Kaldor said: 'I was in the Treasury when cash limits were invented – we had plenty of discussion about them and their operation has proved a very useful tool. But it is a useful tool if it is applied moderately – that is, maintaining a gentle pressure. If you try to use such an instrument in ways which require extreme, not moderate, pressure, it will break down' (1983b, p. 17).
38. It must be noticed that in this passage, as in that previously recalled in which he referred to an undue expansion of consumer credit, Kaldor admitted the possibility that an 'inflation of bank credit' caused a rise in spending.
39. The ability of the banking sector to adjust its balance-sheet to the changing conditions of the market is one element linking Kaldor's analysis to that of Wicksell. Cf. Kaldor (1980, p. 296, fn.; 1981a, p. 19; 1981b, p. 455; and 1982, p. 73, fn.).
40. For Kaldor, banks 'cannot allow themselves to get into a position of being fully stretched' (1982, p. 47).
41. Cf. Kaldor (1980, p. 296 and fn.; 1982, p. 73 and fn.; 1983a, p. 20; and Kaldor and Trevithick, 1981, p. 6).
42. For Kaldor's reference to overdraft facilities, cf. Kaldor (1980, p. 295; 1982, p. 71; 1983a, p. 20); and Kaldor and Trevithick (1981, p. 6).
43. As Kaldor notes, the problems relative to the stability of the demand function for money become irrelevant if the money supply is horizontal. On the contrary, a rising money supply function increases the relevance of the demand for money; cf. A.C. Dow and S.C. Dow (1989), who discuss the possibility of integrating a post-Keynesian analysis of liquidity preference with that of an endogenous money supply.
44. Kaldor explained what he meant on this point by saying that in a credit money economy 'an excess of "actual" over "desired" money balances' (1981a, p. 20, fn. 1) can never occur. As in 1970, he thus meant that the amount of money actually in circulation can differ from the amount of money that the authorities may *desire to supply*, but cannot differ from the amount of money *desired* by the public. Cf. also Kaldor (1980, p. 294; 1981b, pp. 454–5; 1982, pp. 46 and 70; 1983a, p. 21); and Kaldor and Trevithick (1981, p. 7).
45. For a more extended treatment of Keynes's theory, according to which interest rates mainly depend on the policy of the monetary authorities, cf. Panico (1988, pp. 102–41).
46. Rousseas (1986, pp. 96–8) and Targetti (1988, pp. 364–71) for example, propose a supply function of money which is horizontal at first and then, after a certain point, increases in a more than proportional way.
47. The value of the parameter γ can go from zero to infinity and depends on the way the monetary authorities set their priorities on policy objectives. It indicates the degree of endogeneity of the money supply. When $0 < \gamma < \infty$, the money supply is strictly increasing. It is, instead, horizontal, for $\gamma = 0$, and vertical for $\gamma = \infty$.
48. The power of the authorities to stabilize the interest rate, as Kaldor himself seems to suggest, may be lower when r_2^* is fixed at a higher level.

REFERENCES

Arestis, P. (1988) 'Post Keynesian Theory of Money, Credit and Finance', in Arestis, P. (ed.), *Post Keynesian Monetary Economics*, Aldershot: Edward Elgar.

Chick, V. (1986) 'The Evolution of the Banking System and the Theory of Saving Investment and Interest', *Economie et Societé*, **20** (3), Aug/Sep, 111–26.

Cramp, A.B. (1970) 'Does Money Matter?', *Lloyds Bank Review*, October.

Davidson, P. (1972) 'A Keynesian View of Friedman's Theoretical Framework for Monetary Analysis', *Journal of Political Economy*, **80**, Sept/Oct, 864–82.

Davidson, P. (1988) 'Endogenous Money, the Production Process and Inflation Analysis', *Economie Appliquée*, **41** (1), 151–69.

Davidson, P. (1989) 'On the Endogeneity of Money Once More,' *Journal of Post Keynesian Economics*, **11** (3), 488–90.

Davidson, P. and Weintraub, S. (1973) 'Money as Cause and Effect,' *Economic Journal*, **83**, Dec, 1117–32.

Desai, M. (1989) 'The Scourge of the Monetarists: Kaldor on Monetarism and Money', *Cambridge Journal of Economics*, **13**, Mar, 171–82.

Dow, A.C. and Dow, S.C. (1989) 'Endogenous Money Creation and Idle Balances', in J. Pheby (ed.), *New Directions in Post Keynesian Economics*, Aldershot: Edward Elgar.

Dow, J.C.R. (1988) 'Incertezza e processo finanziaro: le conseguenze per il potere della banca centrale', *Moneta e Credito*, (164), 439–55.

Dow, S.C. (1985) *Macroeconomic Thought. A Methodological Approach*, Oxford: Basil Blackwell.

Dow, S.C. (1988) 'Money Supply Endogeneity', *Economie Appliqée*, **41** (1), 19–39.

Dow, S.C. and P.E. Earl (1982) *Money Matters. A Keynesian Approach to Monetary Economics*, Oxford: Martin Robertson.

Fand, D. (1988) 'On the Endogenous Money Supply', *Journal of Post Keynesian Economics*, **10** (3), 386–9.

Gedeon, S.J. (1985–86) 'The Post Keynesian Theory of Money: a Summary and Eastern European Example,' *Journal of Post Keynesian Economics*, **8** (2), 208–21.

Goodhart, C.A.E. (1984) *Monetary Theory and Practice*, London: Macmillan.

Goodhart, C.A.E. (1989a) 'The Conduct of Monetary Policy', *Economic Journal*, **99**, 293–346.

Goodhart, C.A.E. (1989b) 'Has Moore Become too Horizontal?', *Journal of Post Keynesian Economics*, **12** (1), 29–34.

Jarsulic, M. (1989) 'Endogenous Credit and Endogenous Business Cycles', *Journal of Post Keynesian Economics*, **12** (1), 35–48.

Kahn, R.F. (1954) 'Some Notes on Liquidity Preference', *Manchester School of Economics and Social Studies*, **22**, Sep, 229–57.

Kaldor, N. (1939) 'Speculation and Economic Stability', *Review of Economic Studies*, **7**, Oct, 1–27.

Kaldor, N. (1958) 'Monetary Policy, Economic Stability and Growth, a Memorandum submitted to the Committee on the Working of the Monetary System', in *Essays on Economic Policy I*, London: Duckworth [1964].

Kaldor, N. (1960) *Essays on Economic Stability and Growth*, London: Duckworth.

Kaldor, N. (1964) *Essays on Economic Policy I*, London: Duckworth.

Kaldor, N. (1970) *Further Essays on Applied Economics*, London: Duckworth.

Kaldor, N. (1976) 'Inflation and Recession in the World Economy', *Economic Journal*, **86**, Dec, 703–14.

Kaldor, N. (1980) 'Monetarism and UK Monetary Policy', *Cambridge Journal of Economics*, **4**, Dec, 293–318.

Kaldor, N. (1981a) *Origins of the New Monetarism*, Cardiff: University College, Cardiff Press.

Kaldor, N. (1981b) 'Fallacies of Monetarism', *Kredit und Kapital*, **14**, July, 451–62.

Kaldor, N. (1982) *The Scourge of Monetarism*, Oxford: Oxford University Press.

Kaldor, N. (1983a) 'Keynesian Economics after Fifty Years', in Trevithick J. and Worswick D. (eds), *Keynes and the Modern World*, Cambridge: Cambridge University Press.

Kaldor, N. (1983b) *The Economic Consequences of Mrs. Thatcher*, London: Duckworth.

Kaldor, N. (1984) Introduction to the Italian edition of *Il Flagello del Monetarismo*, Torino: Loescher.

Kaldor, N. (1985) 'How Monetarism Failed,' *Challenge*, **28**, May/June, 4–13.

Kaldor, N. (1986) *Ricordi di un economista*, M.C. Marcuzzo (ed.), Milano: Garzanti.

Kaldor, N. and Trevithick, J. (1981) 'A Keynesian Perspective on Money', *Lloyds Bank Review*, (139), Jan, 1–19.

Kennedy, C. (1949–50) 'Period Analysis and the Demand for Money', *Review of Economic Studies*, **16**, 41–9.

Keynes, J.M. (1936) *The General Theory of Employment, Interest and Money*, London: Macmillan.

Laidler, D., (1989) 'Dow and Saville's Critique of Monetary Policy – A Review Essay, *Journal of Economic Literature*, **27**, Sep, 1147–59.

Lavoie, M. (1984) 'The Endogenous Flow of Credit and Post Keynesian Theory of Money', *Journal of Economic Issues*, **19**, Sep, 771–97.

Lavoie, M. (1988) 'Change, Continuity and Originality in Kaldor's Monetary Theory', in E.J. Nell and W. Semmler (eds), *Nicholas Kaldor and Mainstream Economics*, London: Macmillan.

Markowitz, H.M. (1952) 'Portfolio Selection', *Journal of Finance*, **7**, Mar, 77–91.

Meulendyke, A.M. (1989) 'Can the Federal Reserve Influence whether the Money Supply is Endogenous? A Comment on Moore', *Journal of Post Keynesian Economics*, **10**, Spring, 390–97.

Minsky, H.P. (1957) 'Central Banking and Money Market Change', *Quarterly Journal of Economics*, **71** (2), May, 171–87.

Minsky, H.P. (1975), *John Maynard Keynes*, New York: Columbia University Press.

Moore, B.J. (1979) 'The Endogenous Money Stock', *Journal of Post Keynesian Economics*, **2** (1), Fall, 49–70.

Moore, B.J. (1983) 'Unpacking the Post-Keynesian Black Box: Bank Lending and the Money Supply', *Journal of Post Keynesian Economics*, **5** (4), Summer, 537–56.

Moore, B.J. (1987) 'Marx, Keynes, Kalecki and Kaldor on the Rate of Interest as a Monetary Phenomenon', mimeo.

Moore, B.J. (1988a) 'The Endogenous Money Supply', *Journal of Post Keynesian Economics*, **10** (3), Spring, 372–85.

Moore, B.J. (1988b) 'Concluding Comments', *Journal of Post Keynesian Economics*, **10** (3), Spring.

Moore, B.J. (1988c) *Horizontalist and Verticalist. The Macroeconomics of Credit Money*, Cambridge: Cambridge University Press.

Moore, B.J. (1988d) 'Unpacking the Post-Keynesian Black Box: Wages, Bank Lending and the Money Supply', in P. Arestis (ed.), *Post Keynesian Monetary Economics*, Aldershot: Edward Elgar.

Moore, B.J. (1989a) 'On the Endogeneity of Money Once More', *Journal of Post Keynesian Economics*, **11** (3), Spring, 479–87.

Moore, B.J. (1989b) 'A Simple Model of Bank Intermediation', *Journal of Post Keynesian Economics*, **12** (1), Spring, 10–28.

Niggle, C.J. (1989) Review of B. Moore: 'Horizontalists and Verticalists: the Macroeconomics of Credit Money', *Journal of Economic Issues*, **23** (4), Dec, 1181–5.

Panico, C. (1988) *Interest and Profit in the Theories of Value and Distribution*, London: Macmillan.

Robertson, D.H. (1952) *Utility and All That*, London: Macmillan.

Robinson, J.V. (1951) 'The Rate of Interest', in *Collected Economic Papers of Joan Robinson*, vol. 2, Oxford: Blackwell [1960].

Rousseas, S. (1960) 'Velocity Change and the Effectiveness of Monetary Policy, 1951–57', *Review of Economics and Statistics*, **42**, Feb, 27–36.

Rousseas, S. (1986) *Post-Keynesian Monetary Economics*, London: Macmillan.

Rousseas, S. (1989) 'On the Endogeneity of Money Once More', *Journal of Post Keynesian Economics*, **11** (3), Spring, 474–8.

Targetti, F. (1988) *Nicholas Kaldor*, Bologna: Il Mulino.

Thirwall, A.P. (1987) *Nicholas Kaldor*, Brighton: Wheatsheaf Books.

Tobin, J. (1958) 'Liquidity Preference as Behaviour Towards Risk', *Review of Economic Studies*, **25** (67), Feb, 65–86.

Tsiang, S.C. (1943) 'A Note on Speculation and Income Stability', *Economica*, **10**, Nov, 286–96.

Weintraub, S. (1978a) *Capitalism's Inflation and Unemployment Crisis*, Boston: Addison Wesley.

Weintraub, S. (1978b) *Keynes, Keynesians and Monetarism*, Philadelphia: University of Pennsylvania Press.

Weintraub, S. (1981) 'Bedrock on the Money Wage – Money Supply Inflation Controversy', *Banca Nazionale del Lavoro Quarterly Review*, **34**, Dec, 439–46.

Wray, L.R. (1989) Review of B. Moore: 'Horizontalists and Verticalists: the Macroeconomics of Credit Money', *Journal of Economic Issues*, **23** (4), Dec, 1185–9.

4. A Fundamental Controversy about Money: Post-Keynesian and New Monetary Economics

Hans-Michael Trautwein[1]

MONEY MATTERS

Controversies about money are quite common, both in real life and in economic theory. Yet money is so pervasive a phenomenon that controversies about it are hardly ever fundamental in the sense that the necessity of a definite means of payment is under dispute. The functional advantages of money are generally considered self-evident, whereas its influence on real economic activity quite often is not. The belief in the long-run neutrality of money is still at the root of prevalent theories of Neoclassical and Monetarist derivation.

The standard view of money as a requisite, but essentially neutral lubricant of economic activity has been challenged by two different approaches which can be classified as 'post-Keynesian theories of money' and 'New Monetary Economics'. Their perspectives are fundamentally opposed to each other: one sees money as a pivotal determinant of the constructions of market economies, and the other sees it as an outdated obstacle to the proper functioning of market economies. While post-Keynesians emphasize the indispensability of money and dispute its neutrality, New Monetary economists dispute its indispensability and emphasize the neutrality of the unit of account – if the latter only were made independent of any inflationary money issue. Such views are certainly at the extremes of a widening range of theories of money and banking, and they have not attracted very much attention. Yet in my opinion, they deserve more systematic confrontation, since they illuminate some fundamental characteristics of the existing monetary system as well as its potential for evolution.

THE ESSENTIAL FEATURES OF A MONETARY ECONOMY

Post-Keynesian theories of money differ from one another mainly on the relation of credit to money. One line of argumentation emphasizes the *endogeneity* of the money supply by including demand-driven forms of credit in a broad notion of money (cf. Kaldor and Trevithick 1981; Lavoie 1984; Moore 1988). The other line – the one to be investigated here – stresses a fundamental distinction between money and credit in terms of *uncertainty* and *liquidity constraints* (cf. Davidson 1978; Minsky 1975; Riese 1983).[2] The following sketch of a post-Keynesian view of the role of money can accordingly be regarded as a brief and simple synthesis of those 'Fundamentalists' and a few others quoted below. There are considerable differences in focus, methodology and policy implications in the works of these authors.[3] But their different arguments can be twined into one rough thread with regard to their foundations in Keynes's writings and to the essential features of a monetary economy. Like beads on that thread, five propositions summarize the post-Keynesian position for the confrontation with New Monetary Economics.

Proposition 1
Money exists because of a vital need to fix values under conditions of fundamental uncertainty in market relations
In the post-Keynesian view, the need for money is derived from credit and speculation, not from barter (cf. Davidson 1978, p. 147ff; Heinsohn and Steiger 1988, p. 327ff). The antagonistic interdependence of private decisions in market economies generates uncertainty which in turn creates the need to fix values, via contracts and the materialization of liquidity. Money accordingly evolves from the requirement of a standard of value in contractual offers and commitments. Contracts generally require such a standard because they involve either speculation (about future changes in value) or some kind of credit (whenever delivery and payment do not take place at the same instant), or elements of both.

Beyond contracts a demand for the material fixation of value makes itself felt whether or not credit is involved in the transactions. Debtors need means of payment to settle their debts. Other contractors need some security against claims for compensation in case they fail to meet obligations. There is, moreover, the general need all economic agents have for some reserve that gives 'immediate command over goods in general' (Keynes 1936, p. 166), in case their own goods, assets or capacities for work fail to sell. Accordingly, something is required that can be expected to transmit value, without significant cost, from hand to hand and from the present to the future. A specific money matter comes to be distinguished from other stores of value and media of exchange by its stability of value in circulation, thereby qualifying for the role of the standard. The derived function of a general unit of account enhances, in turn, the acceptance of that money matter.

Proposition 2
The functions of money are inseparably intertwined in circular reinforcement; money thereby acquires the property of perfect liquidity

In the post-Keynesian view, money represents liquidity in the sense of certainty of value. All other forms of wealth are marked by a comparative disadvantage in terms of uncertainty, that is, by some degree of illiquidity.[4] The supreme liquidity of money consequently confers on the holding of money an implicit yield of 'potential convenience or security given by this power of disposal' (Keynes 1936, p. 226). This yield is reflected in the rates of interest earned on the holding of other assets as contractual or potential claims on money. The 'price of money' itself is the rate of interest on a money loan, since the latter represents a temporary sacrifice of liquidity for the creditor.

Thus money is an asset in two respects: it has the power to appropriate equivalents in any marketable kind; and it has the power to appropriate surplus in its own kind, simply by a temporary change of hands. Lending money opens a source of permanent real income through the market without engaging in real production, since some of the borrowers' real income is redistributed to the lenders (cf. Heinsohn and Steiger 1988, p. 346ff; Herr 1988, p. 86ff). Borrowing money helps to overcome present liquidity constraints on investment and employment in real production by setting another constraint in the future: the returns on financed investment must exceed the money rate of interest in order to yield profits. That constraint not only binds entrepreneurial debtors. It becomes the dominant opportunity-cost calculus of probabilities in any investment decision because an alternative to profit on real production is established by the nexus of the interest-rate. 'In a "Wall Street" paradigm model, all units are like a banker who maximizes profits under liquidity and solvency constraints' (Minsky 1977, p. 143).

Proposition 3
Money is not only a 'subtle device' for handling uncertainty; it is also a fundamental cause of uncertainty

Keynes stated in one of his 'sundry observations on the nature of capital' that 'the only reason why an asset offers a prospect of yielding during its life services having an aggregate value greater than its initial supply price is because it is *scarce*; and it is kept scarce because of the competition of the rate of interest on money' (Keynes 1936, p. 213). The interest rate on money is of paramount importance in competition for profits on investment because money is different from other assets in one central aspect: its value is not derived from capitalization, but from its function as a standard of capital value and its role as the ultimate asset. Money is an unspecified, omnipotent claim to anything traded in the market while other assets form potential claims to money by capitalizing expected returns to specific processes of production (cf. Spahn 1988, p. 181).[5] Money enjoys an 'extra' yield from liquidity, since the stability of its value is derived in part from the fact that the value of money is independent of the outcomes of particular investments.

Here we have a self-reinforcing circle again, starting from a very trivial point: money must be (kept) scarce simply because it would not be money otherwise; its supply must be comparatively inelastic with respect to interest rate changes (cf. Keynes 1936, p. 241 n.1). The liquidity preference of wealth owners makes the interest rate on money, in turn, comparatively inelastic with respect to changes in the money supply (cf. Keynes 1936, p. 233); hence the central role that liquidity preference plays as a constraint on investment and employment. Since the maximization of profits in a monetary economy implies that yields on money (liquidity premium), on financial assets (interest rates) and on real investment (marginal efficiencies of capital) are equal in equilibrium, real investment can be constrained by competition from money and financial assets to such an extent that involuntary unemployment arises and persists (cf. Keynes 1936, p. 234ff; Hagemann and Steiger 1988, p. 33; Riese 1988, p. 88ff). In this way, the contrived scarcity of money causes uncertainty about the future course of economic activity.

Yet, the credit and cheque clearing facilities of modern banking and payments systems seem to refute the dual inelasticities of supply and substitution which Keynes identified as the essential properties of money (cf. Keynes 1936, chap. 17). The creation of means of payment by bank credit would imply either a high elasticity of production (if they are included in the notion of money), or a high elasticity of substitution (if the notion of money is reduced to 'cash' or 'legal tender'). The concept of contrived scarcity would accordingly not be applicable. Yet it can be made consistent, in a post-Keynesian synthesis, by combination of a narrow definition of money with a cylical view of finance in banking systems.

Proposition 4

The definition of money is confined to the matter that is both the standard of value and the ultimate asset for the settlement of debts. In those capacities it cannot be replaced by private 'near-monies'

From this point of view, only 'currency' or 'legal tender' is money in modern national economies, since it exclusively provides both the standard of value and ultimate assets.[6] It does so because *and only in so far as* the central bank first of all serves the purpose of safeguarding the functionality of the monetary system by keeping the value of money comparatively stable. In this sense, it is held to provide a public good (cf. Riese 1983, p. 111; Spahn 1988, p. 182).[7]

Privately produced financial assets certainly operate as substitutes for money in some of its functions. But, it is argued, they do so only because their issuers (mostly banks) face liquidity constraints in the form of reserve requirements and their own cost of funds. This means that wealth owners and other market agents recognize the legitimacy of those private near-monies only because these promise redeemability. They are accepted as money substitutes because the banks cannot fully substitute them for money. The liquidity – or rather the low 'illiquidity discount' – of demand deposits and other 'liquid assets' is thus derived from inelasticities of supply and substitution of central bank money; and it is held that no financial innovation can lift this basic constraint (cf. Riese 1986, p. 42f; Spahn 1988, p. 185; Herr 1988, p. 83).

The explanation of the finance constraint in terms of requirements of systematic functionality seems to involve circular reasoning, as it explains the substitutability of money by its low elasticity of substitution. Both this explanation and the narrow definition of money are nevertheless justified with regard to the cyclical interaction between the money-supplying central bank and credit-creating commercial banks (and other financial intermediaries). A broader definition would not only blur the liquidity constraints faced by the intermediaries; it would also obscure the causes for instabilities arising from the central dilemma of killing a boom or feeding inflation that the central bank faces in its efforts to preserve the functionality of the monetary system by restricting money supply *and* accommodating credit demand.[8]

Proposition 5

Money and credit complement one another over the cycle of inflationary credit expansion and deflationary liquidity squeezes. The critical phenomena of a monetary economy cannot be avoided by simply abolishing money

In a boom, increasingly speculative leverage financing of production tends to trigger inflation. Every boom accordingly threatens to carry the economy into the narrow straits between Scylla and Charybdis – with inflationary erosion of the monetary system on one side, and debt-deflationary credit crunches on the other. Both kinds of cumulative processes gravely affect the volume of market transactions and of real production. Inflation feeds a 'credit explosion' that, if not stopped by sizable changes in yield prospects, accelerates into hyperinflation which eventually leads to replacement of the currency by a scarcer sort of money – either (partly) by foreign currency or (completely) by a currency reform. If on the other hand, yield prospects suddenly change on a significant scale (due, for example, to unanticipated losses of large debtors, or unexpectedly strong wage increases), a 'credit implosion' will lead to a debt-deflationary revaluation of the current money. Hence, relaxation of the contrived scarcity of money by credit expansion must ultimately rebound upon very inelastic limits of money supply and substitution, one way or the other.

In modern banking systems, the extremes of hyperinflation and depression will generally be averted by central bank action, imposing and relaxing refinance constraints on the commercial banks. Yet, in the post-Keynesian view, the central bank cannot exogenously stabilize the economy by regulating the money supply according to some golden rule. The central bank is seen rather as a stabilizer of financial instability, as an institutional part of the endogenous credit cycle which to some extent can avert profound crises by reversing cumulative processes, not by stopping them altogether. But even in the reversal of such processes the power and the will of the central bank are asymmetrical: it can always kill a boom, but it cannot reanimate business if yield prospects remain uncertain for reasons beyond its influence (cf. Minsky 1977; Davidson 1978, p. 335; Riese 1986, p. 62ff).

All in all, post-Keynesian theories see the critical phenomena of inflation and under-employment, stagflation and depression as 'inherent and inescapable flaws' in monetary economies (Minsky 1985, p. 51); flaws which can be aggravated or alleviated by different kinds of monetary (and other economic) policy, but not altogether avoided, since money cannot be abolished. 'So long as there exists any durable asset, it is capable of possessing monetary attributes and, therefore, of giving rise to the characteristic problems of a monetary economy' (Keynes 1936, p. 294).

THE ESSENTIAL FEATURES OF COMPETITIVE PAYMENTS SYSTEMS

The view of money as the indispensable pivot of market economies is challenged by *laissez-faire* approaches to monetary stability that have come to be labelled 'New Monetary Economics'. This label contains (at least) two diverging lines of argumentation which both start from a Legal Restrictions approach to money and to monetarism. A strictly New Classical line can be made out in attempts to integrate money and monetary policy into dynamic equilibrium models (cf. Sargent and Wallace 1982; Sargent 1987, part II; Hoover 1988, part III). The other line consists of different attempts to develop theories of finance without money by way of irrelevance propositions, models of monetary standards, historical allusions and speculative extrapolation of trends. I discuss this latter approach below, with reference to the Black–Fama–Hall (BFH) system, a competitive payments system outlined by Greenfield and Yeager.[9] Five propositions serve to summarize my account in direct contraposition to the approach described by Post Keynesian theories.

Proposition 1
Money exists because of legal restrictions on financial intermediation
In the specific Legal Restrictions approach of the BFH line, the argumentation starts from competitive accounting systems without any tangible media of exchange. The banks in these imaginary systems provide 'real services' by managing portfolios and carrying out transactions. They offer various sorts of deposits 'tailored to have the characteristics of any form of marketable wealth' (Fama 1980, p. 43).[10] Those deposits would be too heterogenous to serve as a standard of value and unit of account – a role which, instead and in principle, could be played by any standardized good such as tons of fresh cut beef or barrels of crude oil. Both Black and Fama contend that 'purely financial' transactions and portfolio management activities within these systems would not have any specific 'impact on the real sector or on the price level' (Black 1970, p. 19). To this end, Fama explicitly applies the Modigliani–Miller theorem to the banks' decisions regarding the size and composition of their portfolios. Both Black and Fama conclude that there is no need to control deposit creation or other bank activities 'to obtain a stable general equilibrium with respect to prices and real activity' (Fama 1980, p. 39). Money enters into their worlds of finance only through regulations such as bank notes monopolies, reserve requirements, and limitations of deposit interest rates. The basic reason for regulating money into existence appears to be a government's hunt for new forms of taxation (cf. Black 1970, p. 17; Fama 1980, pp. 52, 56).

Legal Restrictions approaches to money have, in general, led to the contention that the Quantity theory and other strands of current monetary theory (including Liquidity Preference theory) are 'narrowly institution-bound' and 'almost completely invalid' under *laissez-faire* conditions, since there will not be anything that meaningfully could be called a quantity of money (cf. Black 1970, pp 9ff, 20; Wallace 1983, p. 4ff). There is obviously no market rationale for base money if its existence is reduced to legal restrictions. The theory of money is accordingly 'simplified' by being replaced with irrelevance propositions of the theory of finance.

Proposition 2
Macroeconomic instability is caused by the fixity of the prices of the media of exchange in the existing monetary system
In the BFH view, macroeconomic problems arise from the fact that the unit of account and the medium of exchange are tied together in the one asset called money. The medium of exchange has a fixed price in terms of the unit of account. Conversely, the unit of account is defined as the *value* of one unit of the dominant medium of exchange. This fixed-value homogeneity of the medium of exchange is seen to be at the roots of inflation, stagflation, deflation and depression (cf. Greenfield and Yeager 1983, p. 309).

Ideally, the unit of account is functionally neutral in the sense that its value is not affected by the volume of transactions carried out in this unit. This neutrality of the standard unit is jeopardized by its 'monetary union' with the medium of exchange. If the supply and demand for money are out of balance, its 'price' and quantity 'cannot adjust to clear a market of its own; instead, its market value is a reciprocal average of the prices of all other things' (Yeager 1968, p. 61). Excess supplies create their own demand in a most critical way since money is the one thing that routinely buys all sorts of commodities. 'Unwanted' money does not go out of existence (as other unwanted assets do), but circulates as a medium of exchange and touches off inflationary processes by repercussions on the unit of account. The excess of liquidity in circulation affects the value of the unit of account instead of the 'unit value' of the medium of exchange. The prices of millions of individual goods and services have to adjust, 'leaving scope for quantities traded and produced to be affected' (Greenfield and Yeager 1983, p. 309).[11] This situation leads logically to the next proposition.

Proposition 3
The functions of money should and need not be intertwined in one specific entity. The unit of account could be defined and kept stable by a standard independent of variations in the purchasing power of the media of exchange
Payments systems with some degree of separation of the means of payment from the unit of account are no academic novelties. There is con-

siderable evidence that such systems have existed and still exist where the monetary sovereignty of governments is eroded (for example, in times of hyperinflation) or not fully established (as in the Middle Ages, or in international trade; cf. Cowen and Kroszner 1987). The separation of monetary functions proposed in the BFH view would however, have to be accomplished by deliberate state intervention, since the unit of account would have to be redefined independently of any particular medium of exchange.

A reference model for such a redefinition has been developed by Hall who, in his search for monetary policies consistent with stable prices and deregulation of the monetary system, explored a multi-composite commodity standard. He proposed to define the dollar in terms of a resource unit containing a combination of standardized commodities whose values have been most stable in terms of the consumer price index over a period of several decades. His example is the ANCAP standard 'comprising 33 cents worth of ammonium nitrate, 12 cents worth of copper, 36 cents worth of aluminium, and 19 cents worth of plywood' (Hall 1982, p. 115). In the BFH system a similar, but more comprehensive standard would define the 'valun' (value unit), entirely independent of any inflationary money issue. The valun would not physically exist as a dominant, homogenous medium of exchange. 'People would not be trying to buy Coca-Cola from slot machines by sticking in sheets of plywood' (Yeager 1989, p. 370). The commodity bundle is thought to provide the standard for the unit of measurement only, just as the orange-red radiation of krypton 86 provides the standard for the metre length by a certain number of wavelengths (cf. Greenfield and Yeager 1983, p. 305).

Greenfield and Yeager emphasize that their system is not based on any sort of commodity reserve money. They exclude the existence of any distinct base money, as the government would be forbidden either to attribute legal tender status to any particular means of payment, or to issue fixed-value obligations suitable as media of exchange. The circulating media of exchange would not be directly convertible claims to the valun bundle as the medium of account; none of them would gain dominance as homogenous means of payment. Therefore, the unit of account would not exist in any definite quantity. The government would be confined to defining the valun and enforcing contracts specified in valuns. Apart from that, it would adopt an attitude of *laissez-faire* toward the financial intermediation of credit and payments.

Cowen and Kroszner (1987, p. 214ff) have argued that a discretionary change of the accounting unit would not be necessary, if equity shares came to dominate value-fixed demand deposits in agents' portfolios. The dollar could then remain an abstract unit of account while disappearing as a means of payment. This obviously implies that – once price relations have been established in the absolute figures of a scale – relative prices will continue to move on this scale even when its standard is abandoned and forgotten. The old scale will do, but only as long as prices do not rise to an extent that makes it impracticable for calculation. The assertion of price stability in a competitive payments system with heterogenous media of exchange is, however, one of the cornerstones in both the original BFH view and the evolutionary approach.

Proposition 4
A separation of monetary functions would permit the development of competitive payments systems, based on transfers of interest-bearing liquid assets
Financial intermediaries in the BFH system would presumably be more similar to mutual funds than to present-day banks.[12]

> The funds would invest in primary securities (business and personal loans and stocks and bonds) and perhaps in real estate and commodities. They would seek to attract customers (owners of their shares) by compiling records of high earnings, safety, and efficiency in administering the payments (checking) system. (Greenfield and Yeager 1983, p. 307)

Holdings in the funds would not have to be fixed in value units – they could rise and fall in value according to earnings, capital gains and losses on the asset portfolios of the funds. For convenient use in payments, however, BFH funds could fix the value of their shares at 1 valun each (as most present-day checkable money-market funds do in dollars). They could take account of gains and losses by adjusting the numbers of shares in each owner's portfolio. Risk-averse customers could keep portfolios with fixed total values which probably would earn less as the fixation of values would have to be provided for by forward transactions in futures markets.

Payments could be made by cheques or electronic transfers of fund shares in the appropriate amounts of valuns. For convenience, a small fraction of bearer shares could circulate as hand-to-hand currency in the form of notes and coins. The use of 'smart cards' (chip cards), point-of-sale systems, and other recent and further innovations in payment techniques is expected to remove the inconveniences of this sophisticated exchange of assets for goods or other assets.[13] The crucial contention is that the means of payment in the BFH system are heterogenous. Currency and demand–deposit-like fixed holdings, 'as well as checkable *equity* holdings . . . would be distinguishable by their private issuers, who individually would face competitive pressures to keep their obligations *meaningful*'

(Greenfield and Yeager 1986, p. 848) by restricting their quantity to the public's demand for holdings at comparatively stable or rising values.

At the clearing house, the intermediaries would have to agree on a range of securities or goods acceptable as redemption assets in settlements of adverse balances. In the BFH view, even those assets cannot be regarded as base money: They have markets of their own where their prices – quoted in terms of non-tradeable standard bundles – can adjust to shifts in demand and supply. Direct convertibility of fund shares and bank notes to valun bundles (or corresponding titles) must nevertheless be excluded from the clearing process. Otherwise, the separation of monetary functions could be jeopardized by arbitrage in the markets of the standard commodities, thus tying their price movements to shifts in the supply and demand for means of payment. Greenfield and Yeager accordingly advocate a system of indirect redeemability: obligations are kept meaningful by claims to 'redemption property *worth* as many standard bundles as the number of units to be settled' (Greenfield and Yeager 1986, p. 848).

Proposition 5
Real capital formation and liquidity preference would not conflict in competitive payments systems with a separate unit of account. *Laissez-faire* **of financial intermediation would promote macroeconomic stability**
The separation of monetary functions in the BFH system is held to have many advantages over present-day monetary systems (cf. Greenfield and Yeager 1983, p. 308ff; Cowen and Kroszner 1987, p. 212ff; Yeager 1989):

1. The system would provide a stable unit of account, independent of shifts in the supply and demand for means of payment.
2. The government would come under financial discipline, since it would lose the power to acquire resources by seigniorage and other kinds of inflation tax.
3. Competition under *laissez-faire* would allow financial intermediaries to innovate to the fullest extent – without 'the socially unproductive instability hitherto associated with continual attempts to wriggle around changing government regulations' (Greenfield and Yeager 1983, p. 308).
4. Competition among intermediaries would create incentives to integrate finance and the payments system by creating assets (like mutual fund shares) that double as checking and investment accounts. Conflicts between liquidity preference and 'profit maximization' would disappear with the distinction between money and capital, since all liquidity would be transformed into capital assets. 'Keynesian' liquidity constraints and depressions would be avoided, since 'indulgence

in liquidity preference, far from obstructing the conveyance of released resources into real capital formation, yields interest or dividends corresponding to that use of resources' (Yeager 1989, p. 375).

5. Competition would exert discipline on the BFH funds, since overissue would depreciate shares and induce shareholders to change funds. Imprudent funds would face increasingly adverse balances at the clearing house. Competitive pressure on the funds would thus contribute to price stability by restraining fund lending and fund share issues to real demand.

6. *Laissez-faire* could prevail, even if particular intermediaries failed in competition. Disordering repercussions would not spread as widely as in present-day banking systems. Self-aggravating runs would be concentrated on the failing institutions as 'no scramble for base money of limited total quality could make suspicion of particular institutions spread to others' (Greenfield and Yeager 1983, p. 308). Moreover, mutual funds could not become insolvent in the same way as banks. As funds issue no liabilities in the strict sense, but equities, they could not normally have liabilities in excess of their assets. Portfolio losses would have to be shared by shareholders, but they would most likely be 'distributed' in less critical ways than in fixed-liabilities banking systems.

The long list of presumed advantages does not entirely blind BFH thinkers to disadvantages of a system with heterogenous means of payment, but they treat those problems as technically solvable calculating difficulties, forming only minor obstacles on the way to making money and monetary disorder obsolete (cf. Cowen and Kroszner 1987, p. 211). Positive writings along the BFH line therefore often give the impression of being ambiguous blends of alternative models for purposes of comparison, proposals for monetary reform, and trend extrapolations of ongoing financial innovations, which are supposed to show the way to 'banking and interest rates in a world without money' (Black 1970).

CONFRONTATION

The controversial issue which I wish to elucidate by a confrontation of post-Keynesian theories and New Monetary Economics is perhaps best captured in Hicks's last book:

> We are on the way to a credit economy, in which any money that does not bear interest has become no more than small change, or petty cash ... Money remains of course a standard of value, in terms of which debts are expressed.

> But money as means of payments is just a debt. The payment of a debt is an exchange of debts. We regard it as payment because the debts have different quality. It is quality from the point of view of the creditor that matters. (Hicks 1989, p. 103f)

The quality of debts is precisely the question to which post-Keynesians and New Monetary economists give extremely different answers. In the post-Keynesian view all debts ultimately relate to money as the supremely liquid matter. The money of our time is made up of debts; but these debts have the distinct quality of being irredeemable debts of the government – as such, they are claims on the economy as a whole. True, these claims are convertible into other governments' fiat monies, and there is competition between national currencies on a global scale; and to some extent, financial innovations also serve to circumvent cash requirements and other regulations of the credit business. But all this does not alter the fundamental post-Keynesian proposition that *money is indispensable in the credit economy*, and that the existence of money fundamentally affects real activity by the way it influences the supply and demand for credit.

This proposition is challenged by the BFH vision of a sophisticated credit exchange system. In that system the different qualities of debts are seen as vehicles for financial stability, if they are freely marketed as media of exchange and evaluated in terms of a *separately defined standard of value*. Implicitly, it is held that free competition in the payments system will not tend to re-establish any sort of outside money. The dichotomy of value theory and monetary theory disappears in the 'credit barter' of the BFH world, and the standard propositions of General Equilibrium theory apply.

Both views pose a lot of questions, of which I will discuss only those relating to first, the circularity of argumentations about the relevance of money, and second, the stability of competitive payments systems without money (for a more extensive discussion see Trautwein 1990, p. 25ff).

Circular Contrapositions

The thread of post-Keynesian theory (as described above) is evidently running in circles. Money cannot be fully replaced because it is supremely liquid because it is notoriously scarce because it cannot fully be substituted ... These 'properties' of money are as much the results of its functions as the functionality of money is explained by its properties; and where one would expect a rationale for the 'ultimate asset' quality of money, another circle starts: uncertainty creates the need for money, and money creates uncertainty.

The BFH system is not free from circularities either. *Laissez-faire* systems with a separation of monetary functions can develop two different circles of valuation, depending on whether the unit of account is defined in terms of a commodity bundle or is purely abstract. If the unit is defined in terms of a comprehensive bundle (in order to avoid returns to convertibility), pressures upon relative prices in the bundle would necessitate readjustments of the nominal prices (or 'basket weights') of some or all items in the bundle, in order to keep the value of the aggregate medium of account equivalent to its originally defined unit (cf. Cowen and Kroszner 1990, p. 37f). The unit of account loses its functional meaning if the aggregate price of the bundle items deviates from 1, or if weights have to be readjusted. Destabilizing repercussions on the structure and level of prices occur if nominal prices of bundle items (to a large extent with low cross-elasticities of demand) have to be readjusted. Efforts to preserve bundle value stability in response to shifts in relative prices might thus have self-reinforcing adverse effects.

Another type of circular valuation problem develops if the unit of account is purely abstract. In such a system (as advocated by Cowen and Kroszner 1987), financial assets would never be anything other than claims on other financial assets, since convertibility into an ultimate good or asset is excluded and only heterogenous assets are allowed to circulate. This could either pose the indeterminacy problems of an infinite circular chain of valuation of assets; or endanger the operationality and stability of a system with a purely abstract unit of account, by significant fluctuations of asset values or by the re-emergence of some ultimate convertible asset (cf. White 1984, p. 710 and 1986, p. 851; Hoover 1988, p. 102f).

Despite the apparent circularity of their arguments, it would be inappropriate to accuse the post-Keynesians of begging the question or to condemn the various BFH thinkers of retreating into infinite regress. The circles deserve a closer look on two controversial points: on the (in)separability of monetary functions and related properties, and on the (in)stability of financial and payments systems devoid of base money.

The post-Keynesian tenet of inseparable links between monetary functions and essential properties implies that the BFH system is untenable because it lacks a perfectly liquid asset. Some sort of base money would always be (re)established in the described circular processes. Mutually reinforcing interrelations between the functions and the properties of money are not exclusively a post-Keynesian theme. It is a 'conventional' view that the supply of money (like language) is a natural monopoly, 'self-reinforced' by external economies of scale in its common use (cf. Klein 1974, p. 447ff; King 1983, p. 132f). In so far as reductions in the costs of information about properties of goods and about exchange ratios give rise to positive externalities, money can also be considered a public good (cf. Yeager 1987, p. 313). Both 'market failure' aspects of positive externalities pertain, however, only to the role of money as the standard of value. As a means of payment it is certainly not a public good, but private property – an object of rivalry and exclusive possession. With this functional distinction in mind, it seems perfectly plausible to propose a clear separation of the public good 'unit of account', required for economic communication and calculation, from the private good 'means of payment', required for actual exchanges of property.

The question remains, nevertheless, whether the natural monopoly argument can be extended to the role of money as means of payment. The controversy accordingly boils down to a dispute about the New Monetary economists' belief in the inherent stability of competitive payments systems based on the separation of the medium of account (standard of value) from the media of exchange and debt settlement.

Stability of BFH Systems
In a *laissez-faire* system where fund shares are the predominant media of exchange, runs on particular funds could destabilize the whole system, according to the scheme's very logic. Risks are shifted from financial intermediaries to their customers, since the liabilities of the intermediaries generally will not be fixed in nominal values. Share depreciation in some fund could therefore lead to unexpectedly large redemption claims. The corresponding loss of assets would tend to be self-aggravating, as parting with the most liquid redemption property would further depreciate fund shares, thereby inducing more holders to leave the fund. Redeemed portfolio assets of the losing fund could lose value due to excess supplies, which in turn would affect share values of other funds with the same kind of assets in their portfolios. Moreover, (re)finance conditions would deteriorate for issuers of assets in excess supply. In this way, even a BFH system would not be protected from contagious liquidity constraints of real activity.

Instead of a scramble for base money, there would be a scramble for appreciating fund shares, perhaps also for fixed-value claims to valun bundles. Though asset runs under floating exchange rates may be more self-restraining, it clearly needs to be proved that such a regime would prevent the autocatalytic emergence of a supremely liquid asset that would evolve into money. If flexibility in the use of heterogenous media of exchange is an essential feature and advantage of the BFH system (as opposed to the disequilibrating inertia in the use of a homogenous medium of exchange), costs of ascertaining the values of particular fund shares have to be taken into account. The more significantly share values fluctuate, the higher are such information costs. Increasing information costs in the face of heterogeneity imply increasing external economies in the use of a single, homogenous means of payment and of perfect substitutes in exchange – by fixation of nominal values at par. A natural monopoly of money cannot then be excluded, in so far as it is a general claim on the economy as a whole rather than on a single fund, firm or individual (cf. King 1983, p. 33).

These objections lose much of their force if the BFH system is conceived to be a fixed-liability free-banking system with a homogenous redemption asset (such as gold or T-bills), and a separate multi-commodity medium of account (cf. Yeager 1989). Competing banks would have to maintain the full valun values of their issues of coins, notes and cheques by way of indirect redeemability. Due to the fixed values of the claims, there is more inertia in noteholding (and respective deposit accounts) than in shareholding. Banks with adverse balances at the clearinghouse would not be stripped of their assets as quickly as funds would, since their demand for redemption assets would not (before default) be reflected in the values of the media of exchange they issue.

Scrambles for redemption assets might send the latters' valun prices up. But there is no inherent incentive to switch from the multi-commodity medium of account to the redemption asset as a medium of account. The positive externalities of an established unit of account clearly prevent this, as long as the relative prices of redemption assets and their traded counterparts can be expressed in it without distortion. Therefore, the standard of value and the means of payment need not be one and the same thing, even if both are natural monopolies in their respective functions as unit of account and redemption asset.

Accordingly, any view of money as one autocatalytically multi-functional entity meets a hard challenge in New Monetary Economics. Yet it is not clear whether or not a BFH system with indirect redeemability would be (largely or entirely) protected from critical monetary phenomena such as liquidity crises and debt deflation. The price level could still be affected by 'credit inflation' and 'credit crunches', even though the prices of the redemption assets (as means of payment) could adjust to shifts in supply and demand on markets of their own. The interdependence of markets and, above all, the interdependence of creditors could necessitate adjustments of the whole price level. It cannot, for instance, be excluded that 'over-issuing' banks first bring about a rise in prices and an expansion of real activities by way of leverage finance, and then cause liquidity and finance constraints by way of contageous credit losses – either incurred by their creditors (depositors, note-holders *et alii*) or by the creditors of other intermediaries in want of the appreciating redemption assets.

It has yet to be shown that occasional scrambles for indirectly valued redemption assets will not (or not to the same extent) cause debt-deflationary pressures on the price level in the way they have done in bygone gold standard systems with direct convertibility. Otherwise, the controversy would end up in two irreconcilable beliefs: Keynes's suspicion of any redemption asset 'giving rise to the characteristic problems of a monetary economy' (1936, p. 294) would still stand up to assertions of smooth equilibration under the disciplinary pressures of free competition in financial intermediation.

NOTES

1. I have benefited from comments by Tyler Cowen, Omar Hamouda, Axel Leijonhufvud, Leland Yeager and participants of the Hohenheim Conference. Any remaining errors are mine.
2. It should be noted, however, that the distinction based on endogeneity and stringency of the money supply in much of the quoted literature is more a matter of emphasis than of clear dividing lines. Minsky's contributions in particular, can be interpreted in both ways.
3. For a longer, more differentiated synthesis of post-Keynesian theories see Trautwein (1990).
4. 'Illiquidity' means the potential loss of capital value if an asset is to be realized – that is, exchanged for money – at short notice. Cf. Hicks (1962) and (1989, p. 62); Trautwein (1990, p. 6 n.13).
5. By an extreme extension of Keynes's 'observation', Riese deduces *all* profits on capital assets from a systemic excess demand for money, forming a market-inherent 'budget constraint' of resource allocation. Productive investments of capital are kept scarce to the extent that 'excess supplies' of physical resources and labour lower their costs to such a degree as to allow prices to yield profits which in equilibrium equal the money rate of interest. Cf. Riese (1983, p. 113f) and (1987, p. 199ff).
6. This definition is emphatically advanced by Riese (1986, p. 40f), Herr (1988, p. 78ff), Spahn (1988, p. 184f). Keynes and the Fundamentalists (Davidson, Minsky *et al.*) have generally used wider and shifting definitions of money, but they have not accounted for them in the light of liquidity preference. Cf. Keynes (1936, p. 167, n.1), Davidson (1978, p. 155ff), Minsky (1985, p. 25).
7. Regulation of the money supply obviously presupposes market failures, such as natural monopolies, negative externalities and public goods. All these cases are implicit in post-Keynesian theories, but rarely explicated (and never set off against the neoclassical underpinnings of these notions). I will return to this in the final section.
8. Lack of space prevents me from elaborating on 'financial instability' theorems and other post-Keynesian theories of the cyclical interaction between borrowers, lenders and the central bank. For a synthesis see Trautwein (1990, p. 9ff).
9. Greenfield and Yeager (1983) have dubbed their system 'BFH' with reference to the seminal essays by Black (1970), Fama (1980) and Hall (1982). It should be mentioned that the use of the label New Monetary Economics for both New Classical and other approaches, rather of Modern Austrian provenance, is suggested by Cowen and Kroszner (1987), but not shared by all of the authors subsumed under that heading.
10. For critical discussions of Black (1970) and Fama (1980) see McCallum (1985) and Hoover (1988, p. 94ff). The more prominent Legal Restrictions approach of Wallace and his collaborators cannot be followed up here. Cf. Wallace (1983); Bryant and Wallace (1984) and, for criticism, White (1987); Hoover (1988, p. 23ff).
11. The same arguments pertain to excess demand for money so as to interpret depression

as an essentially monetary disorder. Yeager (1968, pp. 45, 60ff) in fact refers to Keynes's 'Essential Properties of Money' for this argument.

12. The checkable money-market mutual funds which have evolved in the USA during the seventies and eighties are frequently cited as models for BFH-intermediaries. Cf. Greenfield and Yeager (1983, p. 307f); Cowen and Kroszner (1987).

13. 'There is no tangible money but the inconvenience of barter is nevertheless avoided; transactions are effected by means of signals to an accounting network, with these signals resulting in appropriate credits and debits to the wealth accounts for sellers and buyers' (McCallum 1985, p. 4). For further details and modifying explications see Greenfield and Yeager (1983) and (1986), Cowen and Kroszner (1987), Yeager (1989).

REFERENCES

Black, F. (1970) 'Banking and Interest Rates in a World Without Money – The Effects of Uncontrolled Banking', *Journal of Bank Research*, 1, Autumn, 8–20.

Bryant, J. and Wallace, N. (1984) 'A Price Discrimination Analysis of Monetary Policy', *Review of Economic Studies*, 51, 279–88.

Cowen, T. and Kroszner, R. (1987) 'Neue Entwicklung in den "New Monetary Economics"', *Zeitschrift für Wirtschaftspolitik*, 36, 207–20.

Cowen, T. and Kroszner, R. (1990) 'Commodity Bundle Media of Account: "Black–Fama–Hall" Reform Proposals', George Mason University, unpublished manuscript.

Davidson, P.A. (1978) *Money and the Real World* (2nd edn), London, Basingstoke: Macmillan.

Davidson, P.A. (1979) 'Why Money Matters: Lessons from a Half-Century of Monetary Theory', *Journal of Post Keynesian Economics*, 1, 46–70.

Davidson, Paul A. (1989) 'Keynes and Money', in R. Hill (ed.), *Keynes, Money and Monetarism*, London, Basingstoke: Macmillan, 2–36.

Fama, E. (1980) 'Banking in the Theory of Finance', *Journal of Monetary Economics*, 6, 39–57.

Greenfield, R.L. and Yeager, L.B. (1983) 'A Laissez-Faire Approach to Monetary Stability', *Journal of Money, Credit and Banking*, 15, 302–15.

Greenfield, R.L. and Yeager, L.B. (1986) 'Competitive Payments Systems: Comment', *American Economic Review*, 76, 848–9.

Hagemann, H. and Steiger, O. (1988) 'Keynes' "General Theory" nach fünfzig Jahren', in H. Hagemann and O. Steiger (eds), *Keynes' General Theory nach fünfzig Jahren*, Berlin: Duncker & Humblot, 9–57.

Hall, R.E. (1982) 'Explorations in the Gold Standard and Related Policies for Stabilizing the Dollar', in R. Hall (ed.), *Inflation: Causes and Effects*, Chicago: Chicago University Press, 111–22.

Heinsohn, G. and Steiger, O. (1988) 'Warum Zins? Keynes und die Grundlagen einer monetären Werttheorie', in H. Hagemann and O. Steiger (eds), *Keynes' General Theory nach fünfzig Jahren*, Berlin: Duncker & Humblot, 315–53.

Herr, H. (1988) 'Wege zur Theorie einer monetären Produktionswirtschaft – Der keynesianische Fundamentalismus', *Ökonomie und Gesellschaft*, Jahrbuch 6, 66–98.

Hicks, J. (1962) 'Liquidity', *Economic Journal*, 72, 787–802.

Hicks, J. (1989) *A Market Theory of Money*, Oxford: Oxford University Press.

Hoover, K.D. (1988) *New Classical Economics: A Sceptical Inquiry*, Oxford: Basil Blackwell.

Kaldor, N. and Trevithick, J. (1981) 'A Keynesian Perspective on Money', *Lloyds Bank Review*, **39**, 1–19.

Keynes, J.M. (1936) 'The General Theory of Employment, Interest and Money', *Collected Writings*, vol VII, London, Basingstoke: Macmillan [1973].

King, R.G. (1983) 'On the Economics of Private Money', *Journal of Monetary Economics*, **12**, 127–58.

Klein, B. (1974) 'The Competitive Supply of Money', *Journal of Money, Credit and Banking*, **6**, 423–53.

Lavoie, M. (1984) 'The Endogenous Flow of Credit and the Post Keynesian Theory of Money', *Journal of Economic Issues*, **18**, 771–96.

McCallum, B.T. (1985) 'Bank Deregulation, Accounting Systems of Exchange, and the Unit of Account: A Critical Review', NBER Working Paper, No. 1572.

Minsky, H. (1975) *John Maynard Keynes*, New York: Columbia University Press.

Minsky, H. (1977) 'A Theory of Systemic Fragility', in E.J. Altman and A.W. Sametz (eds), *Financial Crisis – Institutions and Markets in a Fragile Environment*, New York: Wiley & Sons, 138–52.

Minsky, H. (1985) 'The Financial Instability Hypothesis: A Restatement' in P. Arestis and T. Skouras (eds), *Post Keynesian Economic Theory. A Challenge to Neo-Classical Economics*, Brighton: Wheatsheaf, 24–55.

Moore, B. (1988) 'The Endogenous Money Supply', *Journal of Post Keynesian Economics*, **10**, 372–85.

Mott, T. (1989) 'A Post Keynesian Perspective on a "Cashless Competitive Payments System" ', *Journal of Post Keynesian Economics*, **11**, 360–69.

Riese, H. (1983) 'Geldökonomie, Keynes und die Anderen. Kritik der monetären Grundlagen der Orthodoxie', in *Ökonomie und Gesellschaft*, Jahrbuch 1, 103–60.

Riese, H. (1986) *Theorie der Inflation*, Tübingen: J.C.B. Mohr.

Riese, H. (1987) 'Aspekte eines monetären Keynesianismus – Kritik der postkeynesianischen Ökonomie und Gegenentwurf', in *Postkeynesianismus. Ökonomische Theorie in der Tradition von Keynes, Kalecki und Sraffa*, Marburg: Metropolis, 189–206.

Riese, H. (1988) 'Das Verhältnis von monetärer und realwirtschaftlicher Dimension im Keynesianismus', in K-G. Zinn (ed.), *Keynes in nachkeynesscher Sicht – Zum 50. Erscheinungsjahr der 'Allgemeinen Theorie' von J.M. Keynes*, Wiesbaden: Deutscher Universitätsverlag, 73–106.

Sargent, T.J. (1987) *Dynamic Macroeconomic Theory*, Cambridge, MA and London: Harvard University Press.

Sargent, T.J. and Wallace, N. (1982) 'The Real Bills Doctrine vs. the Quantity Theory: A Reconsideration', *Journal of Political Economy*, **90**, 1212–36.

Spahn, H-P. (1988) 'Liquiditätspräferenz, internationales Geld und Notenbankpolitik – Monetärer Keynesianismus und das keynesianische Element im praktizierten Monetarismus', *'Ökonomie und Gesellschaft*, Jahrbuch 6, 178–206.

Trautwein, H-M. (1990) 'Money-Matters in Post Keynesian Theories and New Monetary Economics', Arbeitsbericht Nr. 77 des Fachbereichs Wirtschafts- und Sozialwissenschaften der Universität Lüneburg.

Wallace, N. (1983) 'A Legal Restrictions Theory of the Demand for "Money" and the Role of Monetary Policy', *Federal Reserve Bank of Minneapolis Quarterly Review*, **7**, 1–7.

White, L.H. (1984) 'Competitive Payments Systems and the Unit of Account', *American Economic Review,* **74,** 699–712.

White, L.H. (1986) 'Competitive Payments Systems: Reply', *American Economic Review,* **76,** 850–53.

White, L.H. (1987) 'Accounting for Non-Interest-Bearing Currency: A Critique of the Legal Restrictions Theory of Money', *Journal of Money, Credit and Banking,* **19,** 448–56.

Yeager, L.B. (1968) 'Essential Properties of the Medium of Exchange', *Kyklos,* **21,** 45–69.

Yeager, L.B. (1987) 'Stable Money and Free-Market Currencies', in J.A. Dorn and A.J. Schwartz (eds), *The Search for Stable Money. Essays on Monetary Reform,* Chicago: Chicago University Press, 296–317.

Yeager, L. B. (1989) 'A Competitive Payments System: Some Objections Considered', *Journal of Post Keynesian Economics,* **11,** 370–77.

5. Monetary Theory after Sraffa

Gary Mongiovi and Christof Rühl[1]

> *Of money, wit and wisdom believe*
> *one fourth of what you hear.*
> *(Anonymous)*

INTRODUCTION

The trouble with economists is that they just don't know how to handle money. Few things are more obvious than the fact that monetary institutions and financial assets are crucial elements of a modern market economy. What has proved elusive is a coherent explanation of the role they play. There is no real place for money in the theory of intertemporal general equilibrium, which typically posits the existence of complete contingent futures markets. Temporary equilibrium versions of Walrasian theory can accommodate money – that is, it can assign a positive price to a commodity that has no intrinsic use value – either as a device by which agents preserve flexibility of action in the face of uncertainty, or as an institution that reduces the real cost of exchange; but when money is introduced the existence of an equilibrium cannot generally be established (Hahn 1965, 1981).[2]

The two important lines of aggregate analysis that have descended from Keynes – through Friedman and Phelps on the one hand, and Modigliani, Patinkin and Tobin on the other – both contend that the long period impact of monetary disturbances falls entirely on the price level. But the extensive debates that produced this consensus failed to establish any definitive results regarding the speed of market adjustment or the nature of the monetary transmission mechanism; hence key issues with important policy implications were left unresolved. Indeed, these issues have receded from the forefront of macroeconomic discussion, crowded out (so to speak) by the New Classical research programme. The latter acknowledges that unanticipated monetary disturbances can have a short-period impact on output levels, employment, the growth rate, and so on; but barring circumstances that might generate hysteresis, money is neutral with respect to the long-period behaviour of real variables.

Conventional monetary economics reflects the theoretical tension latent in any attempt to assign a meaningful role to money in a framework which, at the most fundamental level, explains all real magnitudes independently of monetary forces. The past two decades have witnessed the emergence of an alternative post-Keynesian tradition; the leading architects of this approach have called attention to the need for a theoretical framework that can elucidate the connections between monetary and real phenomena.[3] While much of this work exhibits a refreshing concreteness that is rarely found in modern monetary economics, the post-Keynesian research programme has itself so far failed to produce a systematic and convincing account of how money influences real variables. Useful insights about uncertainty and expectations, or the endogeneity of money, or financial fragility, do not in themselves constitute explanations of economic processes. What seems to be missing is an appreciation of the degree to which monetary theory is contingent upon the value and distribution theory that underlies it: what can or cannot be said about money depends to a large extent on what has already been said about how relative prices and incomes are formed.

The aim of this chapter is to contribute to a clarification of the foundations upon which a useful monetary theory can be built. Our principal frame of reference is the classical surplus approach to the theory of value and distribution, as reconstructed by Sraffa (1960). Sraffa, as is well known, was concerned with explaining relative prices and distribution in a static context, and most subsequent writers in that tradition have tended to focus on similar problems; monetary issues have, until recently, been left out of consideration. We note at the outset that neither post-Keynesian analysis nor the surplus approach provides a convincing account of the way monetary and real variables interact, though they fail for different reasons. After a brief review of the problems traditionally raised by monetary theory, we present critical evaluations of these two approaches. In the course of a discussion on the determination of outputs within the surplus approach, we shall consider whether lessons can be drawn from connecting two lines of reasoning that have thus far remained entirely disconnected: the structural description of a market economy implicit in Sraffa's reconstructed classical model; and the behavioural hypothesis of rational expectations which, since its introduction by Muth (1961) only one year later, has come to dominate the macroeconomic literature.

MONEY AND MARGINALIST THEORY

Before considering how money might fit into a heterodox framework, a few words are in order regarding the role which it plays in mainstream theory. The two *bêtes noirs* of Keynesian polemics are Say's Law and the Quantity Theory of Money; rejection of both of these doctrines has come to be regarded as a litmus test of a theory's Keynesian pedigree. But Say's Law is a red herring, and the standard arguments against the Quantity Theory have missed their mark.

Say's Law is so closely identified with the supposition of a tendency toward full employment that its original meaning has been nearly lost. As understood by the classicals, Say's Law asserted that any act of production inevitably gives rise to an amount of demand sufficient to purchase whatever was produced. Its original function was evidently to compensate for the absence of a classical explanation of the magnitude of the social product. By permitting the classicals to suppose that any level of aggregate output would be supported by aggregate spending, the Law of Markets relieved them of the need to consider how that level of output was determined in the first place; hence they could regard the latter as a datum when explaining prices and distribution. Say's Law implies nothing whatsoever about whether the economy tends toward full employment, and it was not deployed by the classicals to derive propositions about the labour market. Moreover, classical theory contains no mechanism which supports the claim that production calls forth a matching level of demand. If an appropriate theory of output had been available to the classicals, they could have abandoned Say's Law (Mongiovi 1990).

The Quantity Theory, on the other hand, is directly rooted in the orthodox explanation of distribution according to which the forces of supply and demand tend to bring about a situation in which any factor with a positive price is fully employed; the subsequent analysis of monetary phenomena takes place within a framework that regards full employment as the normal condition. The equation of exchange $MV = PQ$, which *is* implicit the classical literature, does not in itself imply full employment. It does entail, however, that if the level of real output Q is fixed, an increase in the effective quantity of money MV must give rise to a proportional increase in the level of money prices.

Because they lacked an explanation of outputs, the classicals treated the level of economic activity as parametric in their discussions of distribution and prices; and they accordingly tended to view the relationship between the price level and the volume of the circulating medium in terms similar to those associated with the modern version of the Quantity Theory. But in so far as their analysis of distribution does not entail full employment, there is room for an output theory in which money is non-neutral.[4]

Since the marginalist theory of distribution asserts that under normal conditions the economy tends to operate at full employment, changes in the effective quantity of the circulating medium can, in the long period, influence *only* the level of money prices: *the orthodox theory of distribution implies the Quantity Theory of Money.* Thus, as Green (1982, p. 60) observes, 'the quantity theory of money *as a theory* only took shape with the marginal revolution; . . . classical quantity theory was not a theory at all, but simply a logical consequence of assuming an independent level of output'.

POST-KEYNESIAN MONETARY ECONOMICS

By undermining the explanation of distribution upon which the Quantity Theory is grounded, the Cambridge critique appears to open the way for money to play an active role in the determination of real variables. Several heterodox approaches have yielded promising insights in this direction, without yet providing a fully satisfying account of how money matters. While a thorough survey of these approaches is beyond the scope of the present work, a few remarks concerning their robustness are worth making.

The post-Keynesian literature on money has focused on three themes which, though treated separately here, tend to overlap with one another.

Endogeneity of Money
A number of writers, notably Kaldor (1970, 1982) and Moore (1988), have stressed the endogenous character of money in modern industrial economies. Since money originates in the extension of credit by the banking system, the quantity of money in existence, they contend, will always adjust to accommodate the quantity demanded. When excess reserves are present in the system, any increase in the demand for credit will call forth additional loans – additional *money* – at the current interest rate. And if credit has already been extended to the point where excess reserves are close to zero, the central bank in its capacity as lender of last resort will be compelled in the face of a rise in the demand for credit, to make additional reserves available through the discount window in order 'to ensure that the clearing banks do not become insolvent as a result of lack of liquidity' (Kaldor 1982, p. 47). Nor, the argument goes, can the monetary authorities bring about an expansion of the money supply unless agents had meant to hold more money in the first place, or agents can be induced, by

a prior reduction of interest rates, to hold more money.[5] What the monetary authorities *can* regulate, by fixing the terms at which they extend credit to commercial banks, is the level of interest rates.

The basic point – that the supply of money cannot be fixed independently of the demand for it – is not in dispute. But the analytical importance assigned to this issue appears to be excessive, at least in the light of doctrinal history. For endogenous money was a key element in the monetary writings of Wicksell (1898), Hayek (1931, 1933) and the pre-*General Theory* Keynes (1930), all of whom explained macroeconomic fluctuations in terms of the ability of the banking system to extend credit on demand at a rate of interest below the real rate of return on capital: they were in fact testing the limits of the simple Quantity Theory.[6] The argument of *The General Theory*, on the other hand, proceeds on the supposition that the quantity of money is fixed exogenously by the monetary authorities (Keynes 1936, pp. 246–7). Thus the endogeneity of money was acknowledged, and its consequences analysed, well before the book was written; while Keynes himself never suggested that endogeneity was in any way central to the particular monetary theory of production he had in mind in 1936.[7]

Beyond this, endogeneity in the Kaldor–Moore sense paradoxically appears to rule out the possibility that money can have a systematic influence on real phenomena, in either the long or the short period: if the quantity of money in existence is purely a consequence of the amount of money demanded, the former cannot be said to play a causal role.

Perhaps it is the money rate of interest that matters; then we must consider how it matters. On this point the post-Keynesian literature provides no clear answer. Interest rate changes could be expected to influence the composition of agents' portfolios. But the real economic consequences of a change in the form in which agents wish to hold their wealth are apt to be indirect and of uncertain magnitude and direction. An increase in the interest rate, for example, might induce agents to substitute yield-producing assets (such as bonds) for money; but how this will affect output, employment, real wages, and so on depends upon various elasticities and upon the connections between interest rates and the prices of all assets, including investment goods and shares of common stock. These connections need to be sorted out before a line of causality can be established linking interest rate changes to variations in output and employment via portfolio adjustments; it is not apparent that post-Keynesian theory has in this respect advanced much beyond the Keynesian mainstream of the 1970s, as represented for example by Tobin (1965).

A second possibility is that the interest rate affects real activity directly, through its influence on the level of investment. The difficulty here is that, after Sraffa, there is no theoretical basis for supposing that the interest rate and investment are related in any systematic way. Moreover, as soon as the proposition is accepted that the interest rate regulates investment in the conventional manner, there would remain the need to explain why market forces fail to push the interest rate toward the level compatible with full employment.

The third possibility is that variations in the interest rate entail shifts in income distribution, which in turn have consequences for accumulation, output and employment. Although neither Kaldor nor Moore has anything to say about the distributive impact of interest rate variations, recent work by Pivetti (1985) and Panico (1985) attempts to establish a causal link running from interest rate variations to distribution. This line of work will be considered below.

Money and Uncertainty

Other post-Keynesian writers have stressed the connection between money and fundamental uncertainty.[8] The link has two aspects, both of which derive from the properties of money as a store of value. First, because incomes are paid in money, entrepreneurs cannot be certain that the demand for their products at any particular future date will coincide with the amounts produced. Investment decisions are made in an environment of uncertainty and must be based upon producers' expectations about future levels of demand. At the same time, however, money reduces both the level of uncertainty and its potential to cause damage; money contracts enable agents to anticipate at least some transactions with relative confidence.[9] Furthermore, Hicks (1974) has pointed out that the use of a medium of exchange which also serves as a store of value means that an agent always has the option to delay taking a decision until more information becomes available. Uncertainty can never be entirely removed, and the agent must balance the anticipated benefits of waiting against the potential cost of acting too late; but having the flexibility to 'wait and see' ought to reduce, in some sense, the risks of decision-making under uncertainty.

Much of this makes sense, as far as it takes us; the trouble is that it doesn't take us far at all. The basic issue here is whether *on balance* money is a stabilizing or a destabilizing force; and this question remains unresolved. On the one side, writers like Chick (1983) or Minsky (1975, 1982) insist upon the destabilizing impact of speculation, and call attention to the special role of the speculative demand for money. But this view neglects the existence of a virtual armory of financial instruments – puts, calls, stock options, interest rate swaps, and so forth – that enable agents to hedge themselves against the consequences of unforeseen events.

Interestingly, advocates of the alternative view, that money promotes stability under conditions of uncertainty, have not emphasized the role of such hedging instruments, but tend instead to focus on the money contract as a device for limiting the range of possible states of nature (Davidson 1980; Kregel 1980). Against this position, we might note that the use of money is not a pre-condition for the formation of contracts; the possibility, at least in principle, of non-money contracts weakens any claim that the essential social function of money is to bridge the uncertainty that separates present from future. Moreover, the variability of different price levels for different classes of commodities (which contracts do not generally suppress) would undermine any stabilizing function of contracts. The existence of a contract which fixes the price of one commodity or input while other commodities or inputs are undergoing substantial price changes will alter the positions of the contracting parties in unanticipated ways; and in so far as contracts limit the flexibility with which agents can respond to new circumstances, they will exacerbate rather than dampen the destructive potential of unexpected change.[10]

Even if we accept the claim that contracts suppress uncertainty, the argument is marred by a curious irony: particular significance is assigned to wage contracts, which enable entrepreneurs to take decisions on the supposition that an important element of costs will remain unchanged in money terms for a specified period of time. The real impact of money, on this reasoning, is evidently that it facilitates the formation of contracts which prevent the wage from falling to a level that would clear the labour market. The argument provides a rationale, in terms of monetary institutions, for wage rigidity; but the implicit explanation of unemployment is identical with that of conventional marginalist analysis, an explanation whose validity has been called into question by the capital controversy.

Expectations and uncertainty are pervasive features of social existence; but no useful theory can be built upon unobservable subjective phenomena unless the latter are related unambiguously to the objective stimuli that explain them. This is the main difficulty with placing uncertainty at the centre of monetary theory. The fact that no definitive answer can be given to the question whether monetary institutions reinforce or counteract the destabilizing effects of uncertainty is perhaps only the most obvious manifestation of this problem.

Financial Instability
According to Minsky's (1982, 1986) financial instability hypothesis, firms tend during periods of economic expansion to misjudge the degree to which investment projects can safely be financed by debt. As the expansion continues, this over-confidence (which has been fuelled by steadily

rising profits) can lead to a situation in which firms find themselves dangerously over-leveraged; that is, to a state of financial fragility in which the economy is vulnerable to even a small interruption of the flow of expenditure. Such an interruption is indeed likely to occur, since the leverage position of the economy has set up a situation in which interest rates are bound to rise.

This story, which is both plausible and consistent with casual observation, nevertheless leaves a number of questions unanswered. Why, first of all, do firms allow themselves to become over-leveraged? Surely from past experience management knows the maximum gearing ratio consistent with sound business practice. Textbooks on financial management discuss at length the appropriate levels – generally rules of thumb – of various financial ratios. Any systematic tendency of firms to accumulate levels of debt which threaten their own survival would be a phenomenon which requires explanation. Second, a firm's financial ratios indicate the degree of risk incurred by lenders when they extend credit to it; *ceteris paribus*, firms with high gearing ratios are greater credit risks than firms with low ratios. Lenders might be expected then, to charge higher rates of interest to firms with higher than average gearing ratios. If lenders do behave in this way, the interest rate mechanism should suppress the tendency of firms to become over-leveraged.[11] And if interest rates do not reflect the credit risk associated with individual borrowers – a true cost, for which lending institutions should require compensation – the question of why this is the case must be posed.

MONEY AND THE SURPLUS APPROACH

Recent literature has attempted to develop Sraffa's cryptic observation that distribution might be susceptible of determination by the monetary authorities through their ability to regulate the money rate of interest (Sraffa 1960, p. 33). Sraffa never made clear his views on how the hint ought to be formally developed. One obvious procedure is to introduce interest payments, as an element of cost, into the standard classical price equations; this can be done in two ways.

First, we might follow Pivetti (1985), who argues that competition operates to bring the total rate of profit on capital r^* into equality with the sum of the interest rate i plus a historically rigid normal net rate of return r_n. The price equations then may be written:[12]

$$p = pA(1 + r^*) + wl, \text{ or}$$

$$p = wl[I - A(1 + r^*)]^{-1}, \tag{5.1}$$

where A is a unit input coefficient matrix, l is a row vector of labour input requirements per unit of output; w is the *money* wage; p is a row vector of prices in money terms; and $r^* = (r_n + i)$. If r_n is presumed to be constant in the long run, an increase of i by the monetary authorities will entail an increase in prices, and, with a given money wage, a decline in the real wage rate.[13]

An alternative treatment (Panico 1985) gives much the same result. Let d be a row vector of coefficients which represent the typical levels of debt per unit of output in the various sectors. Since in the long period each sector's revenues must be sufficient to cover interest costs, we have:

$$p = pA(1 + r_n) + wl + id, \text{ or}$$

$$p = [wl + id][I + A(1 + r_n)]^{-1}. \tag{5.2}$$

Here again an increase in i with w and r_n fixed, must lead to an increase of all commodity prices in money terms, and therefore to a decrease in the real wage.

While the models represented by systems (5.1) and (5.2) do expose certain important features of a modern market economy, they ultimately fail as explanations of distribution. The models are intended as explanations of the normal (long-period) distribution pattern, and therefore require that the interest rate fixed by the monetary authorities be permanent, or lasting, in some meaningful sense. But what meaning can be given to a 'lasting change' in the rate of interest when, as Nell (1988) has pointed out, the monetary authorities typically alter the level of interest rates (or try to, anyway) at frequent intervals? Since interest rates are established through the operations of the bond market, there are questions too about the ability of the monetary authorities to sustain the interest rate at a level that is not consistent with the public's assessment of the appropriate value of bonds, which of course depends partly on the profitability (net of interest) of private capital.[14]

There are a number of problems relating to the way debt is modelled, particularly in the second formulation of the argument. Can the level of debt really be supposed to bear any systematic relation to output as, for example, wage costs or material costs do? If not, the elements of d will be difficult to specify in an unambiguous fashion, and moreover, there will be no reason to suppose that they can be regarded as constant with respect to output. If a change in the interest rate did have the impact on distribution that these theories contend, the resulting change in the real wage would entail changes in consumption, and hence in outputs and in the debt coefficients. These coefficients are in fact even more directly dependent on the interest rate; for the degree of indebtedness that any enterprise is willing to sustain must certainly be sensitive to the rate of interest. Beyond all this, the debt coefficients are likely to differ among firms in a given sector, in which case the formulation of system (5.2) will be incompatible with the law of one price.[15]

The main difficulty with the approach, though, lies in the supposition that the money wage *and* the normal rate of net profit are parametric. A general increase in prices in consequence of a rise in the interest rate might be expected to result in higher wage demands by workers. Whether these will be sufficient to fight off a deterioration in their standard of living depends on a range of considerations that cannot be captured in the static price equations. It is conceivable that the rise in money wages could more than offset the increases in the prices of wage goods, so that workers experience an *increased* standard of living. Nor can the long-period effect on the rate of (net) profits be predicted *a priori* since the ability of firms to pass on cost increases is constrained by their need to sell their products. When the point is made that distribution depends upon market power, what is usually meant is the market power of workers versus employers. Here, however, the market power of those who demand goods relative to those who sell them is a crucial consideration. It follows that an increase in the interest rate is as likely to squeeze (net) profits as it is to reduce real wages. The experience of the US economy during the 1980s, for example, appears to be consistent with this view: real wage rates and rates of return in manufacturing industries declined, while the rate of return on financial capital increased.

The models of Pivetti and Panico help to clarify some aspects of the distributional role of finance. But the forces which regulate distribution in a monetary economy are evidently too complex to be reduced to the simple mechanisms described in such models.

THE DETERMINATION OF ACTIVITY LEVELS IN CLASSICAL THEORY

The model associated with Sraffa is concerned with economic statics; it depicts the structure of an economy in a state of rest, with all quantities fixed at their normal levels, and all prices adjusted to their long-period values. Monetary theory, by contrast, has traditionally dealt with issues relating to changing activity levels, to disequilibrium phenomena and to short-run problems. The prospect for 'monetary theory after Sraffa', then, depends upon whether classical analysis can contribute anything to our understanding of the long unresolved issues raised by monetary theory.

The system of equations presented in Parts I and II of *Production of Commodities* summarize what Garegnani (1984) has called the theoretical core of the surplus approach. Three categories of data are taken as parametric in order to determine the set of relative prices consistent with a uniform rate of return: first the technical conditions of production; second, the size and composition of the social product; and third, either the real wage or the profit rate. The long-period position established by these data is generally conceived as a centre of gravitation toward which the economy is pushed by competition.

The core exposes a set of logically necessary and mathematically exact relationships which link relative prices, the real wage and the profit rate, once the fundamental data are specified. The data themselves, on the other hand, are governed by complex social, historical and institutional influences, and therefore do not have the status of logically necessary inferences. The investigation of these influences is accordingly relegated to a separate stage of analysis outside the core. In particular, the forces that regulate the historical trend of variables like output, employment, real wages, and the profit rate, are left to be analysed separately from the forces operating at a *given* stage in the economy's development.

This two-stage analytical method does not imply that theoretical issues lying outside the core are in any sense less significant than those examined within it. On the contrary, in as much as the data are what determine the long-period position, the task of explaining them would appear to occupy an important place in economic analysis.[16] Nor does the classical focus on long-period analysis imply that questions relating to the short period or to economic dynamics are devoid of relevance; the core should in fact provide a useful frame of reference for the analysis of what happens when (as is always the case in reality) the economy is not in a fully adjusted position, including of course the analysis of accumulation and other aspects of economic dynamics. It is precisely in connection with such issues that money acquires significance.

Both the classical and the older neoclassical approaches share the long-period method in which equilibrium configurations of relative prices are conceived as stable attractors. In classical theory, the possibility of establishing a trend rate of growth which is independent of short-run deviations of endogenous variables from their long-period values requires that these deviations be understood as oscillations around the fully adjusted position which acts as a centre of gravity. As in the traditional neoclassical comparison of the business cycle to the movements of a pendulum, any deviation of say, relative prices from their normal values would result in a process of convergence back toward their equilibrium levels.[17] This parallel in *method* has drawn fire from the post-Keynesian camp. The harshest critics would deny altogether the legitimacy of any equilibrium approach, and some go so far as to place classical and neoclassical *theories* on the same footing.[18] A less extreme critique simply questions whether a classical long-period position (as distinct from a Keynesian short run with a given capital stock) can ever be established by an actual historical process (Asimakopulos 1990). While the terms of the debate occasionally appear to be confused, these critical arguments raise sensible questions about the roles money, expectations and uncertainty ought to play within the surplus approach.

Perhaps the most basic distinction between the classical and neoclassical approaches lies in the fact that the prices, activity levels and distribution variables found in classical theory need not exhibit the optimality properties associated with the equilibria determined in neoclassical models. More specifically, the level of activity will not typically be characterized by full employment of labour. Thus the disturbance of a long-period position could plausibly lead to the restoration of an initial position that was not Pareto optimal. At the same time, the system's trend rate of growth is left to be explained at a separate stage of analysis. The question naturally arises whether anything can be said about the recursive effects on the data set when an arbitrarily chosen initial position is disturbed.

Three issues have to be distinguished in order to consider more precisely the problem at hand.

(*i*)   There is first the question whether under ordinary circumstances a unique stable equilibrium can be established within classical theory. At the moment this issue remains unresolved, and we will not pursue it here. In what follows we assume that such an equilibrium can generally be established.

(*ii*) Let us assume the same for a neoclassical system. Once the system's data (preferences, technology and factor endowments) are specified, its growth path will be uniquely determined; the long-run trend will reflect an inherent tendency toward Pareto optimality, whatever the initial position happens to have been; and the position of any variable can be determined at any moment in time, save for random disturbances that might generate short-run fluctuations. The conventional neoclassical growth story is hardly convincing; but the model does give definite results.

What can be said about the trend rate of growth of real output in a system defined along classical lines? Since the system does not exhibit the optimality and full employment properties of the neoclassical growth path, a multitude of growth paths are conceivable from the outset. And since the growth path is not driven by the forces of marginalist theory, the system's overall growth rate would appear to be indeterminate. One might be tempted to interpret the long-period prices and the given outputs as elements of a steady state growth path. Garegnani (1983) has observed that such an assumption begs the central question, which is to explain how the rate of growth is determined in the first place.

(*iii*)   The truly interesting questions arise, however, when we consider the possibility that the data may themselves depend upon the values taken by the dependent variables. Thus we are led to the problem of path dependence. Given the endogenous determination of the growth rate of real output in the marginalist framework, we might consider whether permitting short-period deviations to exert some influence on the fundamental data help us to explain the movement of the classical natural position over time.

   Garegnani (1983) was the first writer to discuss clearly the problem of the determinacy of the classical growth path. Considering the possibility of an alternative to the orthodox explanation of the level of output, he pointed out that to show that the economy fails to attain full employment *in the short run* is 'not the same thing' as demonstrating that the economy does not gravitate around a position that is close to full employment *in the long period* (ibid., p. 76).

   Consider Figure 5.1. Let *A* be an arbitrarily chosen initial position (with *Y* and *t* representing aggregate real output and time), corresponding to the normal utilization of the capital stock that happens to be in existence at time t^*. The line *AB* indicates the trend that real output would follow over time according to basic neoclassical reasoning; the growth rate would be explained, that is, by the saving generated by the income corresponding to the normal utilization of productive capacity. Now let *A'* be a level of aggregate output lower than *A* but corresponding to the same initial level of productive capacity; that is, connected with lower than normal utilization and consequently with a lower level of employment. *A'* might be interpreted as a short-run deviation located on a curve oscillating around the neoclassical trend line *AB*; or we might interpret it as a position on a curve that oscillates about the trend line *A'B'*, lying below and progressively diverging from *AB*. In this case the capital stock would be growing at a lower rate than in neoclassical theory, owing to the initial under-utilization of capacity. It is also possible to argue that a new trend line (such as *A"B"* or *A"B'''*) can depart from each point on *AB* or *A'B'*, according to whether utilization at t^{**} is above or below what would be required to preserve the path in question; more generally, the new trend

Figure 5.1   Classical and neoclassical interpretations of output trends

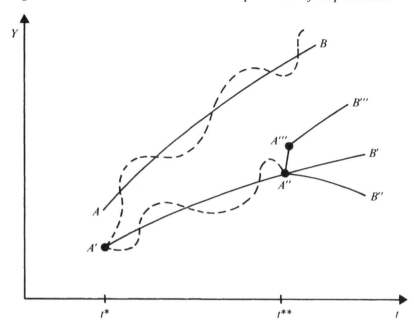

line would be contingent on deviations from the long-run trend as soon as
we allow these deviations to influence the data set.

Let us be clear what is at stake here. A distinction has to be introduced
which, though it is obvious, is often overlooked. The trend lines drawn in
Figure 5.1 can be kept separate for analytical purposes and may be taken
as corresponding loosely to the three issues identified above.

AB shows the conventional neoclassical equilibrium growth path,
which is optimal given preferences, factor endowments and technology.
The same growth path could be established, *as a special case*, by the
equations of a classical surplus model provided that the parameters determined outside the core happen to coincide with the requirements of this
particular trend line.

The line *A'B'*, on the other hand, corresponds to the trend line discussed
under the heading of issue (*ii*) above. Characterized by persistent unemployment, and sub-optimal in comparison with the neoclassical growth
path, *A'B'* represents the path that might be observed within the framework of the surplus approach. Without additional assumptions, the path
A'B', *because it is associated with persistent unemployment*, could never be
the result of neoclassical reasoning. The classical economist, on the other
hand, might interpret *A'B'* as a growth path that exists independently of

short-period deviations, where the latter are possible as long as they represent either temporary disturbances or oscillations around $A'B'$.

The third issue (*iii*) discussed above, is reflected, e.g., in the curve $A''B''$. Unlike the other two curves in Figure 5.1, $A''B''$ is the result of path dependence in which short-run fluctuations may alter the data set. Here the trend itself is governed by fluctuations; it becomes, in other words, an *ex post* notion, an entity which has no existence independent of short-run fluctuations. Under these circumstances, the long- and the short-run cannot be kept analytically distinct when the development of the system over time is under discussion.

The distinction between issues (*ii*) and (*iii*) has special relevance for the gravitational process. If we can assume that the process leads back to the initial (fully adjusted) position, then the growth rate of real output can be determined from whatever forces regulate the parameters which produced the initial position. If, on the other hand, the gravitational process itself alters the data, then neither the initial position (with given parameters), nor a new fully-adjusted position (with new parameters) can be determined without precise knowledge of the changes induced by the adjustment process.[19]

MONEY, EXPECTATIONS AND THE SURPLUS APPROACH

As long as the classical long-period position is perceived as a static configuration of parameters and dependent variables, behavioural assumptions are not really important. Even for comparative static exercises, crude generalizations (such as 'capitalists maximize profits') may suffice. This of course changes as soon as convergence and feedback processes are scrutinized. Any discussion of the connection between short-run adjustments and the secular development of the system requires behavioural assumptions; and these cannot be formulated as long as it remains unclear how agents form their expectations. To argue simply that their behaviour is governed by uncertainty amounts to saying that dynamic processes cannot be discussed systematically.

As compared with the heterodox traditions discussed here, mainstream theory has been more energetic in developing new ideas about individual behaviour, learning processes and the formation of expectations. To a large extent, this impressive creativity has been fuelled by Muth's rational expectations hypothesis (1961). The hypothesis asserts that economic agents form their expectations on the basis of the relevant model of the economy; that is, on the basis of what, to the best of their knowledge, appears to be the most accurate model. In more technical language: the subjective probability distribution of expected outcomes is presumed to coincide with the objective probability distribution associated with the 'true' model of the economy in question. Hence agents act as if they know this model when forming their expectations.[20]

A distinction can be drawn between a 'strong' and a 'weak' form of the hypothesis. In its weak form, the hypothesis implies simply that people 'do the best they can with the information they have' (Hoover 1988, pp. 14–15): information is scarce and agents will efficiently use whatever information is available. This assertion, which Friedman (1979) has labelled the *information exploitation assumption*, can be distinguished from the *information availability assumption*. The latter corresponds to the strong form of the hypothesis, which states that 'people actually know the structure of the model that truly describes the world' (Hoover 1988, p. 15).

The most striking results of the New Classical macroeconomics have been derived from the strong form of the hypothesis. A peculiar characteristic of this line of work is the combination of a continuous-market-clearing assumption with the supposition that agents form expectations rationally. Small wonder then that the outcomes reinforce neoclassical concepts such as the natural rate hypothesis, the vertical Phillips curve, diverse policy ineffectiveness propositions, and so on. This is true both for models (in the tradition of Sargent and Wallace 1975) that conclude that monetary policy is neutral with respect to output and employment even in the short run, and for nominal equilibrium models of the business cycle (in the tradition of Lucas 1972) where agents generate temporary cyclical movements of output and employment in response to misperceived price signals following random disturbances of the money stock.[21] In both instances the results depend on the fact that the position established by the underlying model of the economy is optimal and, given the initial data, will tend to be re-established in the long run. The strong form of the rational expectations hypothesis enables economists to ignore macroeconomic co-ordination problems and adjustment mechanisms (cf. Leijonhufvud 1989). In the first class of models, systematic monetary policy has no real effects (though it can have lasting price level effects) because capital and labour always remain fully employed; in the second, monetary disturbances can have only temporary real effects because agents' best course of action, upon discovering that they had misread the price signals, is to return to the initial position where capital and labour are fully employed.

In Keynes (or Kalecki), short-run underemployment equilibria would never have been understood as representing optimal or efficient positions of the economy. Even in the older business cycle theories of neoclassical

extraction, fluctuations were imagined to take place *around* an optimal
equilibrium growth path such as the one depicted by *AB* in Figure 5.1.
Positions on the broken line were interpreted as deviations from equilibrium, and they would certainly not have been regarded as optimal. By
contrast, the early New Classical models viewed unemployment as a
voluntary response to some perceived change in data; and business cycles
were no longer interpreted as deviations from a social optimum, but as
fluctuations of the equilibrium position itself. In these models, positions
off the trend line *are* Pareto efficient, if only in the sense that no intervention is conceivable which would make anyone better off.

The appeal of the rational expectations hypothesis arises from two
considerations. First, it is sensible to suppose that over time people learn
how the world works, that they do not systematically repeat mistakes, and
that they try to make the best possible use of the information available to
them. The second consideration is the analytical role of the hypothesis as
'a consistency axiom for economic models' (Lucas 1987, p. 13).[22] If it is a
consistency axiom, the hypothesis is model specific; that is, we may talk
sensibly about rational expectations only when we already have a clear
idea how the economy operates.[23] Understood in this way the hypothesis
is compatible with virtually any well-articulated theory of economic reality. And indeed, Tobin (1975) has argued that if agents conceive of the
economy as operating on Keynesian principles, the rational expectations
hypothesis can support Keynesian outcomes. Other writers (for example,
Fischer 1977; Phelps and Taylor 1977; Taylor 1979) arrived at similar
conclusions; but to do so they had to impose certain conditions on their
models – sticky prices, contractual arrangements and the like. The need
for such conditions becomes evident once we consider the structure of
mainstream Keynesian theory. In its weak form the rational expectations
hypothesis implies that agents learn from experience; the model in
question would then converge until it no longer generates Keynesian
outcomes. Its strong form then ultimately requires that the availability of
information be restricted (in order, for example, to ground price rigidities
in rational behaviour) so as to explain why agents do not gradually learn
about opportunities for Pareto improvements and then transform this
knowledge into action.

In an important paper Friedman (1979) has analysed the informational
requirements of the rational expectations hypothesis in relation to the
distinction between the long run and the short run. (Of course he has in
mind the neoclassical long-period position, where the allocation of
resources is optimal, unemployed labour and capital do not exist, and
money is neutral.) Friedman wonders why New Classical models typically
posit conditions which neoclassical monetary theory established long ago

to be properties of long-period equilibrium – the neutrality of money, the vertical Phillips curve, independence of the real and monetary sectors, and so on. The possibility of these conditions holding in the short run, he argues, is contingent on the information availability and not on the information exploitation assumption. The former, in contrast to the latter, represents essentially a long-run concept: it already implies that all variables have converged to their long-run values. In all other cases, which correspond to what have traditionally been considered short-run problems, expectations need not have converged to their long-period values. These other cases can, of course, be modelled by accepting only the information exploitation hypothesis, which allows for processes of adaptation, that is, for learning.

The outcome of the discussion is that the neoclassical policy propositions (regarding, for example, the neutrality of monetary policy) hold in the short run only because properties which had previously been considered pertinent exclusively to the long period have been imposed on models of the short run – in particular the supposition, implicit in the information availability assumption, that all relevant variables (including expectations) have converged to their long-period equilibrium values. If instead the weak form of the rational expectations hypothesis had been employed, a process of learning could not be excluded and the short-run neutrality properties of New Classical models would not hold. It is clear that Friedman's conclusion depends on his definition of the long run as representing an optimal position. Since he has tied the information availability assumption in this manner to the neoclassical properties of long-period equilibrium, he may reasonably conclude:

> Macroeconomic models based on the assumptions of the rational expectations hypothesis do not demonstrate the short-run ineffectiveness of policy … because they are not really short-run models. The information availability assumption of the rational expectations hypothesis implicitly places such models in a long-run equilibrium context in which their [neo]classical properties – including the neutrality of monetary policy – are not surprising. (Friedman 1979, pp. 40–41)

What, however, does this discussion imply about the properties of the long-run growth path in classical surplus theories?

Consider Figure 5.1 and suppose that the system is moving along the trend line $A'B'$. Money may be introduced, in the first instance, purely and simply as a unit of account; then natural prices will be expressed in money terms. All agents in the model are presumed to form their expectations rationally, that is, they regard the surplus approach as the true model of the world in which they live, and they share a common understanding of the forces that determine the growth path of the economy. Let us also suppose that no informational biases exist and that no inside information is available. As long as the system remains in a fully adjusted position, it will exhibit no inherent tendency to change: all agents share the belief that this particular model correctly describes the economy, regardless of whether this state of affairs represents a social optimum. The natural position discussed here, therefore need not be associated with full employment.[24] Two issues can then be investigated: first, whether in general a trend line falling below the optimal growth path and progressively diverging from it (such as path $A'B'$ in Figure 5.1) can be sustained once we allow for random monetary disturbances; and, second, whether random short-run deviations can alter the long-run trend itself (as illustrated by the paths departing from A'').

Suppose that at time t^{**} the system experiences a monetary shock of the sort usually encountered in Lucas-type nominal business cycle models; in other words, suppose there occurs a sudden and unexpected increase in the quantity of money. As in the standard scenario, agents react by increasing production; output and employment rise immediately. In Figure 5.1, following the unanticipated increase in the money supply, the level of aggregate real output will, at t^{**}, jump to A'''. This real effect is due entirely to the conventional mechanism according to which agents misread the general increase in the price level as an increase in their own relative prices. The question is: will a new path result?

In nominal New Classical models the answer is 'no'. As soon as it becomes apparent that the configuration of relative prices has remained unchanged, that is, that people had done more work than they would have done had they realized the price changes were purely nominal, they act to re-establish the initial real position. The obvious precondition for this outcome is that the initial position was optimal in the sense that it was on a neoclassical growth path.

Classical theory ought to give a different result. If the initial situation is not characterized by full employment, a jump to A''' might imply a Pareto improvement.[25] Before the monetary shock occurred, the initial position was sustained because, given the knowledge then available, no agent had any reason to expect that he could benefit by altering his own behaviour. In a classical model, agents' expectations would be formed on the basis of a conception of the economy in which first, unemployment is a normal by-product of the market process; and second, wage concessions do not generally lead to increases in employment. But assuming that points on

$A'''B'''$ are Pareto superior to the initial position, agents will have no reason to return to the original growth path once a random disturbance has placed the economy on $A'''B'''$. In our simple framework, in fact, any such 'positive shock' will move the system to a new position which should be sustained: agents will adjust to what they have incidentally discovered, namely that the economy is capable of sustaining a higher level of output than their model predicted. As long as Pareto improvements are possible and activity-increasing shocks continue to occur, the system will converge toward the full employment growth path. An uninterrupted sequence of positive shocks, sustained over a sufficiently long period of time, could carry the system to the neoclassical path AB, where no further Pareto improvements are possible. There is, in other words, room for misperceptions that result in lasting real effects. But whereas in neoclassical models the Pareto optimal outcome is known to agents from the start, because it is embodied in the model which they use to form their expectations, here agents learn *by experience* that higher output levels can be sustained. They do not know from the start how to live in the best of all possible worlds (they are not even aware of its existence), and hence can discover this world only gradually and accidentally, if at all. The adjustment to paradise will therefore not exhibit the smooth inexorable convergence Friedman attributes to conventional models in which some sort of irrationality (or price rigidity) is embraced and then eliminated by rational expectations. Rather it will proceed in sharp irregular steps (as when the system jumps to A''' in Figure 5.1).

Three additional points merit attention. First, the system might be exposed to activity-decreasing, or negative, random shocks. When a negative shock occurs the system will be pushed toward a lower growth path. In this case, under our simple assumptions, rational individual behaviour would shift the level of aggregate activity back to the level associated with the classical growth path ($A'B'$ in our example).[26] Second, we might ask whether the periodic occurrence of positive and negative shocks will lead agents to discover regularities they had not noticed before, that is, to correct the model they use in forming their expectations. This question cannot be addressed here, though we think it merits serious consideration. Third, the rational expectations hypothesis *per se* is by no means immune to criticism. In a classical setting, with agents forming expectations on the basis of a model in which suboptimal output levels are sustained as a matter of course, the institutional context cannot be ignored; for the latter not only defines the range of admissible action, but also shapes expectations. It is furthermore worth noting that agents are no more homogeneous than capital.

CONCLUDING REMARKS

The observations made above are hardly exhaustive. Indeed, they underscore the pressing need to formulate and test formal hypotheses. If expectations underlie the role money plays in the determination of outputs and distribution, then it is unfortunate that the discussion has been left largely to the mainstream: if the incorporation of behavioural assumptions in structural models is indispensible to an adequate treatment of money, then the modern literature on expectations deserves to be taken seriously.

NOTES

1. We are grateful to Harald Hagemann, Silke Kutschinski, Perry Mehrling, Edward Nell and Christine Rider for helpful comments on earlier drafts.
2. Narrower approaches to monetary theory, such as overlapping generations models or the class of models based on 'finance constraints', are not considered in what follows.
3. See, for example, Kaldor (1970, 1982), Davidson (1972), Minsky (1975, 1982, 1986) and Kregel (1980).
4. Indeed, from Smith onward money was often viewed as a device which not only increases economic efficiency by reducing the transaction costs associated with barter, but which also fosters accumulation by extending the division of labour. In these writings, in particular in Smith, money is not neutral even in the long run (cf. Rühl 1991).
5. The implication here is that the interest rate cannot be regulated by the interaction of the supply of and demand for money. Since agents cannot be forced to swap their government bonds for money when the monetary authorities initiate expansionary open market operations, the supply of money can never exceed the demand for it.
6. This notwithstanding Wicksell's and Hayek's conviction that the Quantity Theory would hold in the long run. So long as there was no reason to question the soundness of the marginalist theory of distribution – and at the time they wrote, there were no compelling arguments against it – the only sensible course, for those who believed that money must somehow matter, was to try to expose the role of money in cyclical fluctuations.
7. Money matters in *The General Theory* precisely because it is *not* endogenous and can therefore influence the rate of interest. Cottrell (1986) shows that a less extreme version of the endogeneity postulate is not only more empirically appropriate, but also leaves room for money supply changes to play an active role in the determination of real variables.
8. The main references are Minsky (1975, 1982, 1986), Kregel (1980), Davidson (1972, 1980) and Chick (1983).
9. Cf. Kregel (1980, p. 45): 'money is the least *un*certain link between the present and the unknown future.'
10. This in fact appears to have been the point that Sraffa was trying to make in his critique of Hayek's trade cycle theory, when he observed that 'Money is not only the medium of exchange, but also a store of value, and the standard in which money debts, and other legal obligations, habits, opinions, conventions, in short all kinds of relations between men are more or less rigidly fixed . . . The money which [Dr Hayek] contemplates is in effect used purely and simply as a medium of exchange. There are no debts, no money-contracts, no wage-agreements, no sticky prices in his suppositions. Thus he is

able to neglect altogether the most obvious effects of a general fall, or rise, of prices.' (Sraffa 1932, pp. 43–4)

11. Thus even when money is fully endogenous, its supply curve need not be horizontal; if banks require higher interest rates as the economy becomes more heavily leveraged, the money supply curve would be depicted as upward sloping.

12. For simplicity, the equations in the text assume that all capital is circulating capital, and that production is characterized by constant returns over the relevant range of output. The interest component of cost reflects not only the cost outlays required to service debt, but also the opportunity cost of holding share capital rather than bonds; thus the interest cost is calculated as a percentage of the value of the entire stock of productive capital, that is, on pA.

13. All money prices will rise; but relative prices, of course, will rise or fall according to the technical conditions of production in the various sectors.

14. Here a curious point of tangency between New Classical economics and the monetary theories of distribution discussed above becomes visible. The accuracy of the former theory's predictions about behavioural adjustments to policy changes depends upon the degree to which the monetary authorities' commitment to the new policy is perceived by agents as credible; that is, the authorities must demonstrate a willingness to pursue the policy for a length of time sufficient to make it worthwhile for agents to modify their behaviour. The parallel element in the monetary theories of distribution examined in the text is the requirement that, in order to effect a lasting change in the profit rate, the monetary authorities must be sufficiently persistent in their pursuit of a specific target rate of interest.

15. A correct treatment would require that the interest costs saved by less heavily indebted firms accrue to them as rents. But this still leaves open the question of what regulates the degree of indebtedness and hence the 'rents' of different producers.

16. Except for his chapter on 'Natural and Market Price', virtually all of Smith's *Wealth of Nations* is concerned with phenomena which lie outside the core. The attention which Marx devoted to crises and accumulation also illustrates the importance of non-core issues in the classical framework, as does Ricardo's analysis of diminishing returns, the effects of machinery on employment, etc. Sraffa made several contributions to monetary economics before 1932 and was fully aware of the importance of money. The fact that he turned to other matters should not be taken to mean that he considered money irrelevant or that his analysis is incompatible with monetary investigations.

17. Any viable alternative to this approach would have to specify precisely how such deviations influence the initial set of data.

18. See for example Minsky (1990, pp. 370–71): 'the result of endogenous instability and a structure of constraints and interventions is a path without an equilibrium or centre of gravity . . . Garegnani works within a framework set up to demonstrate that markets achieve and sustain an equilibrium. Orthodox neoclassical theorists work within a framework set up to demonstrate that markets achieve and sustain an equilibrium. In such set-ups, outside disturbances can only move the economy from an equilibrium. Cycles are generated because overshoots occur in the process of returning to the assumed unique . . . centre of gravity. To Garegnani and neoclassical economists the business cycle is analogous to a pendulum . . . [Surplus theorists have] to stand mute when problems of the path of the economy through time are addressed.'

19. Referring to the possibility that the classical long-period position might be path dependent, Schefold (1990, p. 227) observes that: 'path-dependence in the gravitation process will be the more important, the more distant the comparison, the slower the gravitation and the more the techniques are similar. The possibility of this kind of path-dependence limits the reliability of applications of the theory, but I do not believe that there are sufficient general models of gravitation that would fare better.'

20. Expectations 'tend to be distributed, for the same information set, about the prediction of the theory (or the "objective" probability distribution of outcomes)' (Muth 1961, p. 316).

21. A discussion of the impact of technological shocks – changes in technology – lies

beyond the scope of this chapter, though such shocks are at the heart of New Classical real business cycle theory. The present argument would not be altered by admitting such productivity shocks into the analysis.

22. Cf. Laidler (1986, pp. 45–6): 'For analytical exercises designed to reveal the long run equilibrium properties of economic models, it is of course quite appropriate to attribute to agents within the model knowledge of that same model. Any other basis for expectations formation would, under some condition or other, lead agents into systematic error, causing them to revise their method of forming expectations. Hence it could not be a component of a full equilibrium structure.'

23. '[T]his is why', as Lucas (1987, p. 13) puts it, 'attempts to define rational expectations in a model-free way tend to come out either vacuous ("People do the best they can with the information they have") or silly ("People know the true structure of the world they live in").'

24. A neoclassical economist might feel compelled at this point to provide some explanation of how the economic system could remain stuck in such a position. Such an explanation is not necessary if expectations are formed on the basis of a classical model in which agents interpret unemployment as a normal feature of the economy, and recognize that a general decline of wages need not constitute an effective remedy.

25. In general, except under the special circumstances described here – an increase in nominal prices with relative prices and distribution left unchanged – a movement to a higher growth path in a classical context need not entail a Pareto improvement: higher growth rates are often accompanied by shifts in the distribution of income, so that the condition that 'no one be made worse off' is violated.

26. One of the authors, Mongiovi, has reservations about this conclusion. He would have written instead that 'When a negative shock occurs, the system will move onto a lower growth path and stay on that path until another shock occurs.'

REFERENCES

Asimakopulos, A. (1990) 'Keynes and Sraffa: Visions and Perspectives', and 'Reply', in K. Bharadwaj and B. Schefold (eds), *Essays on Piero Sraffa: Critical Perspectives on the Revival of Classical Theory*, London: Unwin Hyman, 331–45, 358–61.

Chick, V. (1983) *Macroeconomics after Keynes*, Cambridge MA: MIT Press.

Cottrell, A. (1986) 'The Endogeneity of Money and Money Income Causality', *Scottish Journal of Political Economy*, 33, 2–27.

Davidson, P. (1972) *Money and the Real World*, London: Macmillan.

Davidson, P. (1980) 'The Dual-Faceted Nature of the Keynesian Revolution: Money and Money Wages in Unemployment and Production Flow Prices', *Journal of Post Keynesian Economics*, 2, 291–307.

Fischer, S. (1977) 'Long-term Contracts, Rational Expectations and the Optimal Money Supply Rule', *Journal of Political Economy*, 85, 191–206.

Friedman, M. (1979) 'Optimal Expectations and the Extreme Information Assumptions of "Rational Expectations" Macromodels', *Journal of Monetary Economics*, 5, 23–41.

Garegnani, P. (1983) 'Two Routes to Effective Demand: Comment on Kregel,' in J. Kregel (ed.), *Distribution, Effective Demand and International Economic Relations*, London: Macmillan, 69–80.

Garegnani, P. (1984) 'Value and Distribution in the Classical Economists and Marx', *Oxford Economic Papers*, 36, 291–325.

Green, R. (1982) 'Money, Output and Inflation in Classical Economics', *Contributions to Political Economy*, **1**, 59–85.

Hahn, F. (1965) 'On Some Problems of Proving the Existence of an Equilibrium in a Monetary Economy', in F. Hahn and F. Brechling (eds), *The Theory of Interest Rates*, London: Macmillan, 126–35.

Hahn, F. (1981) *Money and Inflation*, Oxford: Basil Blackwell.

Hayek, F.A. (1931) *Prices and Production*, London: Routledge and Sons.

Hayek, F.A. (1933) *Monetary Theory of the Trade Cycle*, London: Routledge and Sons.

Hicks, J. (1974) *The Crisis in Keynesian Economics*, New York: Basic Books.

Hoover, K. (1988) *The New Classical Macroeconomics: A Sceptical Inquiry*, Oxford: Basil Blackwell.

Kaldor, N. (1970) 'The New Monetarism', *Lloyd's Bank Review* (97), 1–18.

Kaldor, N. (1982) *The Scourge of Monetarism*, Oxford: Oxford University Press.

Keynes, J.M. (1930) *A Treatise on Money*, London: Macmillan.

Keynes, J.M. (1936) *The General Theory of Employment, Interest and Money*, London: Macmillan.

Kregel, J. (1980) 'Markets and Institutions as Features of a Capitalistic Production System', *Journal of Post Keynesian Economics*, **3**, 32–48.

Laidler, D. (1986) 'The New Classical Contribution to Macroeconomics', *Banca Nazionale del Lavoro Quarterly Review* (156), 27–55.

Leijonhufvud, A. (1989) 'Recent Developments in Macroeconomics and the New Classical View on Money', *Diskussionsbeitrage zur Gesamtwirtschaflichen Theorie und Politik*, new series (13), Bremen: University of Bremen.

Lucas, R. (1972) 'Expectations and the Neutrality of Money', *Journal of Economic Theory*, **4**, 103–24.

Lucas, R. (1975) 'An Equilibrium Model of the Business Cycle', *Journal of Political Economy*, **83**, 1113–44.

Lucas, R. (1987) *Models of the Business Cycle*, Oxford: Basil Blackwell.

Minsky, H. (1975) *John Maynard Keynes*, New York: Columbia University Press.

Minsky, H. (1982) *Can 'It' Happen Again*, Armonk, NY: M.E. Sharpe.

Minsky, H. (1986) *Stabilizing an Unstable Economy*, New Haven: Yale University Press.

Minsky, H. (1990) 'Sraffa and Keynes: Effective Demand in the Long Run' and 'Reply', in K. Bharadwaj and B. Schefold (eds), *Essays on Piero Sraffa: Critical Perspectives on the Revival of Classical Theory*, London: Unwin Hyman, 362–71.

Mongiovi, G. (1990) 'Notes on Say's Law, Classical Economics and the Theory of Effective Demand', *Contributions to Political Economy*, **9**, 69–82.

Moore, B. (1988) *Horizontalists and Verticalists*, Cambridge: Cambridge University Press.

Muth, J. (1961) 'Rational Expectations and the Theory of Price Movements', *Econometrica*, **29**, 315–35.

Nell, E. (1988) 'Does the Rate of Interest Determine the Rate of Profit?' *Political Economy: Studies in the Surplus Approach*, **4**, 263–8.

Panico, C. (1985) 'Market Forces and the Relation Between the Rates of Interest and Profit', *Contributions to Political Economy*, **4**, 37–60.

Phelps, E. and Taylor, J. (1977) 'Stabilizing Powers of Monetary Policy Under Rational Expectations', *Journal of Political Economy*, **85**, 163–90.

Pivetti, M. (1985) 'On the Monetary Explanation of Distribution', *Political Economy: Studies in the Surplus Approach*, **1**, 73–103.

Rühl, C. (1991) 'Geldkreislauf, Einkommenskreislauf und Effektive Nachfrage: Die Rolle des Geldes im "Wohlstand der Nationen",' *Jahrbucher fur Ökonomie und Gesellschaft*, **9**, 273–333.

Sargent, T. and Wallace, N. (1975) ' "Rational" Expectations, the Optimal Monetary Instrument and the Optimal Money Supply Rule', *Journal of Political Economy*, **83**, 241–54.

Schefold, B. (1990) 'On Changes in the Composition of Output', and 'Reply', in K. Bharadwaj and B. Schefold (eds), *Essays on Piero Sraffa: Critical Perspectives on the Revival of Classical Theory*, London: Unwin Hyman, 178–203, 220–28.

Sraffa, P. (1932) 'Dr Hayek on Money and Capital', *Economic Journal*, **42**, 42–53.

Sraffa, P. (1960) *Production of Commodities by Means of Commodities*, Cambridge: Cambridge University Press.

Taylor, J. (1979) 'Staggered Wage Setting in a Macro Model', *American Economic Review*, **69**, 108–13.

Tobin, J. (1965) 'The Theory of Portfolio Selection', in F. Hahn and F. Brechling (eds), *The Theory of Interest Rates*, London: Macmillan, 3–51.

Tobin, J. (1975) *Asset Accumulation and Economic Activity*, Oxford: Basil Blackwell.

Wicksell, K. (1898) *Geldzins und Guterpreise*, Aalen: Scientia Verlag [1968].

6. The Policy Implications of Classical Monetary Theory: Between the Two Hands

Arie Arnon

INTRODUCTION

Classical monetary theory was as divisive as modern theories of money, credit and banking. The views on money and credit held by political economists writing in the one hundred years after Adam Smith ranged, not surprisingly, from 'money (and credit) are a veil' to 'money (and credit) matter'. In this chapter we will describe four of the most important trends during the classical period, focusing attention on their policy implications. We will limit ourselves to the analysis of convertible regimes, starting from Smith's views, moving on to those of Ricardo and then to the Currency and Banking Schools.[1]

In analysing the policy implications of each trend we will distinguish between two different aims of intervention. One is the 'safety-net' target of intervention, according to which responsibility for the safety of the banks and the continued functioning of the system is to be delegated to a special agent – the monetary authority. This agent is supposed to keep the fragile banking system intact, and, in fact guarantee, to some degree at least, the banks' solvency. This form of intervention, known later as the 'Lender of Last Resort' function of central banks, is a *passive* form of intervention. The second, *active* form of intervention, is not just intended to secure the working of the financial system but aims also to achieve some macro-targets through monetary tools.[2] In both the passive and active forms of intervention, the monetary authorities have to analyse, decide and act. However, whereas in the latter the authorities take the initiative, in the former they do not. In both cases the decisions can be taken either according to a pre-specified rule or at the authorities' discretion. As we shall see both passive and active monetary policies were discussed, at least superficially, by classical political economists.

Some of the classicals preferred not to intervene at all, leaving everything – from maintaining the confidence of individuals in the banking system to the determination of the price level – to the invisible hand. The only type of intervention that the 'free trade' camp accepted took the form of *setting the rules of the game* (for example, convertibility of notes). The visible hand camp, which supported intervention, either to achieve the stability of the financial system or in order to influence macro-variables, was fighting an uphill battle. The influence of the visible hand theorists was limited during the classical period and it was not until Bagehot (1873) that a systematic, visible hand view was generally accepted. However, we should keep in mind that even then the recommended Lender of Last Resort policy was a *passive* form of intervention. It was well into the twentieth century before a theory justifying an active policy was generally, but by no means unanimously, accepted (see Toniolo 1988).

This chapter will explore the degree to which the passive and active forms of policy intervention were discussed during the classical period. One should keep in mind that while both forms of intervention were actually used, the various discussions were *not* based on clear and coherent theoretical formulations regarding either active or passive policies.

SMITH'S INVISIBLE HAND POSITION

Adam Smith, the founding father of classical economics, is also a natural point of departure for a discussion of classical monetary theory. In *The Wealth of Nations* (Book I, ch. iv, 'The Origins and Use of Money'), Smith discusses money before he approached his main subject, the division of labour. Smith saw money as a necessary condition for the development of the division of labour and thus for the growth and creation of wealth.[3] He described the evolution of commodity money, and justified the use of money by the efficiency of a monetary economy in comparison with barter. Not until Book II did Smith examine a system in which convertible bank notes exist alongside commodity money. Here Smith emphasized that reducing the quantity of commodity money (mainly gold coins) will improve production by transforming 'dead stock' into 'productive capital'. This is the role of the banks.

Smith described the well-known process which led to a system based on fractional reserves, a process which started when convertible bank notes were substituted for coins in circulation. He insisted that the right quantity in circulation is that which would have circulated if coins were the only medium of circulation. This principle was later to become famous as the Currency Principle. As long as coins continued to circulate alongside convertible notes issued by the various banks, there would be no danger of surplus in the internal circulation, since the surplus would be exported, just as in the case of a pure commodity money circulation. However, Smith argued further that even if the entire circulation were composed of convertible bank notes, which cannot function as international money, the right quantity could still be maintained as long as the many competing issuing banks acted in a responsible manner.

Smith examined the banking system and found that convertible notes entered circulation either directly, through exchange of gold, or through bank loans. In return for these loans the banks received assets which were supposed to guarantee repayment. Smith thought that as long as the quantity of notes in circulation corresponded to the needs of entrepreneurs for money to answer 'occasional demand', there would be no surplus in circulation. Such desired correspondence could be achieved by the simultaneous use of two methods. First, banks issuing notes should give loans against 'real bills', defined as bills which represent real transactions, that is sales of commodities on credit, between two respected dealers, who agree to transfer money and repay the debt within a short period. This is the essence of Smith's well-known Real Bills Doctrine.[4] The second method he recommended, known as 'cash accounts', was popular in Scotland, and in Smith's view had contributed to the development of the Scottish economy in the previous 25 years. In modern terms, this method involves the opening of a credit line by the bank to a dealer able to provide 'two persons of undoubted credit and good landed estate to become surety for him' (Smith 1776, p. 316). The bank allows the dealer to withdraw any sum up to this limit whenever he wants – an authorized overdraft.

As long as the banks follow both methods – discounting only real bills and opening cash accounts – the *right quantity of notes* in circulation will be maintained. Smith noted that these methods are exactly those which follow from the banks' own self-interest (Smith 1776, pp. 319–20). However, he does not clarify why the quantity of notes so issued will correspond to the 'ready money . . . for answering occasional demand' mentioned above.

Smith's opposition to notes of low denomination was the only limitation he imposed on the principle of free trade in banking assuming convertibility and the lending policy described above. The main justification for this position was the protection of the weak. Since consumers cannot be expected to distinguish between 'responsible' and 'mean' bankers, they should be protected against bankruptcies by provisions which would ensure that transactions between consumers and dealers – which involve small sums – be conducted in coins alone.[5]

It is important to note that Smith distinguished, albeit not systematically, between money and credit. In his terms, coin is money and convertible bank notes are called paper money (p. 310). These latter have a dual function. On the one hand, they are substitutes for coins and thus function as money; but on the other hand they are issued by the banks as loans and thus function as credit. However, in spite of this, it is clear that for Smith notes function primarily as money, that is, they were first and foremost a close substitute for coins. The right quantity of commodity money is determined by the distribution of precious metals in the world. The right quantity of convertible bank notes is determined so that, together with the quantity of coins in circulation, it will equal the right quantity of a pure commodity money circulation. Thus the banks, under the above-mentioned weak limitations, can be left to compete both in discounting real bills and in opening credit lines. In other words, *Smith accepted competition in both money and credit* and thus saw no need for the intervention of any central body in determining the right quantity of money or of credit.

One should note that the Bank of England was a private bank and should thus be subject to the same principles of competition which applied to any bank. However, Smith recognized that it was not just a private bank, but also an 'engine of state', dealing with state debts and taxes, whose actions sometimes resulted in overstock of banknotes in circulation through no fault of its own managers. The Bank of England also assumed responsibility for the miscalculations of other banks since it had to convert their notes into gold when they overissued (Smith 1776, p. 322). Although Smith was not explicit on the application of the Real Bills Doctrine to the Bank of England, this does not change his general support for free trade and opposition to central banking. Increases in the number of banks and in the competition between them contribute to greater caution on the part of the bankers, to less danger of 'malicious runs' and to greater protection for the public. Smith's conclusion is clear: *subject to convertibility* and limitations on low denomination notes he saw banking as one of the trades and, as always, supported competition. In a passage that might be endorsed today by the new Free Banking School supporters, Smith stated:

> This free competition too obliges all bankers to be more liberal in their dealings with their customers, lest their rivals should carry them away. In general, if any branch of trade, or any division of labour, be advantageous to the public, the freer and more general the competition, it will always be the more so. (Smith 1776, p. 350)

Smith's theory assumes that a mixed convertible circulation, one based on commodity money, needs no regulation or control. The quantity of money will always be the right one. The quantity of money is demand determined, that is, money is an endogenous variable, while the quality, or value of money is not related, in the long run, to the quantity. At the roots of this approach, one will find the argument that the quality of commodity money, that is, its value, is determined by conditions in the markets of goods. Therefore, the value of the circulating medium will always be equal to what it is supposed to be, regardless of the bankers' actions. This is not a short-run analysis. In the short run additional money will overflow the channels of circulation and, under Smith's assumptions (full employment, open economy and fixed exchange rate), will 'spill over' and cause an outflow of gold.

This argument is different from, but consistent with, what is known as the price-specie-flow mechanism (sometimes called Hume's mechanism).[6] This mechanism, which is not presented explicitly in the *Wealth of Nations* but was known to Smith,[7] can be described as follows. As long as the currencies in the countries involved in trade were metal coins and convertible notes, and international payments were made in gold, price changes and specie flows would act as equilibrating forces. In international trade there is a tendency to equate imports and exports through price changes in the trading countries. If, for example, exports exceed imports, excluding gold, then gold will flow into England. This will cause price rises in England (and possibly a fall in prices in the 'rest of the world'); the consequences will be a decrease in exports from England and an increase in its imports. Smith, for some reason, ignored the price-specie-flow mechanism and in particular its dependence on changes in relative price levels, and favoured an explanation based on a more direct effect. However, as Laidler (1981) argues, Hume's mechanism 'could easily have been incorporated' into Smith's treatment. Table 6.1 summarizes Smith's position.

RICARDO'S (1824) VISIBLE HAND POSITION

Ricardo's pamphlets on monetary issues were written mainly during the Restriction Period, when notes were inconvertible. For our purposes, his views on a convertible system are more interesting. These are summarized in his 1824 text written after the Resumption, when notes were made convertible again.[8] In this posthumously published *Plan for a National Bank* Ricardo first distinguished between the two functions of a bank: to issue notes and to act as an intermediary. Furthermore, he believed that these functions should be carried out by two distinct bodies, directed by different principles. The first body, labelled the Issuing Department (of the Bank of England) should be the sole issuing bank responsible for the creation (and destruction) of convertible notes. It would be guided by a

Table 6.1   Summary of classical economic regimes

| | Institutional framework facing individual banks | | | Responsibilities delegated to the monetary authority | | | |
| | | | | Passive policy (Lender of last resort) | | Active policy | |
	Convertibility of notes	Free to issue notes	Free to advance credit	Rule	Discretion	Rule	Discretion
Smith (1776)	+	+	+	−	−	−	−
Ricardo (1824)	+	−	+	−	+	−	+
Currency School (1844)	+	−	+	−	−	−	−
Banking School (1844)	+	+	−	−	+	−	+

strict rule: always exchange gold for notes and notes for gold at a given rate of exchange. The amount of notes would be the correct one, since these would be given only 'in exchange for gold at the price of £3 17s 10½d per ounce,' and *not against discounts.* Thus, 'regulating their issues by the price of gold, the commissioners would never err' (Ricardo 1951–73, IV, p. 293). The commissioners in charge of the Issuing Department do not have to lend to the government, which should finance itself. In addition, Ricardo demanded that *country bank notes be withdrawn from circulation* (Ricardo 1951–73, IV, p. 287, the seventh proposition). Thus for the first time since Ricardo started writing on monetary issues he clearly *rejected competition in issuing notes.* The second body, the Banking Department, should be free to act as any non-issuing bank: to maximize profits by lending the funds it can raise.

Ricardo's proposals, which called for a change in the institutional framework under which the banks then operated, led to an effective monopoly in issuing notes. It seemed that the directors in charge of this monopoly, who were guided by the above rules, were to have no responsibility apart from handling their own banking business. However, in the following passage Ricardo allowed the Bank's directors certain *discretionary* activities with its securities.

If the circulation of London should be redundant, it will show itself by the

increased price of bullion, and the fall in the foreign exchanges, precisely as a
redundancy is now shown; and the remedy is also the same as that now in
operation; viz. a reduction of circulation, which is brought about by a reduction of the paper circulation. That reduction may take place two ways; either by
the sale of Exchequer bills in the market, and the cancelling of the paper money
which is obtained from them, – or by giving gold in exchange for the paper,
cancelling the paper as before, and exporting the gold. (Ricardo 1951–73, IV,
pp. 296–7)

The first method is a well-known procedure in central banking – open
market operations – and is clearly incompatible with competition in
banking in general and with the Real Bills Doctrine in particular. Only
here, possibly after examining the practical working of the resumed convertible system, did Ricardo arrive at conclusions quite contrary to those
of the spirit of the Real Bills Doctrine, arguing that the quantity of notes
should *not* be determined through competition between issuers.

Furthermore, while his proposals paved the way to the monopolization
of note issuing, Ricardo also rejected the simple rule described above for
the determination of the quantity of notes. Thus, Ricardo's position in
this last text differed significantly not only from his own earlier views, but
also from those of the Currency School which we will describe next. Not
only did he explicitly reject both competition and a strict rule as appropriate methods for determining the quantity of notes, but he also openly
recommended discretion. Thus, his system is closer to modern central
banking practice than it is to the automatic mechanism characteristic of
the Currency School's proposals, which left almost no place for discretion
in either money or credit. Ricardo was moving toward a rejection of the
application of the invisible hand mechanism to money and credit and
adopting what was basically a visible hand theory.[9] See Table 6.1 for a
summary of this position.

THE SURPRISING SIMILARITY BETWEEN THE CURRENCY SCHOOL AND SMITH

The Currency School rejected the Real Bills Doctrine for money. They
agreed with Thornton's argument that discounting 'good bills' would not
necessarily insure the 'just' quantity in circulation. Bankers would find it
difficult to distinguish 'bona fide' good bills, since good bills could also be
created by fictitious deals between merchants. Criticism of Smith's formulation of the Real Bills Doctrine does not necessarily imply rejection of the
general position that the quantity should be determined by market forces.
However, the Currency School's strong distrust of bankers also led them

to reject competition in note issuing. As a result, they sought an alternative method for determining the quantity of convertible notes in circulation and they adopted Ricardo's Plan, albeit with no discretion. Their position is most clearly expressed in the 1844 Bank Act, the enactment of which also marked the Currency School's victory in their debates with the Banking School. According to the provisions of the Act, every change in the quantity of Bank of England notes would equal the change in the amount of precious metals in the reserves of the Issue Department. This change would *not* depend on the banking system's discretionary actions, but on the public will; thus bankers were freed from all responsibility other than obeying the Act. The Act thus provided an *automatic mechanism* for controlling the money supply – coins plus convertible banknotes. Its advocates did not think it important to control aggregates other than notes, and while they rejected the Real Bills Doctrine and competition for notes, they *accepted competition for credit*.

Thus, the Currency School held a strange position. Although their rejection of competition for money should have led them to accept some form of visible hand policy and central banking, they clung to the alternative solution of 'rules', even in the years following the Bank Act, when a succession of crises (1848, 1857, 1866) necessitated discretion. Thus, as shown in Table 6.1, their positions on both passive and active policies were identical to those of Smith, though for altogether different reasons. While Smith rejected the Quantity Theory and accepted the arguments for the endogeneity of the money supply, the Currency School supported the Quantity Theory and viewed the money supply as exogenous.

THE BANKING SCHOOL VISIBLE HAND POSITION

Although the Banking School's strong commitment to free trade and their acceptance of the Real Bills Doctrine for money (that is, notes) has led many[10] to locate them in the Smithian tradition, their position concerning credit complicates the picture. Tooke, the leading Banking School theorist, rejected in 1844 both the Real Bills Doctrine and competition for credit, a position which he developed in later years and which should have led him to endorse some form of visible hand policy regarding credit. However, no such policy was ever fully developed. Tooke had a unique attitude among the classicals towards the relation between credit and the real economic world. While he rejected the possibility that credit creates wealth or capital, he accepted its influence on short-term phenomena in the economy. When the economy is on the rise, credit expansion will only aggravate the price rises while the task of the banking system then is to contract loans. On the other hand, during downward waves, expansionist policies by the banks, including the use of the rate of interest as a policy measure, would encourage the economy. There exists no automatic mechanism by which the banks can control and 'fine-tune' the waves. However, led by the Bank of England, they can and should, act as stabilizers in the economy after their managers have determined the direction of the waves.

Before the Lords' Committee of 1848 which enquired into the Causes of the Distress, Tooke pointed out his rivals' inconsistency with regard to credit legislation:

> Would not your Evidence rather go to show that a Restriction should be imposed upon the Bank of England in respect to the Management of its Banking as well as its Issue Department? To be consistent it would. The only Mode in which any restriction could be imposed upon the Banking Department would be to say that for their liabilities they should hold a certain Amount of Bullion; but that would be the consistent Course; it would however be perfectly impracticable. I only point out the Inconsistency. I never could understand, from the Moment it was proposed, why there should be a different Guarantee to the Public for Notes of the Bank as compared with its other Obligations. (Parliamentary Papers Q.3136, p. 352)

However, at this stage Tooke did not go all the way with this conclusion by recommending, as he should, the desirability of controlling credit. On the contrary, he recommended complete discretion to the competitive bankers, leaving no one responsible for the outcome of the various decisions.

The rationale behind this invisible hand position was that in 1844 Tooke thought it to be his task to prevent over-legislation and what he considered to be unnecessary interference in the banking system. His method was to discredit the Currency School, but not to build a counter argument or complete system. Perhaps the reason was that he did not have an alternative, and believed that 'trial and error' as a method to remedy the present system was the best solution. This view was to be changed during the next ten years, in favour of a visible hand position.

Following the 1844 Banking Act, the directors of the Bank of England assumed that they were free in their 'Banking Business' like any other joint-stock bank. This mistake, argued Tooke, was even greater than their imposition of an erroneous rule on issuing notes because the Bank overlooked its central role in the payments system and its ability to influence the exchanges, the state of credit and most of all, convertibility. Paradoxically, after 1844 the Bank directors were restricted in their actions in areas over which they had no power whatsoever, while at the same time having complete freedom where their discretionary actions were most influential.

> As a general proposition, it may be laid down, and has been shown, that the Issue Department is (as it was before 1844) *acted upon by* the Public; – while the Banking Department continues (as it did before 1844) to *act upon the Public*. Thus producing a result *the very reverse* of that contemplated by the propounders of the scheme of separation. If, then, the due regulation of the currency, in any intelligible sense of the expression, depends, as it undoubtedly does, upon the Banking Department and not upon the Issue Department, it is the height of inconsistency to restrict the latter, and to leave the former wholly at the discretion of the Directors. (Tooke and Newmarch 1857, Vol. V, pp. 546–7)

The natural next step was to suggest some form of credit policy. This was done, implicitly and indirectly, by leaving total discretion to the Bank's directors regarding all their liabilities. It is in this light that one should understand Tooke's efforts during his last ten years to improve the management of the Bank.

In terms of our framework, this position locates Tooke's mature views of the 1850s as accepting the need for a visible hand in banking. However, close as he was to formulating a central banking policy on credit, a full discussion of such a policy is missing. It is clear that the Bank's policies should have been responsive to the prevailing economic conditions, but no specific 'model' regarding targets and tools was available. It was thus left entirely to the intuition of the directors, in the best tradition of complete discretion, to shape their different reactions under various circumstances. Moreover, it is probable that Tooke had in mind a passive form of intervention rather than an active one. Table 6.1 summarizes the Banking School position.

THE CLASSICS AND THE POST-KEYNESIANS: FROM THE ENDOGENEITY OF MONEY TO MONETARY POLICY

The above analysis of classical thinking on monetary policy reveals the obvious; many viewpoints could be found among the classicals on major issues such as the Quantity Theory and the exogeneity of money. While Ricardo and the Currency School were strong supporters of the Quantity Theory, Smith and the Banking School were closer to the post-Keynesians. However, one has to be careful here. The accepted definition of money in those days was very narrow; it included only coins and notes in circulation. If deposits are added to the money aggregates, even the Currency School would become half-hearted regarding their position in favour of money exogeneity.

The different positions regarding monetary policy are more revealing.

While Smith believed in free trade in banking for both money and credit, and rejected any use of a visible hand, the Currency School reached the same conclusion via a very different route. They supported the monopolization of note issuing, thus paving the way to the modern structure of banking, while leaving the directors of the issuing body no discretion at all. Contrary to Smith, they believed in the importance of the quantity of money for prices, but trusted free market forces to do the job. At the same time, they underestimated the importance of credit and at best, thought it to be controlled by market forces as well.

Ricardo and Tooke played with the idea of central banking policy. I believe that what they had in mind was a passive form of intervention, that is, intervention aimed at defending the system. However, it seems that they were both very close to endorsing active intervention as well. The various trends within post-Keynesian monetary theory share Smith's and Tooke's positions regarding the endogeneity of money (Moore 1988; Rousseas 1986; Kaldor 1982). Post-Keynesians contend that the banking system, including the central bank, does not *control* the quantity of money; it is instead determined by the demand, by the 'needs of trade,' which every reasonable central bank is compelled to accommodate. Furthermore, like their classical predecessors, post-Keynesians have thus far neglected to elaborate on the difficult and crucial question of controlling credit flows. As Rousseas (1986, p. 110) put it, this is a 'problem most Post-Keynesian monetary theorists have ignored'.

NOTES

1. The analysis of inconvertible regimes would complicate the picture, of course, and is beyond the scope of this chapter. The four trends mentioned all assumed convertability. Others which did not, like the anti-Bullionists and the Birmingham School are excluded from this discussion.
2. Goodhart's distinction (1988, pp. 5–8) between the micro and macro rôles of a central bank is very similar to the passive – active distinction.
3. On Smith's monetary thought see Laidler (1981), Vickers (1975) and Hollander (1911).
4. 'When a bank discounts to a merchant a real bill of exchange drawn by a real debtor, and which, as soon as it becomes due, is really paid by that debtor; it only advances to him a part of the value which he would otherwise be obliged to keep by him unemployed and in ready money for answering occasional demands . . . The coffers of the bank, so far as its dealings are confined to such customers, resemble a water pond, from which, though a stream is continually running in . . . the pond keeps always equally, or nearly equally full' (Smith, 1776, pp. 322–3). For a critical review see Mints (1945).
5. Smith was aware that this limits free trade and 'may no doubt, be considered as in some respect a violation of natural liberty'. However, he justified it thus: 'But those exertions of natural liberty of a few individuals, which might endanger the security of the whole society, are, and ought to be, restrained by the laws of all governments; of the most free, as well as of the most despotical. The obligation of building party walls, in order to prevent the communication of fire, is a violation of natural liberty, exactly of the same

kind with the regulations of the banking trade which are proposed.' (Smith 1776, pp. 344–5)

6. According to Viner (1937) this mechanism was known before Hume. It was exposed clearly by David Hume in 1752 in his *Political Discourse*.

7. For a detailed study arguing for the existence of Hume's mechanism in the *Wealth of Nations* see Eagly (1970). However, see also Petrella (1968), Bloomfield (1975) and Laidler (1981), who all seem to agree on the absence of the mechanism from this text.

8. The source of this section is Ricardo's *Collected Works and Correspondence*, edited by Sraffa in 11 volumes (1951–1973) References to this edition use Roman numbers for the volume, followed by the page number.

   Ricardo's most important texts on monetary questions are: *The High Price of Bullion* (1810, III, pp. 45–127); *Reply to Mr. Bosanquet* (1811, III, pp. 45–127); *Proposals for an Economical and Secure Currency* (1816, IV, pp. 43–141); and the *Plan for the Establishment of a National Bank* (1824, IV, pp. 271–300).

   There is a vast literature on Ricardo's works. The main works used, apart from Sraffa's excellent introductions are: Blaug (1958), Hollander (1979) and Sayers (1953). See also Arnon (1987).

9. For a detailed study of the changes in Ricardo's views see Arnon (1987).

10. See Schumpeter (1954, p. 731); Corry (1962, pp. 75–8); Mints (1945, pp. 93–4, 99–111, 131); Laidler (1981, p. 198); see also Arnon (1984).

REFERENCES

Arestis, P. (1988) *Post Keynesian Monetary Economics*, Aldershot: Edward Elgar.

Arnon, A. (1984) 'The Transformation in Thomas Tooke's Monetary Theory Reconsidered', *History of Political Economy*, 16, 311–26.

Arnon, A. (1987) 'Banking Between the Invisible and Visible Hands: A Reinterpretation of Ricardo's Place Within the Classical School', *Oxford Economic Papers*, 39, 268–81.

Arnon, A. (1990) *Thomas Tooke: Pioneer of Monetary Theory*, Aldershot: Edward Elgar, and Ann Arbor, MI: University of Michigan Press.

Ashton, T.S. and R.S. Sayers (eds) (1953) *Papers in English Monetary History*, Oxford: Clarendon Press.

Blaug, M. (1958) *Ricardian Economics: A Historical Study* Conneticut: Greenwood Press [1976].

Bloomfield, A.I. (1975) 'Adam Smith and the Theory of International Trade,' in A.S. Skinner and T. Wilson (eds), *Essays on Adam Smith*, Oxford: Clarendon Press, 455–82.

Corry, B.A. (1962) *Money, Saving and Investment in English Economics 1800–1850*, London: Macmillan.

Eagly, R.V. (1970) 'Adam Smith and the Specie-Flow Doctrine', *Scottish Journal of Political Economy*, 17, 61–8.

Fetter, F.W. (1965) *Development of British Monetary Orthodoxy, 1797–1875*, Cambridge, MA: Harvard University Press.

Goodhart, C. (1988) *The Evolution of Central Banks*, Second edn, Cambridge, MA: MIT Press.

Hicks, J.R. (1967) *Critical Essays in Monetary Theory*, Oxford: Clarendon Press.

Hollander, J.H. (1911) 'The Developments of the Theory of Money from Adam Smith to David Ricardo', *Quarterly Journal of Economics*, 25, 426–70.

Hollander, S. (1979) *The Economics of David Ricardo*, London: Heinemann.

Kaldor, N. (1982) *The Scourge of Monetarism*, Oxford: Oxford University Press.

Laidler, D. (1981) 'Adam Smith as a Monetary Economist', *Canadian Journal of Economics*, **14**, 185–200.

Mints, L.W. (1945) *A History of Banking Theory in Great Britain and the United States*, Chicago: University of Chicago Press.

Moore, B. (1988) *Horizontalists and Verticalists: The Macroeconomics of Credit Money*, New York: Cambridge University Press.

Parliamentary Papers (1848) 'Report from the Secret Committee of the House of Lords appointed to inquire into the causes of the distress which has for some time prevailed among the commercial classes, and how far it has been affected by the laws for regulating the issue of banks notes payable on demand together with the Minutes of Evidence', pp. 1847–8, VIII, pt III.

Petrella, F. (1968) 'Adam Smith's Rejection of Hume's Price-Specie-Flow Mechanism: A Minor Mystery Resolved', *Southern Economic Journal*, **34**, 365–74.

Ricardo, D. (1951–1973) *Works and Correspondence of David Ricardo*, ed. P. Sraffa, 11 vols, Cambridge: Cambridge University Press.

Rousseas, S. (1986) *Post Keynesian Monetary Economics*, London: Macmillan.

Sayers, R.S. (1953) 'Ricardo's Views on Monetary Questions', in T.S. Ashton and R.S. Sayers (eds), *Papers in English Monetary History*, Oxford: Clarendon Press, 76–95.

Schumpeter, J.A. (1954) *History of Economic Analysis*, London: Allen & Unwin.

Smith, A. (1776) *An Inquiry into the Nature and Causes of the Wealth of Nations*, ed. E. Cannan, Chicago: Chicago University Press [1976].

Thornton, H. (1802) *An Enquiry into the Nature and Effects of the Paper Credit of Great Britain*, (Introduction F.A. von Hayek), New York: Farrer & Rinehart [1939].

Toniolo, G. (1988) *Central Banks' Independence in Historical Perspective*, New York: Walter de Grugter.

Tooke, T. (1844) *An Inquiry into the Currency Principle: The Connection of the Currency with Prices and the Expediency of a Separation of Issue from Banking*, London: Longman, Brown, Green, Longmans.

Tooke, T. and Newmarch, W. (1857) *A History of Prices and of the State of the Circulation from 1848–1856*, vols V, VI, London: Longman, Brown, Green, Longmans.

Vickers, D. (1975) 'Adam Smith and the Status of the Theory of Money', in A.S. Skinner and T. Wilson, *Essays on Adam Smith*, Oxford: Clarendon Press, 428–503.

Viner, J. (1937) *Studies in the Theory of International Trade*, New York: Harper.

7. Structuralism and the Debate on Latin-American Inflation in the 1980s

Juan Carlos Moreno Brid[1]

INTRODUCTION

Structuralism has traditionally occupied an important position in the debate on macroeconomics in Latin America. However, with few exceptions (*inter alia* Seers and Hirschman) its relevance for development theory has been ignored elsewhere. Recently this has begun to change as heterodox programmes were put in practice to curtail inflation in Argentina, Brazil and Mexico. These programmes, soon identified as structuralist experiments in macroeconomic policy, are often considered the most innovative contributions to stabilization theory in decades (Ocampo 1987). They marked the beginning of a heated debate on anti-inflationary policies.

This chapter presents the structuralist view on Latin-American inflation and contrasts it with some opposing views. It should be recalled that one of the contributions of structuralism to economic development theory is precisely its analysis of inflation (Arndt 1985; Rodriguez 1980). The chapter is arranged in three sections. The first section explores some problems faced in trying to define structuralist macroeconomics. The next section examines the structuralist theory of inflation and contrasts it with the main alternative interpretations of Latin-America's inflation in the 1980s. The third section presents some final comments and conclusions.

STRUCTURALIST MACROECONOMICS

To arrive at a clear and concise definition of a school of economic thought is a complicated affair and a source of controversy. The task is particularly hard in the case of structuralist economics, given the commitment of the latter to a multidisciplinary perspective. For structuralism, economic development theory must consider the specific historical, sociological and institutional frameworks (Rodriguez 1980). Though its emphasis on a multidimensional approach enriches the analysis and policy recommendations, it makes structuralist macroeconomics most difficult to define.

In addition, Latin-American structuralism has been driven more by policy issues than by the analysis of fundamental principles of economic theory (Jameson 1986). This bias has sometimes raised the question of whether there is a unified theoretical framework for structuralist macroeconomics (Chenery 1975).

Another difficulty in reaching a clear definition of structuralism lies in the fact that other schools have explicitly recognized the importance of economic structure. For instance, current literature on development frequently refers to 'structural adjustment' without precisely defining it. Diversity of criteria has led to its use for different, sometimes opposing, economic policies. For example, the World Bank's view of 'structural adjustment policy' stands for a set of measures intended to remove constraints on the free functioning of markets. However, strong critics of the Bank's position also favour 'structural adjustment policies', meaning direct state intervention to boost productivity in selected productive sectors (Fajnzylber 1983; ECLAC 1990).

Structuralist economics has found it difficult to overcome this ambiguity and vagueness. Many of its ideas are couched in somewhat loose terms. 'The structuralist sees the world as inflexible. Change is inhibited by bottlenecks and constraints ... In economic terms, the supply of most things is inelastic. Such general inflexibility was thought to apply particularly to LDCs' (Little 1982, p. 20). Little's conception does not present a clearcut definition. However, it regards structuralism as an approach which stands apart from conventional general equilibrium perspectives. At the same time, it reminds us of structuralism's orientation to the problems of less developed economies. This orientation in turn, may explain why structuralist critiques of conventional theory have centred on its irrelevance for semi-industrial, less developed economies. Taylor describes the structuralist approach in the following terms:

> An economy has structure if its institutions and the behavior of its members make some patterns of resource allocation and evolution substantially more likely than others. Economic analysis is structuralist when it takes those factors as the foundation stones for its theories. (Taylor 1983, p. 3)

Arndt (1988) has pointed out that one of the main traits of structuralism is its emphasis on the relative incompleteness of markets in less developed economies.

In summary, structuralist economics may be characterized as a school based on inductive reasoning from stylized facts, which recognizes the importance of sociopolitical and institutional factors as well as the influence of 'norms' on the behaviour of economic agents. In addition, its basic unit of analysis seems to be, not the isolated consumer or producer, but social group interaction.

THE STRUCTURALIST THEORY OF INFLATION IN THE 1980s

The heterodox theory of inflation is a modern version of the Latin-American structuralist school. Noyola presented the first consistent account of the structuralist approach to inflation:

> Inflation is not a monetary phenomenon, but the outcome of disequilibria on the real side of the economy which express themselves through a rise in the overall price level. The origin of inflation in the real side of the economy is more evident in less developed countries than in industrialised ones. (Noyola 1956, p. 604)

He explicitly differentiated the structuralist theory of inflation from the Keynesian one, as the former does not consider an overall excess demand to be the ultimate cause of inflation. Formally, the structuralist theory distinguishes two forces at work in any inflationary process – structural and inertial. Behind this distinction is the idea that inflation originates in the former element, while the latter perpetuates it. We proceed to take a closer look at them. Since the inertial element is usually not treated in detail, we devote somewhat more attention to it.

The Origins of Inflation
For structuralism, inflation has its fundamental origin in two characteristics of the economy: rigidities in the production system, and conflict on income distribution. Among the first group, structuralism considers bottlenecks and rigidities in the export and food production sectors as factors causing inflation in less developed economies (LDCs). The semi-feudal agriculture and land tenure systems found in LDCs make it virtually impossible for food production to increase at the rates required by demographic expansion. These structural difficulties build inflationary pressure into LDC economies via an upward trend in foodstuff prices. At the same time, the export earnings of these economies are highly unstable due to wide fluctuations in quantities exported and in the prices of export goods. Moreover, differences in the production structures of the developed and the less developed economies prevent LDC exports from generating the

foreign exchange required to cover their import needs. This balance of payments constraint creates additional inflationary pressure via currency depreciations.

The idea of conflict as a structural element at the origin of inflation does not seem to require much elaboration. Struggle among different social groups for bigger shares of the national income pushes money wage rates and prices upwards. If the ensuing distribution of income is not generally accepted, further rounds of price and wage hikes may occur. The process may stabilize or it may lead to an increasing inflation rate.

Inertial Inflation

As a starting point, we may define inertial inflation as a situation where prices follow patterns that are independent of the actual conditions of supply and demand. This idea has as its theoretical foundations the distinction between *anticipated* and *unanticipated* price variations. In practice, inflation is never fully anticipated. The inability of agents to forecast prices with accuracy makes it difficult for them to protect themselves against the effects of inflation. Producers conduct their business in a context of uncertainty. They make decisions concerning prices, volumes and types of products without perfect knowledge of the future course of demand, inflation or economic policy. Nor are they fully knowledgeable about the current relative prices of all goods in the market. Available information is far from perfect and is subject to high acquisition costs. How do they set prices under these circumstances?

Okun (1981), though not a structuralist himself, has shed considerable light on price-setting mechanisms. By focusing on transaction costs in different markets, he has shown that because of uncertainty, rational behaviour on the part of producers may entail a policy of stable prices in response to short-term demand fluctuations. He makes a fundamental distinction between auction and customer markets. The former are characterized by homogeneous products and low information costs relative to market prices. The latter, on the other hand, have more heterogeneous products and higher information costs. Inherently higher transaction costs are an incentive for buyers and sellers in customer markets to maintain a continuous relation with one another. Buyers seek to reduce the cost of searching for reliable suppliers; and sellers try to keep prices relatively stable in order to remain on the customer's list of suppliers. As a result, short-term changes in demand in customer markets lead to changes in output volumes rather than in prices. That is, prices tend to be relatively stable, to show a certain inertia.

Empirical studies have shown that price variance increases with the rate of inflation (Alberro 1987); thus it seems reasonable to assume that uncertainty increases with inflation. The greater uncertainty and higher search costs associated with increased inflation stimulate the introduction of indexation mechanisms in the price-setting process. These mechanisms are formal or informal rules linking price movements to previous changes in certain key prices. Thus, pricing in a context of uncertainty may build an inertial element into inflation. The assumption of an inertial momentum in price changes differentiates the heterodox theory of inflation from the conventional one. The former explicitly states that inflation can be independent of excess demand in the market in question. Conventional theory, on the other hand, holds that any variation in prices is determined exclusively by supply and demand. According to conventional microeconomics, *nominal* schemes of price indexation lack a rational basis. This view endorses only those mechanisms of indexation which assure constant income in *real* terms. It is obvious that any indexation scheme based on the previous price changes of a predetermined basket of goods cannot guarantee a constant income in real terms during the present period. As Blinder (1984, pp. 417–18) puts it: 'Since rational maximizing agents should care only about real wages and relative prices, microtheory will at best, explain real rigidities, not nominal ones.'

But the consistency of inertial inflation with rational economic behaviour can easily be seen with the help of Game Theory, in a 'prisoner's dilemma' situation. Consider a situation of persistent inflation and assume that each individual agent would prefer price stability. However, none of them would choose to postpone an increase in his own sales price, given uncertainty as to the behaviour of others. Each one is willing to maintain stable prices once inflation has been controlled. Unless someone – the government? – can guarantee overall price stability, rational behaviour on the part of individual agents will perpetuate inflation.

Empirical evidence supports the hypothesis of inertial inflation. A number of studies of pricing in the manufacturing sector have repeatedly concluded that changes in demand do not account, to a significant degree, for changes in prices. A recent comprehensive survey of applied studies on this issue concluded that 'studies differ in their coverage, level of aggregation and span of time. However, they all seem to point to the slow adjustment of prices and a more rapid adjustment of outputs, when the demand level changes in the short run' (Nadiri 1986, p. 5).

It should be emphasized that structuralism's notion of inertia goes beyond a statistical hypothesis regarding the significance of the autoregressive behaviour of inflation. If so interpreted, it is consistent with schools of economics antagonistic to the structuralist position. For example, the Rational Expectations School acknowledges the existence of a statistically significant relation between current and lagged rates of inflation. However, it denies that such a relation implies that inflation has inertial behaviour. As one of its most well-known advocates has stated, the 'rational expectations school rejects the idea that the inflationary process has an inherent momentum' (Sargent 1982, p. 42). In this view, inertial inflation is a spurious phenomenon that originates in the systematic application of economic policies inconsistent with zero inflation. Thus, the lack of credible anti-inflationary policies strengthens expectations of persistent inflation and leads to the adoption of behavioural patterns which perpetuate it. It is evident then, that the rational expectations and the structuralist conceptions of inertia would lead to different policies to combat inflation.

THE DEBATE ON LATIN-AMERICAN INFLATION IN THE 1980s

The structuralist theory of inflation as presented above provided the analytical framework for the heterodox programme applied in Argentina and Brazil. They were aimed at reducing inflation through the unconventional use of a number of policy instruments, among them a de-indexation of contracts, a full freeze on prices and wages through direct controls and monetary reform. These programmes differed in a fundamental way from those traditionally espoused by the International Monetary Fund. In particular, they assured that the control of inflation was compatible with output and employment expansion, and they regarded traditional stabilization policies as unsatisfactory in so far as these policies entailed an unnecessary contraction in economic activity (Ibarra 1987).

Heterodox programmes were not as successful in practice as their advocates expected. The 'Cruzado Plan' in Brazil and the 'Austral Plan' in Argentina, the most well-known experiments along this line, failed to produce a permanent reduction in inflation. Their failure has encouraged calls for a rejection of the structuralist theory of inflation and a return to conventional policies, in hopes of extinguishing inflation once and for all. But such action would be wrong.

The main participants in the debate on Latin-American inflation in the 1980s can be classified into two groups which, with some over-simplification, we designate *Mainstream* and *Heterodox*. Both groups acknowledge the existence of an inertial element in Latin-American inflation (in the sense defined by the structuralist school reviewed above). However, they clash on the issue of the fundamental origins of inflation. For those close to the mainstream perspective, the origin of inflation in Brazil and Argentina is to be found in the public sector deficit (cf. Sanginés 1987, p. 162; Dornbusch and Simonsen 1986, p. 277). For heterodox economists, inflation is caused by the conflict over income distribution: it is the 'non-cooperative adjustment of the distribution conflict' (Bacha 1986; cf. also Modiano 1987, p. 229).

Divergence regarding the origin of inflation gave rise to different evaluations of the objectives and results of the heterodox programmes. According to the mainstream view, the heterodox programme was aimed at suppressing both the inertial and the structural elements of inflation. Incomes policy was to be the instrument to fulfil the first objective, while an austere fiscal policy would suppress the structural element. For the heterodox, the programme was much more limited in scope and its objective was simply to do away with inertial inflation. In this sense, it neglected to deal with the structural element of inflation as it supposed that the prevailing distribution of income was generally accepted. Clearly, if the distribution conflict was exacerbated, the programme would be unable to maintain low rates of inflation for any length of time. Discontent of groups having price or wage setting capacity concerning their shares in national income would boost inflation, once price controls were lifted.

The difference between the interpretations may be better appreciated through the following expression:

$$\hat{P} = \hat{P}(-1) + a\,(G-T) + b\,(Y-y) \tag{7.1}$$

where $\hat{P}$ = current inflation
$\hat{P}(-1)$ = lagged inflation
$G-T$ = real public sector deficit
Y = target real income for the previous period
y = actual real income obtained in the previous period

In this expression only one sector is assumed to have the ability to affect the rate of inflation if income expectations are not satisfied. Reaction functions of different social groups to declines in relative incomes may be included to derive algebraic models of more realistic inflationary processes (Olivera 1964). The algebraic expression captures the main elements of both views. The extreme mainstream position considers the parameter b to be insignificant. The extreme heterodox position views the parameter a as irrelevant. Clearly, both assume an inertial element in inflation through the introduction of the lagged term $\hat{P}(-1)$.

The mainstream formulation resembles an augmented Phillips curve, with adaptive expectations, in which the cyclical position of the economy is reflected in the fiscal deficit. This explains why its followers find no difference between the orthodox and heterodox views: ultimately, in the two models inflation is a consequence of excess demand. The heterodox interpretation of the formulation incorporates the structuralist idea of distributional conflict as a source of inflation, but the equation does not reflect the equally important structuralist idea that rigidities and bottlenecks are also potential sources of inflation. Clearly, a more complicated model would be needed to do full justice to the heterodox view. Note also that due to the relative incompleteness of markets and the importance of rigidities in LDCs, reductions in public investment expenditure may end up increasing inflationary pressures if they tighten bottlenecks in the economy.

It should be pointed out that both the heterodox and the mainstream positions view the nominal public sector deficit or surplus as an inadequate measure of fiscal pressure on aggregate demand. Nevertheless, the mainstream approach holds that the public sector budget – adjusted for inflation – should be either balanced or in surplus if price increases are to be curtailed.

On the other hand, the heterodox approach affirms that a public sector deficit, even if adjusted for inflation, is not necessarily incompatible with anti-inflationary policies. The optimum level of the public sector budget depends on the degree of capacity utilization and the short-term target levels of income and employment. If the economy is far below full employment, a deficit may be necessary. But unless income is given, it does not follow that a public deficit leads to an imbalance in the private sector's portfolio. If private income is increasing, the public deficit can be financed without crowding other assets out of the portfolio held by the private sector. An equilibrium situation may be compatible with a public sector deficit which is constant or even increasing in real terms.

Fiscal austerity is sometimes justified in terms of its impact on inflationary expectations. A public sector surplus would indicate that in the future inflation is to decrease. Though the argument may be valid a priori, emphasis on the link between the public deficit and inflation via expectations leads into a dark alley. In practice, it is not clear which indicator of fiscal stance is used to form expectations regarding inflation. Given the length of time during which the nominal deficit has been highlighted as a source of inflation, it is difficult to believe that all agents will form their expectations according to the operating or primary deficits.

CONCLUSIONS

In this chapter we have presented different views of the Latin-American inflation problem and have shown that, although structuralism is difficult to define with precision, it offers a consistent theoretical framework for an examination of the inflationary process in Latin America. The distinction between structural elements causing inflation and inertial elements serving to perpetuate it constitutes a sound platform for analysis and policy design.

The presence of inertial inflation suggests that in highly inflationary conditions, stabilization policy should consider specific measures designed to break existing indexation mechanisms that perpetuate the situation. The importance of distributional conflict as a source of inflation must not be underestimated. Although most studies on conflict and inflation consider only two social groups, workers and capitalists, a more detailed breakdown may be necessary to understand the current Latin-American inflation problem. A useful disaggregation would additionally include the public sector and international creditors. It is hardly a coincidence that the debt crisis and the outburst of inflation occurred at the same time in Latin America. In this sense, the resurgence of inflation seems to call into question the coherence of a stabilization strategy that seeks to hold down inflation while simultaneously transferring substantial shares of income abroad as debt service.

Finally, the structuralist focus on rigidities and bottlenecks as a source of inflation may contribute to an explanation of why inflation tends to be higher and more persistent in LDCs. An important factor along this line is the relation between public expenditure and inflation. While for mainstream economics the relation is simple and direct, for structuralism it is not necessarily so. Given the relative incompleteness of markets in LDCs and the importance of structural rigidities, cuts in public expenditure may even increase inflationary pressures in the economy. Much more work is needed to substantiate these claims, but we believe that the structuralist theory of inflation represents a contribution in the right direction.

NOTE

1. The author gratefully acknowledges the helpful comments of Gary Mongiovi, Martin Puchet, Claudia Schatán, Christof Rühl, and an anonymous referee.

REFERENCES

Alberro, J.L. (1987) 'La dinámica de los precios relativos en un ambiente inflacionario', *Estudios Económicos*, Special issue (Oct.).
Arndt, H.W. (1985) 'The Origins of Structuralism', *World Development*, **13** (2).

Arndt, H.W. (1988) 'Market Failure and Underdevelopment', *World Development*, **16** (2).

Bacha, E.L. (1986) 'A Inercia e o Conflito: o Plano Cruzado e seus Desafios', Rio de Janeiro: Department of Economics, PUC. (mimeo).

Blinder, A. (1984) 'Comment on Perry', *American Economic Review*, Papers and Proceedings, **74**, 417–18.

Chenery, H. (1975) 'The Structuralist Approach to Development Policy', *American Economic Review*, **65**, 311–16.

Dornbusch, R. and Simonsen, M.H. (1986) 'Estabilización de la inflación con el apoyo de una política de ingresos', *El Trimestre Económico*, **54** (2).

ECLAC (1990) *Transformación productiva con equidad*, Santiago de Chile.

Fajnzylber, F. (1983) *La industrialización trunca en América Latina*, Mexico: Nueva Imagen.

Hirschman, A. (1980) 'La matriz social y la política de la inflación: Elaboración sobre la experiencia latinoamericana', *El Trimestre Económico*, July–Sept.

Ibarra, D. (1987) 'Política y economía en América Latina: el transfondo de los programas heterodoxos de estabilización', *Estudios Económicos*, Special issue (Oct.).

Jameson, K. (1986) 'Latin American Structuralism: A Methodological Perspective', *World Development*, **14** (2).

Little, I.M.D. (1982) *Economic Development: Theory, Policy and International Relations*, New York: Basic Books.

Modiano, E.M. (1987) 'El Plan Cruzado: bases teóricas ye limitaciones prácticas.', *El Trimestre Económico*, **54**, Special issue.

Nadiri, M.I. (1986) 'Price Inertia and Inflation: Evidence and Theoretical Rationale', National Bureau of Economic Research, Working Paper no. 2022, Sept.

Noyola, J. (1956) 'El desarrollo económico y la inflación en México y en otros paises latinoamericanos', *Investigación Económica*, **16** (4).

Ocampo. J.A. (1987) 'Una Evoluacion comparativa de quatro planes antiinflatonarios recientes', *El Trimestre Economico*, **54**, Special issue.

Okun, A.M. (1981) *Prices and Quantities: A Macroeconomic Analysis*, New York: The Brookings Institution.

Olivera, J.H.G. (1964) 'On structural inflation and Latin American structuralism', *Oxford Economic Papers*, **16** (3).

Rodriguez, O. (1980) *La teoría del subdesarrollo de la CEPAL, Mexico*: Siglo XXI editores.

Sanginés, A. (1987) '¿Ortodoxia o heterodoxia? la estabilización de la economía boliviana (1985–1986)', *Estudios Económicos*, Special issue, Oct.

Sargent, T.J. (1982) 'The End of Four Big Inflations' in R.E. Hall (ed.), *Inflation: Causes and Effects*, Chicago: NBER and The University of Chicago Press.

Seers, D. (1962), 'A Theory of Inflation and Growth in Underdeveloped Economies Based on the Experience of Latin America', *Oxford Economic Papers*, **14** (2).

Taylor, L. (1983) *Structuralist Macroeconomics*, Basic Books: New York.

PART II

Macroeconomic Fluctuations and Business Cycles

8. Neo-Austrian Traverse Analysis and Austrian Business Cycle Theory

Christian Gehrke

'The difference between a money and a barter economy is the essential ingredient in any analysis of economic fluctuations' (O'Driscoll and Rizzo 1985, p. 201).

'It is not true that by getting rid of money, one is automatically in "equilibrium" . . . Monetary disorders may indeed be superimposed upon other disorders; but the other disorders are more fundamental' (Hicks 1973, pp. 133–4).

INTRODUCTION

Renewed interest in Austrian economics has recently produced several contributions attempting a revival of the Austrian business cycle theory that originated in the work of Mises and Hayek during the 1920s and 1930s.[1] In the course of this revival the famous debates of the early 1930s involving Hayek, Keynes, Sraffa and others have been re-examined.[2] Sir John Hicks, a close observer of these controversies (though he did not actively participate) has recently recalled his 'state of thinking' during the years he spent at the LSE as a member of the Robbins circle:

> We seemed, at the start, to share a common viewpoint, or even, one might say, a common faith. Some of us, especially Hayek, have in later years maintained that faith; others, such as Kaldor, Abba Lerner, George Shackle and myself, have departed from it, to a greater or less extent . . . The faith in question was a belief in the free market, or 'price-mechanism' – that a competitive system, free of all 'interferences', by government or by monopolistic combinations, of capital or of labour, would easily find an 'equilibrium' . . . Hayek, when he joined us, was to introduce into this doctrine an important qualification – that money (somehow) must be kept 'neutral', in order that the mechanism should work smoothly. (Hicks 1982, p. 3)

As is well known, non-neutral money was a key element in Hayek's explanation of business cycles, which in 1931 Hicks found 'immensely exciting, but also very puzzling' (Hicks 1982, p. 6). In his first attempt to come to grips with it, in a paper published in German in 1933, Hicks introduced the notion of 'intertemporal equilibrium' (which, however, he borrowed from Hayek (1928)). Referring to that paper, Hicks recently recalled:

> Hayek was making us think of the productive process as a process in time, inputs coming before outputs; but his completest, and most logical account of intertemporal relations was confined to a model of 'perfect foresight'. In his *Prices and Production* ... things were allowed to go wrong, but only for monetary reasons; it was only because of monetary disturbances that an exception was allowed to the rule that market forces must tend to establish an equilibrium'. (Hicks 1979, p. 199)

To Hicks the notion of 'intertemporal equilibrium' was synonymous with 'perfect foresight equilibrium'; and though he 'saw as yet no need to abandon the Hayek construction', he felt that

> it would clearly be necessary to devise a better concept of equilibrium, one which would serve to isolate specifically monetary disturbances, but which was not burdened by that terribly unrealistic *perfect foresight*. And it would clearly be necessary to devise a better theory of the behaviour of an economy which was not in equilibrium. (Hicks 1982, p. 7)

In 1967 Hicks made a second attempt to disentangle the 'inner mystery' of Hayek's theory. This time his principle conclusion was that it had been 'extremely misleading' as a cycle theory but that it contained 'an interesting analysis of the adjustment of an economy to changes in the rate of genuine saving' (Hicks 1967, p. 210). Hayek's theory, Hicks proposed, should not be viewed as a cycle theory, but as a theory of disproportional growth.[3]

Finally, in 1973, Hicks developed a theory of disproportional growth or traverse, which he based on a neo-Austrian model of production. In a certain sense, therefore, Hicks's *Capital and Time* can be viewed as the final outcome of his attempts to 'devise a better theory of the behaviour of an economy which was not in equilibrium'. Hicks's investigation of traverse processes, although not designed to serve as a cycle theory, nevertheless turns out to be particularly relevant for his evaluation of Hayek's contribution to business cycle theory. Seemingly it served the purpose of removing his discomfort at having abandoned the Hayek construction in the mid 1930s without having been able to spell out its defects clearly.

This chapter assesses the connections between the Austrian cycle theory and the neo-Austrian traverse theory. It will be argued that the latter, although it shares many common elements with the former and even arrives at Hayekian phenomena, nevertheless provides a basis for rejecting the Austrian explanation of business cycles. First, the main features of the Austrian cycle theory are briefly summarized. This is followed by a detailed description of the method adopted by Hicks for the analysis of traverse processes and an overview of the main results achieved in neo-Austrian traverse theory. Finally, the main conclusions are summarized.

AUSTRIAN BUSINESS CYCLE THEORY

There are a number of expositions of the Austrian business cycle theory and, according to Garrison (1989, p. 3), none of these versions should be regarded as 'canonical'. The following sketch relies exclusively on Hayek's writings (1929, 1931, 1939, 1941, 1969) and thus makes no claim to being paradigmatic; rather I shall emphasize those features of the theory which are relevant for a comparison with Hicksian traverse analysis.

Hayek's business cycle theory is commonly characterized as a monetary overinvestment theory, employing a monetary impulse and a real propagation mechanism. It is built on the twin pillars of Austrian capital theory and Wicksell's distinction between the 'natural' and the 'market' rate of interest.

The most significant characteristic of the Austrian theory of capital is the attention given to the complementarity relationships among technical possibilities belonging to different moments of time. To the Austrians both the duration and the timing of production are essential features of capitalistic production. Given the time-consuming nature of productive activities, capital goods can be associated with earlier or later stages in the productive process, so that higher-order and lower-order capital goods must be perceived as intertemporal complements. At any moment of time, then, the capital structure consists of an assortment of various capital goods characterized by different degrees of durability, specificity, substitutability and complementarity, both at a point of time and over time. Although in his *Pure Theory of Capital* (1941), Hayek cautioned against any attempt to represent the structure of capital by a one-dimensional magnitude such as the 'degree of roundaboutness', the 'quantity of waiting' or the 'length of the period of production', he nevertheless uses these notions in his business cycle theory. The structure of production, taken as a whole, is then assumed to be characterized by a longer or shorter period of production, a greater or lesser degree of roundaboutness, according to whether the rate of interest is low or high.[4]

Consequently, changes in the structure of production are linked to changes in the rate of interest.

Austrian business cycle theory makes a crucial distinction between interest rate changes attributable to changes in intertemporal preferences and interest rate changes due to monetary disturbances. In *Prices and Production* Hayek starts by assuming that the system is initially in long-run equilibrium. The market rate of interest equals the natural rate, and the degree of roundaboutness corresponds to consumers' time preference, that is, the volume of voluntary savings is matched by a similar demand for additional capital. He then traces out a new equilibrium that is reached when a change in time preference (an increase in voluntary savings) takes place. Rather than concentrating on the transition (or traverse) to the new equilibrium, he merely describes the outcome: the increase in voluntary savings reduces the market rate of interest which makes it profitable to lengthen the period of production. Since consumers voluntarily sacrifice part of their claims on output, they will be willing to wait till the new, longer methods yield extra consumption at lower prices in the new equilibrium. The transition to the new equilibrium, Hayek maintains, does not cause any significant problems, such as cyclical adjustments.

When the market rate of interest falls because of a monetary injection, Hayek continues, the initial consequences are similar to what happens when the propensity to save increases. More specifically, the theory maintains that since a lower rate of interest lengthens the desirable investment period for the production of any consumer good, entrepreneurs will invest the extra credit money in earlier stages of production rather than in later stages close to final consumption goods output. Therefore the prices of capital goods specific to these earlier stages will be bid up and this price signal in turn induces a redirection of unspecific resources away from later stages towards these earlier ones. In contrast to the case of a change in voluntary savings, however, a shortage of consumer goods and later-stage capital goods must sooner or later emerge and the prices of these goods will in turn start to rise. As long as money wages lag behind the rise in consumer prices, 'forced saving' will be imposed upon consumers and if the monetary (credit) expansion continues, economic activity will be encouraged throughout.

The competition of entrepreneurs for factors of production will drive up wages in proportion to the increase in money, and, unless banks are able (or willing) to expand credit infinitely, the market rate of interest will sooner or later start to rise *pari passu* with factor prices. The desired degree of roundaboutness therefore becomes shorter again and unspecific resources are shifted back towards later stages of production. The rise in costs, while affecting both earlier and later stages, is matched by an increase in demand only for the latter's output. The reversal in relative prices results in an excess capacity in sectors producing durable capital goods in the earlier stages. With the return to shorter periods of production many of the early-stage capital goods, highly specific and designed to participate in longer production processes, become either underutilized or completely useless. And since labour is complementary to capital, the liquidation or abandonment of these highly specific instruments of production is bound to result in workers becoming unemployed.

The Austrian explanation of trade cycles is thus based on the proposition that economic fluctuations must ultimately be due to 'wrong' price signals encouraging entrepreneurs to take 'false' investment decisions. Hayek maintains that a free market system with 'neutral money' would smoothly adjust to any changes in real data, whereas monetary disturbances lead entrepreneurs to choose unsustainably 'long' or 'roundabout' methods of production. Here, Hayek's work on the nature and significance of the competitive price system in market economies can be seen to be closely related to his explanation of industrial fluctuations. For, if one agrees with Hayek's view of (relative) prices transmitting signals (information) that facilitate coordination, that is, if agents' actions in response to price signals are viewed as equilibrating processes, then cycles can be interpreted as inevitable consequences of agents' *misled* equilibrating processes.

NEO-AUSTRIAN TRAVERSE ANALYSIS

The term 'traverse analysis' denotes a branch of growth theory which originated in the 1960s and 1970s. Its object is the study of an economy which was disturbed from a long-run equilibrium growth path by a change in one of the exogenous determinants of growth, such as technical progress, or the supply of labour or natural resources.

The pioneering studies[5] in the field of traverse analysis have been carried out by A. Lowe (1976) and J. Hicks (1965, 1973). Despite the similarity in their object of analysis, there is a fundamental difference in the methods adopted by Hicks and Lowe: whereas Lowe based his study on a circular model of production and aimed at determining the structural and behavioural requirements for 'efficient' traverse paths,[6] Hicks tried to develop a *descriptive* theory of traverse, depicting the 'actual' paths followed by the (model) economy. Hicks first set out his theory of traverse in the context of a two-sectoral model (1965), but then switched to a neo-Austrian model of production for its further development (1970, 1973).

According to Hicks, the Austrian view of production as a transformation of original factors into consumer goods is especially suited to the study of disequilibrium paths, because it relegates the role of the means of production to that of intermediate products, integrated and subsumed within the elementary processes, without explicitly showing up. As is well known, the specific version of Austrian capital theory introduced by Böhm-Bawerk links a sequence of original inputs to the emergence of a final product at a single moment of time (a flow input/point output model), and hence does not admit of taking durable means of production into account. In contrast to this, the neo-Austrian version proposed by Hicks (1970, 1973) treats the elementary production process as one which transforms a stream of original inputs into a stream of final output (flow input/flow output). Thus the neo-Austrian model, while it still conceives of the production process as a completely vertically-integrated activity, does take durable capital goods into account. Since durable capital goods 'contribute, not just to one unit of output, at one date, but to a sequence of units of output, at a sequence of dates' (Hicks 1973, p. 8) their existence invokes intertemporal joint production of final output.

In the Hicksian model an elementary production process is represented by a sequence $\{l(t); b(t)\}_0^d$; where $l(t)$ denotes the flow of primary inputs in fixed proportions – labour, for short; and $b(t)$ the flow of consumption goods (a consumption bundle in fixed proportions); t denotes the time measured from the start of the process and d the physical life of the process. It is assumed that the available technology comprises several elementary processes, each of which can be activated at any level under constant returns to scale (denoting by T historical or calendar time, $x(T-t)$ represents the rate of starts of processes at $(T-t)$). Furthermore it is assumed that processes have no scrap value when terminated and can be costlessly truncated. The centrality of time in productive activity is expressed by the fact that each process consists of a primary phase, in which final output is zero (a 'machine' is being constructed by applying primary inputs) and a secondary phase, in which $b(t)$ is (semi)positive (the 'machine', together with primary inputs, is utilized to produce final output). The problem of 'choice of technique' is solved, in familiar manner, by deriving and comparing $w-r$ relations ('efficiency curves' in Hicks's terminology). This choice involves not only the process (the technique), but also its length; in other words, for each process the optimal date of truncation must be determined.[7]

Now, in long-run equilibrium (a steady state) the economy must be fully adjusted to the available technology, in the sense that of the available processes only the cost minimizing one(s) is (are) activated. Furthermore, on a steady state path the 'age structure' of the activated processes must be such that a constant (or a constantly growing) flow of aggregate outputs and inputs is achieved, which implies a constant (or a constantly growing) rate of starts.

The Hicksian analysis starts out from such a configuration. A technical innovation, occurring at time 0, is the causal factor which pushes the economy onto a traverse path. With static expectations and under competitive conditions, the new method will be adopted for all newly activated processes whenever it yields a higher rate of profit at the going wage rate. On the assumption that the market rate of interest is instantaneously adjusted to the new profit rate, the optimal truncation date for old type processes, started before date 0 and still operated, might change.[8] Thus the economy will embark on a transitional path in the course of which the old technique is gradually replaced by the new one.

Hicks's treatment of this transitional phase consists of considering two different kinds of traverse paths, to which he assigns the labels 'Full Employment' and 'Fixwage' path respectively. To determine the Full Employment path it is necessary to assume that the system functions at 'Full Performance' and that the real wage rate adjusts instantaneously to keep the available labour force continuously fully employed. The full performance condition implies that the existing productive capacity is at every moment fully utilized[9] *and* that all final output in excess of the requirements for utilizing the existing capacity is used to start new processes. Put briefly: full performance implies the non-existence of effective demand failures in that it guarantees continuous saving–investment equality.

The fixwage-path is an application of Hicksian fixprice theory. If the real wage rate is assumed to be fixed exogenously, the rate of starts of new processes is again determined by assuming Full Performance. In this case adjustment takes place by variations in employment, whereas in the flexprice case the wage rate adjusts to clear the labour market. In either case the final product market always clears, as does the capital market.

On these assumptions the rate of starts of new processes on the two different traverse paths (and consequently the development of output, employment and so on) can be determined sequentially. Hicks's sequence analysis approach, by drawing attention to the deviations between the 'actual' course of the economic system and the corresponding long-run equilibrium path, provides a case for the counterfactual approach to sequential causality: the macroeconomic effects of a change in technology are depicted by comparing the entire sequence of the traverse paths with the sequence of the path which the economy would have followed in the absence of this change (Zamagni 1984).

Some Results of Neo-Austrian Traverse Theory

One of the most interesting results is Hicks's demonstration that the introduction of more 'mechanized' processes (processes using relatively more inputs in the construction phase, relatively fewer inputs in the utilization phase) must either lead to a temporary fall in the real wage rate (full employment path) or to a temporary fall in the level of employment (fixwage path), relative to the reference path (the path the economy would have followed in the absence of the innovation). This result confirms the famous Ricardian proposition, according to which a 'transformation of circulating capital into fixed capital' causes an adverse, but temporary, effect on employment.[10] Gozzi and Zamagni (1982) and Violi (1982, 1984a) have demonstrated that a similar effect can also occur in the opposite case of 'less mechanized' processes being introduced. This slightly surprising result can be easily explained by taking note of the fact that Ricardo's 'machinery effect' is due to a temporary fall in the 'gross produce'. Since the introduction of an innovation always disturbs the 'synchronized' age structure of the existing capital stock and therefore changes the time structure of aggregate inputs and outputs, we cannot rule out the existence of a time phase in the course of the traverse in which the final output flow forthcoming (the 'gross produce') is reduced below its reference level, irrespective of the particular form taken by technical change.

When the possibility of 'shortening' or 'lengthening' the duration of the construction phase is taken into account,[11] some interesting phenomena with regard to business cycle theory can be studied. On the full employment path, shortening (lengthening) leads to considerable upward (downward) 'jumps' in the rate of starts in the course of the traverse. These 'jumps' are due to the fact that the new processes contribute earlier (later) to the final product flow than did the old ones so that more (less) resources for the start of processes become available at particular dates. These 'jumps' invoke 'secondary jumps' at later dates (echo effects): first when the processes activated at an excessively high (low) rate reach the utilization phase and secondly when they are terminated. This phenomenon is known in business cycle theory as a 'pure reinvestment cycle'.[12]

However, a more interesting phenomenon occurs on the fixwage path in the case of a lengthening of the construction phase. Formally its emergence is indicated by a negative solution for the rate of starts, during a certain interval of time in the course of the traverse. This means not only that during this time phase no new process can be activated but also that some of those which had been started in the past must be stopped. In other words, the existing capacity cannot be fully utilized. It is obvious that the underutilization of productive capacity is due, in the present context, neither to a deficiency of effective demand nor to any lack of scarce resources (which are left completely out of consideration), but to the diacronic complementarity of the capital structure. Put differently, in the period under consideration the flow of final output currently forthcoming falls short of the requirements for the full utilization of the durable equipment that has been built up. Thus Hicks's neo-Austrian traverse analysis seems to reinforce Hayek's claim, that

> the existence of unused capacity is . . . by no means a proof that there exists an excess of capital and that consumption is insufficient: on the contrary, it is a symptom that we are unable to use the fixed plant to the full extent because the current demand for consumer's goods is too urgent to permit us to invest current productive services in the long processes for which . . . the necessary durable equipment is available. (Hayek 1931, p. 96)

However, it is important to note that despite this common element Hicks's traverse analysis does not support Hayek's explanation of business cycles:

> The relevance, to economic fluctuations, of the time-structure of production was the discovery of Professor Hayek; that there is such a relevance our present analysis confirms . . . Where . . . I do not go along with him (or with what he said in 1931) is in the view that the disturbances in question have a monetary origin. He had not emancipated himself from the delusion . . . that with money removed 'in a state of barter' everything would somehow fit. One of my objects in writing this book has been to kill that delusion. (Hicks, 1973, p. 133)

There is some irony in realizing that Hicks, in order 'to kill that delusion', harks back to an important feature of Hayek's own theory, namely discoordinated time structures of inputs and outputs arising from conversions of the capital structure. Hicks maintains, as Sraffa (1932a) did in his dispute with Hayek, that a barter economy can get out of equilibrium as much as a monetary economy. But unlike Sraffa, who tried to make his case against Hayek by considering an increase in voluntary savings not matched by an increase in planned investment, Hicks does not invoke a saving–investment mismatch. Indeed, in the Hicksian model real saving always flows most safely into real investment, because investment (the start of new processes) is made in terms of consumer goods. Thus, when in $T = 0$ the decision to switch to the new technology is being made, no change in the volume of aggregate savings or investment is taking place.

In *Capital and Time* (1973) Hicks's analysis was mainly confined to a very simplified technology, the so-called 'standard case', for which convergence of the traverse paths to a new long-run equilibrium, or steady-state path can be demonstrated. His analysis has therefore frequently been misunderstood as an attempt to defend 'the central neoclassical notion of general equilibrium ... in particular its modern extension, "steady growth". He tries to show that ... there are strong forces impelling the system towards a new steady growth path whenever a former equilibrium has been disturbed by technical change' (Lachmann 1973, p. 196). This criticism was echoed by Harcourt (1975), who furthermore took Hicks to task for disregarding 'Keynesian' obstacles to full employment equilibrium. In his reply to Harcourt, Hicks clarifies the scope of neo-Austrian traverse analysis:

> It is quite beside the point to argue that the assumptions which are made for my Full Employment path are unrealistic. They are meant to be unrealistic. I have deliberately removed a number of obvious obstacles to the smooth working of an economy, in order to see, if these are the only obstacles. I have cut out money; I have cut out monopolies . . . I have cut out government . . . [I]f I were a real neo-classic, I should then be jumping to the conclusion that of course my economy would be working quite smoothly . . . [But the] results which emerge confirm my suspicion that convergence may not be smooth at all. (Hicks 1975, p. 365)

It is indeed only under very restrictive assumptions on technology that convergence can be assured.[13]

Hicks's pioneering work inspired a number of studies which, while adhering to his method of analysing traverse paths as sequences of temporary equilibria, aimed at generalizing the analysis by relaxing the restrictive assumptions on technology. Thus Violi (1984a,b) demonstrated, in the context of a more general neo-Austrian fixwage model of traverse, that the emergence of a 'Hayek-crisis' is not confined to the case of 'longer and more mechanized methods' being introduced, but can also occur in consequence of introducing a 'less mechanized' method of production. The moment and duration of its occurrence depends, of course, on the exact specification of the time profiles of both the old and the new processes.

The most interesting contributions were provided by Belloc (1980) and Violi (1982), who developed a non-vertically integrated neo-Austrian production model to take account of inter-industry relationships. On the basis of these studies some authors have argued for the superiority of the neo-Austrian approach over the von Neumann–Sraffa approach in the analysis of traverse processes. This position, however, has been conclusively refuted by Baldone (1984), who demonstrated that (on similar assumptions) the method of analysis employed in these studies would be equally applicable to inter-industry production models. Yet Baldone (1984, sec. 4) also demonstrated that the Hicksian full-performance hypothesis will necessarily have to be modified in the context of more general production models (which can either be of the neo-Austrian variety or of the inter-industry type) and that introducing plausible modifications will leave the traverse paths indeterminate.

NEO-AUSTRIAN TRAVERSE ANALYSIS AND AUSTRIAN BUSINESS CYCLE THEORY: A CONCLUDING ASSESSMENT

Our investigation of the connections between the Austrian cycle theory and the neo-Austrian theory of traverse processes has shown that the latter, although it shares a number of common elements with the former, nevertheless provides a case for rejecting the Austrian explanation of economic fluctuations. Both theories derive cyclical fluctuations in economic activity from intertemporally disco-ordinated capital structures, but neo-Austrian analyses of traverses show that the latter can be triggered by non-monetary causes.

Despite the fundamentally divergent conclusions with regard to the role of monetary factors in the explanation of business cycles, there are a number of striking similarities between the two theories. On a methodological level, both approaches attempt to elucidate causal processes by analysing sequences rather than equilibrium positions. The Hicksian method of sequence analysis indeed bears some resemblance to the method adopted by Hayek in the 1930s, although the latter never formalized his cycle theory. Both approaches take as their starting point a long-run equilibrium position. The sequence described by the theory is then traced back to some causal factor introduced to this state.

With regard to the explanation of industrial fluctuations, both approaches set aside 'Keynesian' effective demand failures and instead focus attention on the importance of, first, the temporal structure of productive processes and, second, the intertemporal complementarities implied by capitalistic production, as major sources of macroeconomic malfunctioning. The existence of intertemporal complementarities implies the possibility of intertemporal disco-ordination in the time structure of aggregate inputs and outputs, resulting in a Hayekian over-investment crisis. What emerges from neo-Austrian traverse analysis is a clear picture of the complications involved in co-ordinating activities intertemporarily when a major innovation necessitates a restructuring of an economy's capital stock. Neo-Austrian traverse analyses thus seem to provide a basis for challenging the Austrian assessment of the general ability of a 'free market system' to function smoothly when monetary disturbances are absent.

The neo-Austrian results do, of course, rely on a number of restrictive behavioural and technological assumptions. As Hahn (1990) recently pointed out, in Hicksian traverse theory the assumption about expectations formation is the crucial element for evaluating the validity of his results. To base the analysis of traverse processes on the assumption of static expectations, as Hicks and his followers do, can obviously be no more than a first step. Yet it remains to be shown that the problems of intertemporal discoordination envisaged by Hicks vanish when more sophisticated hypotheses on expectations formation are introduced.

NOTES

1. The classical references are Mises' *Theory of Money and Credit* (1912) and Hayek's *Monetary Theory and the Trade Cycle* (1929), *Prices and Production* (1931) and *Profits, Interest and Investment* (1939). The more recent contributions to Austrian business cycle theory include Garrison (1985, 1986, 1989), O'Driscoll (1977, 1979), O'Driscoll and Rizzo (1985) and Wood (1984).
2. For a survey of the literature that emerged from the Hayek–Keynes controversy see Moss and Vaughn (1986); for a reconstruction of the Hayek–Sraffa debate (Hayek 1932; Sraffa 1932a, 1932b) see Desai (1982), McCloughry (1982) and Mongiovi (1990).
3. For a similar view see Streissler (1969). Hayek himself never saw his theory as anything but an explanation of business cycles (cf. Hayek 1969).
4. In *Prices and Production* (1931) the relevant characteristics of the structure of production are represented by Hayek's famous triangles, in which the base measures the money value of the output of consumer goods and the height represents the time dimension of the structure of production, the degree of roundaboutness. Slices of the triangle perpendicular to the time axis indicate the different stages of production.
5. Magnan de Bornier (1980) notes that rudimentary treatments of the traverse problem can be found both in the works of the classical political economists – most notably in Ricardo's famous chapter 'On Machinery' – and in several contributions to trade cycle theory made in the 1920s and 1930s (most notably in Hayek's, Robertson's and Lundberg's contributions). Similarly, the literature on problems of 'transition between techniques' which emerged in the 1960s in the context of the debate in capital theory (for example, Samuelson 1966, Solow 1967, Spaventa 1973) can be regarded as precursory.
6. Lowe's general conclusion is that 'free market systems' are not endowed with a mechanism to guide them towards 'efficient traverse paths'.
7. It should be noted that in a neo-Austrian framework, contrary to what was asserted by Hicks, neither the phenomenon of the 'reswitching of processes' (or techniques) nor the phenomenon of the 'reswitching of process lengths' (return of the same truncation period) can be regarded as 'curious' or 'exceptional'. See Hagemann and Kurz (1976).
8. It should be noted that the rise in the rate of profit which accompanies the introduction of the new process is the effect and not the cause of its introduction.
9. Processes that have been started will be carried through, albeit their truncation date might be changed.
10. The confusion of the secondary literature on Ricardo's machinery chapter seems ineradicable. Hayek (1941, appendix II) only added to this confusion by asserting 'that the original Ricardian contention about the effect of such a conversion on the size of the "gross produce" rested on a confusion . . . but that in the way in which the proposition was used by later writers, as an explanation of crisis, that is as referring to a temporary phenomenon during periods of transition, it described a real phenomenon.' The studies of Hicks (1973), Violi (1982), Zamagni (1984) and Kurz (1984) have made clear that

Ricardo dealt with precisely those 'periods of transition'; that his numerical example contains a capital shortage theory of *temporary* technological unemployment and that there is nowhere in his chapter any evidence to be found in support of the view that Ricardo's proposition was that the introduction of machinery will lead to permanent technological unemployment. Surprisingly, in two recent articles Samuelson (1988, 1989) claims to have vindicated Ricardo by producing numerical examples that lead to a new long-run equilibrium with permanently unemployed labour.

11. See Hicks (1973, chap. 11).
12. See Nardini (1990), who shows that this phenomenon can also occur on a fixwage path in a slightly modified Hicksian model. See also Einarsen (1938) who traced the history of business cycle explanations based on this phenomenon.
13. See Violi (1984a) and Zamagni (1984).

REFERENCES

Baldone, S. (1984) 'Integrazione verticale, struttura temporale dei processi produttivi e transizione fra le tecniche', *Economia Politica*, 1, 79–105.

Belloc, B. (1980) *Croissance economique et adaptation du capital productif*, Paris: Economica.

Desai, M. (1982) 'The Task of Monetary Theory: The Hayek–Sraffa Debate in a Modern Perspective', in M. Baranzini (ed.), *Advances in Economic Theory*, Oxford: Basil Blackwell.

Einarsen, J. (1938) *Reinvestment Cycles and their Manifestation in the Norwegian Shipping Industry*, Oslo: J.C. Grundersen.

Garrison, R.W. (1985) 'A Subjectivist Theory of a Capital-using Economy', in G.P. O'Driscoll and M.J. Rizzo (eds), *The Economics of Time and Ignorance*, Oxford: Basil Blackwell.

Garrison, R.W. (1986) 'Hayekian Trade Cycle Theory: A Reappraisal', *Cato Journal*, 6, 37–53.

Garrison, R.W. (1989) 'The Austrian Theory of the Business Cycle in the Light of Modern Macroeconomics', *The Review of Austrian Economics*, 3, 3–29.

Gozzi, G. and Zamagni, S. (1982) 'Crescita non uniforme e struttura produttiva: un modello di traversa a salario fisso', *Giornale degli Economisti ed Annali di Economia*, 41, 305–45.

Hagemann, H. and Kurz, H.D. (1976) 'The Return of the same Truncation Period and Reswitching of Techniques in Neo-Austrian and More General Models', *Kyklos*, 29, 678–708.

Hahn, F. (1990) 'John Hicks the Theorist', *Economic Journal*, 100, 539–49.

Harcourt, G. (1975), 'Decline and Rise: The Revival of (Classical) Political Economy', *The Economic Record*, 51, 339–56.

Hayek, F.A. von (1928) 'Das intertemporale Gleichgewichtssystem der Preise und die Bewegungen des "Geldwertes" ', *Weltwirtschaftliches Archiv*, 28 (II), 33–76.

Hayek, F.A. von (1929) *Geldtheorie und Konjunkturtheorie*, Vienna and Leipzig: Hölder–Pichler–Tempsky; [1933], *Monetary Theory and the Trade Cycle*, London: Jonathan Cape.

Hayek, F.A. von (1931) *Prices and Production*, London: Routledge and Kegan Paul.

Hayek, F.A. von (1932) 'Dr Hayek on Money and Capital: A Reply', *Economic Journal*, 42, 237–49.

Hayek, F.A. von (1939) *Profits, Interest and Investment*, London: Routledge and Kegan Paul.

Hayek, F.A. von (1941) *The Pure Theory of Capital*, London: Routledge and Kegan Paul.

Hayek, F.A. von (1969) 'Three Elucidations of the Ricardo Effect', *Journal of Political Economy*, **77**, 274–85.

Hicks, J. (1933) 'Gleichgewicht und Konjunktur', *Zeitschrift für Nationalökonomie*, **4**, 441–55; [1980] 'Equilibrium and the Trade Cycle', *Economic Inquiry*, **18**, 523–34.

Hicks, J. (1965) *Capital and Growth*, Oxford: Clarendon Press.

Hicks, J. (1967) 'The Hayek Story', in *Critical Essays in Monetary Theory*, Oxford: Oxford University Press, 203–15.

Hicks, J. (1970) 'A Neo-Austrian Growth Theory', *Economic Journal*, **80**, 257–81.

Hicks, J. (1973) *Capital and Time: A Neo-Austrian Theory*, Oxford: Oxford University Press.

Hicks, J. (1975) 'Revival of Political Economy: The Old and the New', *The Economic Record*, **51**, 365–67.

Hicks, J. (1979) 'The Formation of an Economist', *Banca Nazionale del Lavoro Quarterly Review*, **32**.

Hicks, J. (1982) 'Introductory: LSE and the Robbins Circle', in *Money, Interest and Wages*, Oxford: Basil Blackwell.

Kurz, H.D. (1984) 'Ricardo and Lowe on Machinery', *Eastern Economic Journal*, **10**, 211–29.

Lachmann, L.M. (1973) 'Sir John Hicks as a Neo-Austrian', *South African Journal of Economics*, **41**, 195–207.

Lowe, A. (1976) *The Path of Economic Growth*, Cambridge: Cambridge University Press.

Magnan de Bornier, J. (1980) *Capital et Desequilibre de la Croissance. Essai sur l'Economie de la Traverse*, Paris: Economia.

McCloughry, R. (1982) 'Neutrality and Monetary Equilibrium: A Note on Desai', in M. Baranzini (ed.), *Advances in Economic Theory*, Oxford: Basil Blackwell.

Mises, L. von (1912) *The Theory of Money and Credit*, New Haven: Yale University Press [1953].

Mongiovi, G. (1990) 'Keynes, Hayek and Sraffa: On the Origins of Chapter 17 of the General Theory', *Economie Appliquée*, **42**, 131–56.

Moss, L.S. and Vaughn, K.I. (1986) 'Hayek's Ricardo Effect: A Second Look', *History of Political Economy*, **18**, 545–65.

Nardini, F. (1990) 'Cycle-Trend Dynamics in a Fixwage Neo-Austrian Model of Traverse', *Structural Change and Economic Dynamics*, **1**, 165–94.

O'Driscoll, G.P. (1977) *Economics as a Coordination Problem: The Contribution of Friedrich A. Hayek*, Kansas: Sheed Andrews.

O'Driscoll, G.P. (1979) 'Rational Expectations, Politics, and Stagflation', in M.J. Rizzo (ed.), *Time, Uncertainty, and Disequilibrium*, Lexington: Lexington Books, 153–76.

O'Driscoll, G.P. and Rizzo, M.J. (1985) *The Economics of Time and Ignorance*, Oxford: Basil Blackwell.

Samuelson, P.A. (1966) 'A Summing Up', *Quarterly Journal of Economics*, **80**, 568–89.

Samuelson, P.A. (1988) 'Mathematical Vindication of Ricardo on Machinery', *Journal of Political Economy*, **96**, 274–82.

Samuelson, P.A. (1989) 'Ricardo was Right!', *Scandinavian Journal of Economics*, **91**, 47–62.

Solow, R.M. (1967) 'The Interest Rate and Transition between Techniques', in C.H. Feinstein (ed.) *Socialism, Capitalism and Economic Growth*, Cambridge: Cambridge University Press.

Spaventa, L. (1973) 'Notes on Problems of Transition between Techniques', in J.A. Mirrlees and N.H. Stern (eds), *Models of Economic Growth*, London: Macmillan, 168–92.

Sraffa, P. (1932a) 'Dr Hayek on Money and Capital', *Economic Journal*, **42**, 42–53.

Sraffa, P. (1932b) 'A Rejoinder', *Economic Journal*, **42**, 249–51.

Streissler, E. (1969) 'Hayek on Growth: A Reconsideration of his Early Theoretical Work', in E. Streissler *et al.* (eds), *Roads to Freedom*, London: Routledge and Kegan Paul, 245–85.

Violi, R. (1982) *L'economia della traversa: struttura del capitale e crescita non uniforme*, thesis: Università di Parma.

Violi, R. (1984a) 'Sentiero di traversa e convergenza', *Giornale degli Economisti ed Annali di Economia*, **43**, 153–78.

Violi, R. (1984b) 'I processi dinamici di transizione indotti dall'innovazione tecnologica', *Annali della Fondazione Luigi Einaudi*, **18**, 53–96.

Wood, J.S. (1984) 'Some Refinements in Austrian Trade-cycle Theory', *Managerial and Decision Economics*, **5**, 141–9.

Zamagni, S. (1984) 'Ricardo and Hayek Effects in a Fixwage Model of Traverse', in D.A. Collard *et al.* (eds), *Economic Theory and Hicksian Themes*, Oxford: Oxford University Press, 135–51.

9. Austrian and Post Keynesian Interest Rate Theory: Some Unexpected Parallels

Fiona C. Maclachlan

O'Driscoll and Rizzo (1985, p. 9) have drawn attention to some methodological similarities between the Mises-inspired modern Austrian school and the fundamentalist Post Keynesian school. Standing apart from the mainstream in modern economic theory, both schools are more interested in elucidating causal processes in historical time, than in deriving the conditions of a general equilibrium. In addition, both schools emphasize the economic implications of decisions formed in an environment of non-probabilistic uncertainty. This emphasis leads them to reject a large class of models which assume either that economic agents believe themselves to have perfect knowledge, or that they believe themselves to have knowledge of probability distributions determining uncertain outcomes.

Given the similarities in approach, one naturally wonders if the two schools arrive at similar theoretical results. One would at least expect theories from the two schools to be comparable in a way that would make dialogue a fruitful exercise. Dialogue between schools employing fundamentally different methodologies tends to drift out of economics and into the realm of philosophy – a subject on which few economists are competent to speak. The modern Austrians and the Post Keynesians, however, should be able to bypass methodological discussion and concentrate on substantive issues in economic theory.

Our focus will be on the theory of the rate of interest as represented by at least some members of the two schools. The theory of interest is one of the most controversial topics in economics – not just between schools but within them as well. Many think, for instance, that Böhm-Bawerk's theory of interest is central to the Austrian corpus of thought, and yet both Menger[1] and Mises rejected it. Similarly, within the Post Keynesian school, there is controversy about the interpretation and the validity of Keynes's liquidity preference theory. While earlier Post Keynesians appeared to endorse the theory as Keynes set it out (for example, Kahn 1954), contemporary endogenous money theorists are critical (Moore 1988). In order to simplify our discussion, therefore, we shall focus on a single, fairly well-defined theory from each school – a theory that might not necessarily be held by all, or even by the majority, of the school's members. From the modern Austrian school, we look at the pure time preference theory of interest. The theory originates with the American economist Frank A. Fetter (1904) but was propagated within the Austrian school, first by Ludwig von Mises (1949), and later by his students Murray Rothbard (1962) and Israel Kirzner (1983, 1990). From the Post Keynesian school we focus on the interpretation of Keynes's liquidity preference theory that is probably best represented by the work of G.L.S. Shackle (1949, 1972, 1974). Unlike the standard interpretation of liquidity preference as it appears in the IS–LM model, the Post Keynesian interpretation places importance on the insights of Chapter 17 of the *General Theory* and in Keynes's later articles (for example, 1937).

The pure time preference and the liquidity preference theories of interest appear to have been developed independently of one another, and yet we find some notable parallels. Members of both schools might be encouraged to find that similar insights were reached from two different directions. The parallels do not extend far, however, before divergence sets in. The divergence is especially evident when conclusions are drawn about the role of the interest rate in intertemporal co-ordination. These conclusions, in turn, suggest very different recommendations for macroeconomic policy.

Our aim is to explore the parallels and pinpoint exactly where the divergence between the two theories emerges. We find that much of the disparity between the ideas of the two schools regarding the working of the macroeconomy springs from subtle theoretical differences in the theory of interest. Only after these differences have been discussed and resolved can one hope for profitable debate between the two schools on issues such as the business cycle and the saving–investment relation.

PARALLELS

A notable parallel between the two schools is their shared refusal to view the productivity of capital as a direct causal determinant of the interest rate. The refusal separates their work from mainstream neoclassical interest rate theory, as well as from a classical Ricardian treatment (Ricardo 1817, p. 198; Robinson 1956, p. 395).[2] For the Austrians, the insight goes back to Böhm-Bawerk's (1884, pp. 88–95) refutation of what he called 'naïve' productivity theories. He identified two strands of thought, both of which he considered invalid. One strand says that interest arises because capital is capable of producing a surplus value; that is, when a given amount of money is invested in a capitalistic mode of production, a greater amount of money can be got at the end of it. Böhm-Bawerk's objection parallels the Austrian objection to all cost of production theories of value. 'A factor of production can never be an ultimate source of value' he writes. 'Wherever value makes its appearance, it has its ultimate cause in the relation of human needs to the means of satisfying them' (Böhm-Bawerk 1884, p. 94). From an Austrian perspective, explaining interest by means of the value productivity of capital appears to beg the question of why capital has value productivity in the first place. Just as he rejects the Marxist assumption that labour creates value, the Austrian rejects the assumption that capital has a similar power.

The second line of argument that Böhm-Bawerk attempts to refute is that interest is to be explained by the *physical* productivity of capital. He admits that it is true that labour assisted by capital is capable of producing more than labour alone. But, he argues, this technological fact by itself cannot explain the emergence of surplus value.

> I readily admit and understand that with the assistance of a boat and net one catches 30 fish a day, while without this capital one would have caught only 3. I readily admit and understand, furthermore, that the 30 fish are of higher value than the 3 were. But that the 30 fish must be worth more *than the pro rata portion of boat and net which is worn out in catching them* is an assumption which the conditions of the problem do not prepare us for, or even cause to appear tenable, to say nothing of making it obvious. (Böhm-Bawerk 1884, p. 93)

The question that Böhm-Bawerk poses is why the value of the output from a capitalistic production process exceeds the total sum value of the inputs. If a profit is to be made by combining various inputs to yield an output of greater value, why is this profit not eliminated through the operation of the market process – either through a rise in the price of the inputs as competitors bid for them, or through a fall in the price of the output as more of it is produced and a lower price clears the market?

For Böhm-Bawerk, the refutation of the two variants of the naïve productivity theory does not close the door entirely on the possibility of a theory of interest incorporating the influence of the productivity of capital, as he attempts to demonstrate with his own theory. For the pure time preference theorists however, the refutations are taken to apply to all productivity theories and Böhm-Bawerk's theory of interest is thought to constitute a surprising reversion (Fetter 1902, pp. 185–7).

Böhm-Bawerk's critique of productivity theories leads to what has become a distinctively Austrian approach to the problem of interest. In explaining interest, the Austrian seeks to answer the question of what prevents competitive forces from eliminating the surplus value that is derived through capitalistic production. The Austrian approach to the problem contrasts with that of interest rate theorists, who view capital as a scarce productive factor, analogous to labour and land. For these theorists the question of why competitive forces do not eliminate interest is like asking why the same forces do not eliminate the wage. If the question were asked, the answer would have to be that capital, like labour, is scarce; and that because the theory is meant to explain distribution and not accumulation, the reason for its scarcity need not be addressed. The Austrian might agree that the scarcity of capital explains a surplus value, but he wants to know what keeps it scarce.

Given the way they pose the problem, the Austrians have reason to share with the Cambridge UK critics of neoclassical distribution theory, a distrust of theories of interest that begin with the specification of a production function containing an aggregate measure of capital, or even a vector of individual capital goods. What underlies the Austrians' distrust, however, is not a perception that such a theory involves logical error, but simply that it does not address the problem in a useful way.

The Post Keynesians are not as explicit as the Austrians about why they reject productivity explanations. Still, one can find in Keynes's writings hints that suggest strong parallels with the Böhm-Bawerkian critique. Keynes writes in the *General Theory*, for instance, that

> it is much preferable to speak of capital as having a yield over the course of its life in excess of its original cost, than as being *productive*. For the only reason why an asset offers a prospect of yielding during its life services having an aggregate value greater than its initial value is because it is *scarce*; and it is kept scarce because of competition of the rate of interest. (Keynes 1936, p. 213)

Here Keynes dismisses the capital productivity theory by asserting that the surplus value that emerges when capital is employed is a consequence and not the cause of interest. If interest exists for some other reason, then capital will necessarily yield a surplus value. Keynes's line of reasoning is consistent with that of Böhm-Bawerk. Böhm-Bawerk argues that the value productivity of capital cannot explain interest because value productivity itself needs explanation: one cannot simply assert that capital has the power to create value. Keynes takes the objection one step further in maintaining that the explanation for surplus value lies in the existence of interest. Thus, to say that value productivity is the explanation for interest is to argue in a circle. In describing the intellectual process that led to his discovery of the liquidity preference theory, Keynes admits that the same

problem of circular reasoning caused him to reject the possibility of a
physical productivity theory as well:

> One naturally began by supposing that the rate of interest must be determined
> in some sense by productivity – that it was, perhaps, simply the monetary
> equivalent of the marginal efficiency of capital, the latter being independently
> fixed by physical and technical considerations in conjunction with expected
> demand. It was only when this line of approach led repeatedly to what seemed
> to be circular reasoning, that I hit on what I now think to be the true explana-
> tion. (Keynes 1937, p. 212)

Böhm-Bawerk had concluded that to maintain that physical productivity
leads to the emergence of surplus value 'is an assumption which the
conditions of the problem do not prepare us for, or even cause to appear
tenable'. Keynes evidently had come to the same conclusion. The only
way, he thought, to derive surplus value from the physical productivity of
capital is to suppose the value of capital is less than the sum of the profits
it generates. But to do so amounts to assuming what is to be explained –
hence his complaint about circular reasoning.

Just as Keynes's objections to productivity theories parallel those of the
Austrians, the way in which he poses the problem of interest is remarkably
similar. In Chapter 17 of the *General Theory*, he introduces the concept of
own-rates of return on different goods, each own-rate being determined by
the sum of its marginal efficiency and liquidity premium, minus its carrying cost. He observes that there is a tendency for own-rates measured in
terms of a common standard to converge on a single rate, and that there is
a tendency for the marginal efficiency of capital goods to decline as capital
accumulates. Then, just as Böhm-Bawerk asks what prevents the erosion
of the surplus value generated by capitalistic production processes,
Keynes poses the question of what prevents the marginal efficiency of
capital from falling to zero. It is only in posing the question in this way
that he is led to his path-breaking conclusion that it is the liquidity
premium on money that determines the level at which the other own-rates
settle.

The way in which one poses a question should affect the answer that one
finds for it. We have seen that the Austrian pure time preference theorists
following Böhm-Bawerk, and the Post Keynesian liquidity preference
theorists following Keynes, share a similar starting point for their analyses
of the interest rate problem. Even if starting in the same place does not
guarantee that they will reach the same destination, at least it makes
possible a comparison of their routes and discussion about which is the
better way to go.

DIVERGENCE

A divergence between the pure time preference and the liquidity preference theory that arises from the start is the use by the pure time preference theorists of the theoretical construct of an originary or natural rate of interest. The originary rate is distinguished from the monetary or actual rate which is determined in the money loan market, and which is viewed as a reflection of the originary rate together with monetary influences. For the pure time preference theorist, the first step in establishing a theory of interest is to explain the originary rate. Once originary interest is explained, then the complicating influences of money can be introduced. Since the originary rate is supposed to be free of monetary influences, the standard procedure is to abstract from money in order to explain it.

For the liquidity preference theorist, on the other hand, money plays a central role in the explanation of interest and no distinction is made between an originary and a monetary rate.[3] Keynes's conclusion is that it is the own-rate on the good whose liquidity premium is most in excess of its carrying costs that sets the level to which the other own-rates adjust. The good that fits such a description is, of course, money. If the pure time preference theorist insists on abstracting from money in the first instance, then he precludes the possibility of arriving at the Keynesian conclusion. From the first step they take towards solving the problem about whose nature they both agree, the Austrian and the Keynesian appear to be moving in different directions.

There is some evidence, however, that the originary/monetary dichotomy is not always strictly maintained by the pure time preference theorists. For instance, they contend that Böhm-Bawerk was wrong to assert that the technological superiority of present goods over future goods helps to account for the existence of originary interest – that is, for the fact that future goods exchange for present goods at a discount. To employ Samuelson's (1981) example, Böhm-Bawerk would agree that if a present bushel of rice ripens into one and a tenth bushels next year, then one present bushel would exchange for more than one future bushels. No assumption of time preference is necessary to achieve the result. A present bushel represents one bushel now or one and a tenth bushels later, whereas a future bushel only represents one bushel at a later date. Given free disposal, the present bushel will always be preferred and so will exchange for more than one future bushel.

Kirzner, however, is not convinced that the rice example proves that interest will emerge:

> The interest problem would begin, in the context of the rice example, only if in

fact the 'value' of the 100 units of 1987 rice is somehow lower than that of 110 units of 1988 rice. *Then* we would have the possibility of a sum of abstract capital value serving as a financial source somehow generating a flow of *greater* subsequent value. (Kirzner 1990, pp. 121–2)

To make sense of the above passage, we have to assume that unlike Böhm-Bawerk, Kirzner is not abstracting from money. Consider his reference to the value of rice. For an Austrian, the objective value of a good is simply a rate of exchange. If present rice exchanges for future rice, then as we have seen, only the assumption of free disposal is necessary to prove that a rice rate of interest will emerge. It is only when a loan contract is made in terms of another good, that rice productivity does not imply the emergence of interest. Kirzner's reference to a 'financial source somehow generating a flow of *greater* subsequent value' suggests that he is thinking of money value and of loan contracts negotiated in terms of money. It is true that the same line of reasoning could be employed to show that rice productivity does not imply the emergence of interest when loan contracts are negotiated in terms of potatoes. But the question then arises why a potato rate of interest is any more pertinent to the problem of interest than a rice rate of interest. A money rate of interest is clearly more pertinent because loan contracts are, in fact, made in terms of money. If, however, one insists on abstracting from money and chooses to frame the theory solely in terms of real goods in order to explain a natural or originary rate of interest, then one must confront the question of the choice of goods in terms of which the loan contracts are to be denominated.

Another instance in which the pure time preference theorist does not consistently abstract from money and the money rate of interest occurs when both Rothbard (1962, vol. I, p. 326) and Kirzner (1990, p. 116) attempt to justify the notion that time preference is positive. They both make use of the common-sense observation that dollars in the present are preferred to dollars in the future. Rothbard writes:

> *Money* is clearly the present good *par excellence*. For . . . the money commodity is the one completely marketable good in the entire society. It is the open sesame to exchange for consumption goods at any time that its owner desires . . . Furthermore, since money is the medium for *all* exchanges, it is also the medium for exchanges on the time market. (Rothbard 1962, vol. I, p. 320)

Rothbard then proceeds to develop his pure time preference theory, focusing on the rate of exchange between present and future money. The liquidity preference theorist would readily agree with the observation that present dollars are generally preferred to future dollars but he would say the reason behind the preference is the liquidity of money. Money today allows one to enjoy the option of consuming (or investing) now or later;

but a claim to money tomorrow limits one's options today. Thus if one prefers more options to fewer, present dollars will be preferred. The liquidity preference theorist would argue, however, that one cannot infer from the fact that present dollars are preferred to future dollars that present *goods* are generally preferred to future *goods*. Most goods are either subject to spoilage or involve substantial storage costs. Moreover, unlike money they are difficult to exchange for other goods, and the rate at which they will exchange is less certain. Thus a person who anticipates an unproductive old age and who wishes to even out his consumption stream through time will not necessarily prefer present goods over future goods. We find that the example Rothbard and Kirzner employ can be used to argue for the existence of a positive rate of interest on money loans, but it cannot be used to argue for the existence of a preference for present over future goods generating a positive rate of originary interest.

The ambiguity in the pure time preference theory about the role of money is related to the central difference between the two theories. This concerns the nature of the preference that is supposed to determine the rate of interest. The theories are parallel in giving causal significance to a subjective preference, but when we delve further and ask about the motivation behind the preference, we find two very disparate notions. Normally economists do not inquire into the reasons behind preferences; rather, they relegate such investigations to the field of psychology or sociology. In this case, however, the reasons have important economic implications.

In making a comparison between the two theories it is useful to employ Shackle's (1949, pp. 101ff.) distinction between the two types of satisfaction that can be derived from a good: consumer satisfaction and possessor satisfaction. A preference for present over future consumer satisfaction brings to mind the actions of a profligate running up charges on his credit card in order to derive immediate gratification from expendable goods and services. A preference for present over future possessor satisfaction, on the other hand, could be associated with a thrifty individual who saves most of his income and merely prefers to possess the vehicle in which he does his saving sooner rather than later.

The pure time preference theorists specify only vaguely the motivation behind time preference. Mises (1949, p. 523) writes of the preference for present over future 'want-satisfaction'; Rothbard (1962, vol. I, p. 326) writes of the preference for present over future goods; and Kirzner (1990, p. 116) writes of people's preference to 'achieve their goals sooner rather than later'. But in illustrating their notion of time preference with the preference for present over future dollars, Rothbard and Kirzner suggest that the preference for present over future possessor satisfaction plays some role in their conception of time preference. They would not deem it so obvious that present dollars are preferable to future dollars if there were a restriction that the dollars must be spent on consumption in the period in which they are received. People who anticipate being less well provided for in the future, under these circumstances, would probably prefer the future dollars. It is because dollars represent a vehicle for transferring purchasing power through time and give one the option of making a purchase now or in the future that they are preferred sooner rather than later, by the thrifty and profligate alike. One is led to infer, therefore, that possessor satisfaction plays at least some role in the Austrian notion of time preference.

Yet when one turns to the Austrian theory of the business cycle which appears to be endorsed by the pure time preference theorists,[4] it appears that it is the preference for present over future *consumer* satisfaction only that is linked to the interest rate. According to the Austrian theory of the business cycle, a fall in the interest rate can mean one of two things. It can mean there has been an increase in the willingness to save, that is, a reduction in the preference for present relative to future consumer satisfaction, sending an appropriate signal to producers to lengthen the period of production. Alternatively, it can mean that the money supply has been artificially expanded, sending an inappropriate signal to lengthen the production period. In the first case there has been a fall in both the originary and the monetary rate of interest and no disruption to the general level of economic activity takes place: the reduction in the demand for consumer goods caused by the increased propensity to save is matched by an increase in the demand for producer goods. In the second case in which there was an artificial expansion of the money supply, there is a fall only in the monetary rate. This will send a false signal, lead to disco-ordination between saving and investment, and ultimately to a business cycle.

Now, suppose it was the case that the pure time preference theorists allowed that a change in the intensity of desire for present over future *possessor* satisfaction of dollars could be associated with a fall in the interest rate. Then there would be an inconsistency with the Austrian theory of the business cycle. A change in the intensity of desire for present possessor satisfaction for dollars need not imply either a change in saving or any artificial alteration in the money supply. It would seem that the fall would have to be regarded as 'natural' since it arises from individual preferences, and yet unlike a fall due to a decrease in the preference for present *consumer* satisfaction, it is not appropriate that the period of production be lengthened and that producers spend more on higher order goods. Since the demand for consumer goods is not necessarily changed, a lengthening of the period of production in this case might create a situation of excess demand.

It appears that within the Austrian theory of the business cycle, the possibility of a change in the preference for present over future possessor satisfaction was not considered as a factor affecting the originary rate of interest. Austrian pure time preference theorists, then, have to admit either that the time preference to which they ascribe the central causal role in the determination of the interest rate is only a preference for present over future consumer satisfaction; or that their theory of interest is inconsistent with the notion underlying the Austrian theory of the business cycle that the interest rate serves to co-ordinate saving and investment. If they choose to equate time preference with the preference for present over future consumer satisfaction, they must answer critics who contend that in a world in which loans were made only for purposes of consumption, the loanable funds market would probably clear at a negative rate of interest. The amount of borrowing for current consumption tends to be small, relative to the amount of saving. Thus it seems unlikely that the preference for present over future consumption can explain a positive rate of interest. If they choose the second route and abandon the idea that the interest rate co-ordinates saving and investment, then their pure time preference theory has much in common with the liquidity preference theory.

The liquidity preference theorist is clearer on the nature of the motivation responsible for the interest rate. Liquidity preference is associated with a type of possessor satisfaction that is derived from holding liquid assets. Liquidity gives to the holder of such assets an assurance that a generalized purchasing power can be carried through time, allowing him to defer decisions and to keep his options open. Keynes (1936, p. 166) writes that the 'psychological time-preferences of an individual require two distinct sets of decisions.' These are first, the decision about how much to save, and second, the decision about which assets to buy with one's savings. The first set of decisions involves a judgement about one's desire for consumer satisfaction, while the latter will involve judgements about the possessor satisfaction obtainable from different assets. Keynes is explicit in saying that liquidity preference relates only to the latter set of decisions; he thus divorces the liquidity preference concept from the idea of a preference for present over future consumption.

The liquidity preference theory of interest implies that the interest rate cannot be relied on to co-ordinate saving and investment as it does in the Austrian theory, and provides a theoretical justification for aggregate demand management. Early on, Keynes (1934, p. 489) isolated the orthodox theory of the interest rate as the 'fatal flaw' in the economic justification for *laissez-faire*. According to the liquidity preference theory the rate of interest can change due to a change in expectations or in perceptions of uncertainty, without any change in either productivity or thrift. The interest rate is divorced from real factors and therefore cannot be relied upon to regulate them.

CONCLUSION

Our comparison of the Austrian pure time preference theory of interest and the Post Keynesian liquidity preference theory has brought to light some notable similarities. Both theories avoid the tricky problem of defining a factor of production whose price is the rate of interest. Rather than viewing interest as some kind of objective productivity return, both schools hypothesize that it arises solely as the result of a subjective preference. The fact that capitalistic production yields output valued more highly than the sum of the value of the inputs is believed to be the consequence rather than the cause of interest. In denying the productivity of capital any direct causal role in the determination of the interest rate, both sets of theorists find themselves standing apart from a long and dominant tradition in economics. The two schools might be reassured by the fact that they share their unpopular position and that similar insights have been drawn from two seemingly independent traditions.

However, after having arrived at the same basic insight that a subjective preference is what explains the existence of interest, the two schools veer off in different directions. The Austrians maintain the long-held distinction between a monetary and a natural or originary rate of interest. With the distinction goes the idea that monetary influences are transitory and non-essential. For the liquidity preference theorists, on the other hand, money with its unique properties plays centre stage in the explanation. Both sets of theorists agree that a present dollar is preferable to a future dollar and that this preference translates into a rate of interest. The difference between them is in the motivation that is supposed to lie behind the preference.

In their exposition of the theory of interest, pure time preference theorists are vague about the motivation. We argue, however, that if their theory is to be consistent with the Austrian idea that the interest rate serves to co-ordinate saving and investment, then the motivation behind the preference for present over future dollars has to be a preference for present over future consumer satisfaction. For the liquidity preference theorist, on the other hand, the motivation that is supposed to lie behind the emergence of interest is unrelated to any preference for present over future consumer satisfaction. Rather it relates to the evaluation of alternative vehicles for saving. For the purposes of saving, present dollars are preferable to promises of future dollars because their greater degree of liquidity entails a wider range of options over future action.

What would seem a rather subtle theoretical difference between the two theories is seen to have important implications for macroeconomic theory. The modern Austrian school is led to the sanguine conclusion that the interest rate, unaltered by 'artificial' monetary policy, will serve to co-ordinate saving and investment so that a change in one will lead to a change in the other without disrupting the level of aggregate demand. If consumers decide to save more, resources released from the production of consumer goods will be directed into the production of investment goods. For the Post Keynesians on the other hand, a downturn caused by underconsumption is at least a theoretical possibility. Moreover, while the Austrian concludes that intervention on the part of the monetary authority will only thwart the co-ordinating influence of the interest rate, the Post Keynesian can argue that discretionary monetary policy can be beneficial in counteracting the effect on the interest rate of the actions of speculative wealth holders.

Both the pure time preference theory and the liquidity preference theory of interest are far from being completely developed. As they stand at the moment, both are susceptible to serious criticisms. The pure time preference theorist must account for the fact that the amount of borrowing done to finance current consumption is only a tiny fraction of the amount that is saved, a fact that suggests that time preference alone would cause the loanable funds market to clear at a negative rate of interest. What is required is some account of the complete causal chain through which the preference for present over future consumption is linked to the rate of interest appearing in the loanable funds market.

Similarly the liquidity preference theorist needs to be more convincing on the role of real or non-monetary factors in the determination of the interest rate. Many economists are willing to accept that liquidity preference can dominate over real factors in the short-run, but few are convinced that the factors of productivity and thrift are completely irrelevant (see, for example, Leijonhufvud 1968, pp. 213–14). Keynes's Chapter 17 analysis, despite its suggestive ingenuity, has proven unpersuasive in sustaining the conclusion that only the liquidity premium on money determines the interest rate.

The main criticism of both theories is not that they are demonstrably wrong but that they are incompletely specified. While both raise many questions and doubts that need to be answered, the idea from which they both begin – that interest is the expression of a subjective valuation unrelated to any objective productivity return – remains a promising start.

NOTES

1. According to Schumpeter (1954, p. 847, fn. 8), Menger described Böhm-Bawerk's theory as one of the 'greatest errors ever committed'.
2. Sraffa (1960, p. 33) is, of course, an important exception.
3. However, that does not preclude the liquidity preference theorist from making a distinction between a nominal and a real rate of interest, where the real rate is defined as the nominal rate, less an expected or actual rate of inflation.
4. The Austrian business cycle theory is presented without criticism in Mises (1949), Rothbard (1962), and Kirzner (1987).

REFERENCES

Böhm-Bawerk, E. (1884) *Capital and Interest*, vol. 1, *History and Critique of Interest Theories*, trans. George D. Hunke and Hans F. Senholz (1959), South Holland, Illinois: Libertarian Press.

Fetter, F.A. (1902) 'The "Roundabout Process" in Interest Theory', in Murray Rothbard (ed.) (1977), *Capital, Interest and Rent: Essays in the Theory of Distribution*, Kansas City: Sheed, Andrews and McMeel.

Fetter, F.A. (1904) *Principles of Economics*, New York: Century Co.

Fetter, F.A. (1914) 'Interest Theories, Old and New,' in Rothbard (ed.) (1977), *Capital, Interest and Rent: Essays in the Theory of Distribution*, Kansas City: Sheed, Andrews and McMeel.

Kahn, R. (1954) 'Some Notes on Liquidity Preference', *Manchester School of Economic and Social Studies*, **22**, 229–57.

Keynes, J.M. (1934) 'Poverty in Plenty: Is the Economic System Self-Adjusting', in Donald Moggridge (ed.) (1973), *The Collected Writings of John Maynard Keynes*, vol. XIII, London: Macmillan, 485–92.

Keynes, J.M. (1936) *The General Theory of Employment, Interest and Money*, London: Macmillan.

Keynes, J.M. (1937) 'Alternative Theories of the Rate of Interest,' in Donald Moggridge (ed.) (1973), *The Collected Writings of John Maynard Keynes*, vol. XIV, London: Macmillan, 201–14.

Kirzner, I.M. (1983) 'Pure-Time Preference Theory: A Postscript to the "Grand Debate" ', New York: C.V. Starr Center for Applied Economics, Department of Economics, New York University.

Kirzner, I.M. (1987) 'Austrian School of Economics' in J. Eatwell, M. Milgate, and P.N. Newman (eds), *The New Palgrave: Dictionary of Economics*, vol. I, New York: The Stockton Press, 145–51.

Kirzner, I.M. (1990) 'The Pure Time-Preference Theory of Interest: An Attempt at Clarification', in L.H. Rockwell (ed.), *The Meaning of Ludwig von Mises*, Auburn, Alabama: The Ludwig von Mises Institute.

Leijonhufvud, A. (1968) *On Keynesian Economics and the Economics of Keynes: A Study in Monetary Theory*, New York: Oxford University Press.

Mises, L. von (1949) *Human Action: A Treatise on Economics*, New Haven: Yale University Press.

Moore, B.J. (1988) *Horizontalists and Verticalists: The Macroeconomics of Credit Money*, New York: Cambridge University Press.

O'Driscoll, G.P. and Rizzo, M.J. (1985) *The Economics of Time and Ignorance*, New York: Basil Blackwell.
Ricardo, D. (1817) *The Principles of Political Economy and Taxation*, New York: Dutton [1973].
Robinson, J. (1956) *The Accumulation of Capital*, London: Macmillan.
Rothbard, M.N. (1962) *Man, Economy and State*, Los Angeles: Nash Publishing.
Samuelson, P.A. (1981) 'Schumpeter as an Economic Theorist', in H. Frisch (ed.) *Schumpeterian Economics*, New York: Praeger Publishers.
Shackle, G.L.S. (1949) 'The Nature of Interest Rates', *Oxford Economic Papers* (NS vol. 1), 100–120.
Shackle, G.L.S. (1972) *Epistemics and Economics*, Cambridge: Cambridge University Press.
Shackle, G.L.S. (1974) *Keynesian Kaleidics*, Edinburgh, Scotland: Edinburgh University Press.
Schumpter, J.A. (1954) *History of Economic Analysis*, New York: Oxford University Press.
Sraffa, P. (1960) *Production of Commodities by Means of Commodities*, Cambridge: Cambridge University Press.

PART III

Growth Theory, Investment and Technological Change

10. Technological Competition and the Determinants of Investment Spending

Chidem Kurdas

SCOPE AND PURPOSE

Joseph Schumpeter objected to perfect competition as an ideal. He argued that perfect competition, the necessary condition of static allocational efficiency, does not promote growth. He described capitalist growth as an evolutionary process kept in motion by new products, technologies, markets, and forms of organization. Neoclassical economics, in taking perfect competition as the ideal, is concerned with 'how capitalism administers existing structures', whereas 'the relevant problem is how it creates and destroys them' (Schumpeter 1950, p. 84). This observation is particularly applicable to neoclassical investment theory. The explanation of investment in terms of the interest rate and the expected marginal return on capital in effect leaves out technical change, 'the propelling factor of modern capitalism' (Schumpeter 1950, p. 102, n.20). In view of the immense structural change in economies worldwide in the last half century, most economists do not contest the relevance of the Schumpeterian vision to modern growth. According to Arrow, for example, 'steady states are essentially an impossibility' (1989, p. 149), because of the pattern of change in demand known as Engels Laws. The composition of demand changes over time as incomes grow, initially from primary to manufactured products, and more recently from manufactured products to services. It is generally conceded that neoclassical theory is least successful in dealing with secular phenomena. The theory takes preferences and technology as exogenous data, and elucidates the allocation of resources on the basis of this data. Nevertheless, the explanation of investment that is rooted in this theory continues to be used in empirical studies.

The topic of this chapter is investment in non-human capital. This includes research and development spending as well as investment in plant

and equipment.[1] The purpose is first, to show that the neoclassical investment model, as it stands, is incomplete, and as a result it cannot explain
investment in new technologies. The second, constructive purpose is to
identify the factors that do influence such investment spending. The
following critical discussion, therefore, looks first at the accepted model.
When investment involves new technology the marginal product of capital
is not pre-ordained, because the future production function is not exogenously given. The parameters of production will be developed during the
learning process set in motion by the investments in research, development
and tangible capital. The only way to understand the return on investment
is to study this process. The variables that play a role in the process are
then presented, their interaction along the product cycle is discussed, and
finally some macro implications of investment decisions based on these
variables are suggested.

THE NEOCLASSICAL THEORY OF BUSINESS INVESTMENT

According to neoclassical theory, the demand for capital, like the demand
for any other commodity, is a function of its relative price, all else being
equal. The demand for capital is determined by its rental cost, that is, the
real interest rate.[2] The reasoning behind this relationship follows basic
neoclassical production theory. The marginal product of capital diminishes with the amount of capital used to produce a given level of output.
The profit maximizing firm chooses to acquire more capital as long as the
marginal contribution of a unit of capital exceeds its marginal cost. The
'desired' capital stock is reached at the point where the value of the
marginal product of capital is equal to its marginal cost.

Obviously, for a given level of output, the lower the cost, that is, the
lower the real interest rate, the larger the desired capital stock. And the
higher the expected level of output, the higher the expected marginal
product of a certain level of capital. In short, according to this reasoning,
the desired capital stock varies inversely with cost of capital and directly
with expected output:

$$K^* = k(i,o) \text{ where } k_i < 0; k_0 > 0. \tag{10.1}$$

This determination is applied both to the firm and the aggregate demand
for capital.

There is the additional question of how quickly the firm adjusts its
actual capital stock to the desired level. Neoclassical theory in itself does

not provide an explanation of the speed of adjustment.[3] So empirical studies of investment spending extend equation 10.1 with a version of the accelerator, namely the capital stock adjustment principle (Dornbusch and Fischer 1984, p. 216; Clark 1979). According to this principle, the short-run change in capital stock depends on the difference between the existing and desired capital stocks:

$$I_t = \o (K^* - K_{t-1}) \text{ where } \o > 0 \qquad (10.2)$$

The neoclassical explanation of the demand for capital, in particular the inverse relationship between capital intensity and the interest rate, has been attacked on capital theoretic grounds (Garegnani 1970). The argument presented here is based on a different line of criticism.[4] It will be argued that the empirical relevance of the neoclassical approach to investment spending is limited by the underlying blueprint view of technology.

The problem can be seen in simple terms. The marginal product of capital is determined by the production function. Since the investment decision is made *ex ante*, the production function has to exist as a blueprint before production begins. Investments that involve new technology, or lead to learning by doing, violate this postulate. Studies of technical change show that such change is an ongoing learning process. It starts with research, and goes on with development and production, with learning by doing and learning by using taking place along the way (Rosenberg 1982).[5] Furthermore, investment in R & D brings new products and processes that may not have been expected at the outset. The investments in research, development and productive capacity are the beginning of this learning process, and the technology thus brought into being does not exist when the investments are contemplated. Furthermore, the changes in technology are endogenous, they are a function of the investments made. If investment spending is (partly) a function of the marginal product of capital, the latter is also a function of investment spending.

The learning process brings increases in productivity long after the initial investments were made, and the changes in productivity lead to changes in price and in market growth. The issue is not simply whether decision makers can estimate the marginal product of capital before the event. It is rather that productivity is a result of the decisions made along the way, not as given at the outset: the outcome of investment is path-dependent. The path has to be taken into account if the determinants of investment are to be understood.

The two-way dependency between capital formation and technical change has been pointed out by several economists (for example, Nelson 1973, 1981; Abromovitz 1989).[6] Michael Boskin (1988, p. 74), speculates that 'investment and innovation are interdependent and that interdependence increases the elasticity of output with respect to capital inputs.' Spending on plant and equipment is influenced by the supply side and demand side ripples caused by new technologies. The expected profitability depends both on future production coefficients and expected sales. These in turn are conditioned by the technology. Demand for the product is a function of existing substitutes and complements, and shifts when new substitute or complementary products come into being. The future level of output, both at the firm and the aggregate levels, is a function of these changes. So the outcome of the investment depends on the technology, while the technology is conditioned by capital formation.

The neoclassical investment model is incomplete because it leaves out the endogenous determination of output and productivity levels, variables that are dependent on investment. The model postulates an exogenously given relationship between future output and productivity. Equations 10.1 and 10.2 are actually only part of an unspecified simultaneous equation system which determines the rate of capital formation together with the secular growth rate of output. Equation 10.1 cannot be interpreted as a reduced form because the relationships between investment, technical change and market growth have not been specified and included in the model.

The salient behavioural mechanism for the neoclassical model of the firm is optimization against externally given constraints. The firm buys its inputs, including technology, and sells its product(s), in markets described in terms of degree of competition. Competition is defined according to how much power individual producers can exert over the price. In the extreme case of perfect competition the firm has no power over the price of its product. The firm's function is to allocate resources efficiently, given technology and preferences.

An alternative to the neoclassical model of the firm has emerged from studies in technical change and business history.[7] The modern corporation that figures in this alternative view seeks diversification and increase of its market share. To gain competitive advantage it searches for knowledge about new commodities and production techniques. These search and selection activities are more crucial for its long run survival and success than the allocation of given resources with given technology (Nelson and Winter 1982a). Satisficing rather than maximization is the behavioural rule for the corporation (Simon 1959). The constraints that the corporation faces are not external to it, but partially a result of its own past decisions about production, investment, research and development. The investment model that applies to the static, homogeneous, and simple neoclassical firm does not apply to the growth-oriented and complex institution that is the modern corporation. Rather than an optimization calculus, this view sees business investment motivated by the kind of competitive pressure that 'strikes not at the margins of the profits and outputs of the existing firms but at their foundations and their very lives' (Schumpeter 1950, p. 84).

In sectors and economies that are relatively stagnant, in which little technical and structural change is going on, information about past production applies to the future. The future rate of return on capital can then be inferred from the past rate of return. The explanation of investment can stop at equations 10.1 and 10.2, since the past is whatever it happens to be, and the information that it provides is not affected by the forces set into motion by the investment itself. An investment decision concerning a future that will diverge from that past is another matter. The model criticized here may come to its own when there is little or no change in products, markets and technologies. The stagnant conditions make it possible to project the existing rate of return into the future, rendering superfluous any other explanation of the expected return. Under conditions of structural, organizational and technical change the initial productivity of capital and level of output do not provide the information to determine the future outcome of the investment.

Aggregated over all industries the numerous investment decisions mean new technologies, a new configuration of consumer preferences, and higher levels of national income. These outcomes in turn condition capital formation at the macroeconomic level. Historically, fast growth rates in capitalist economies have been due to the virtuous circle of interaction between investment in research, physical capital formation, technical knowledge and practice, and demand. The return on investment depends on this interactive process, because it depends on the market growth that follows technological change and on the eventual form the technology takes. The neoclassical investment model, having abstracted from the changes that accompany accumulation, has no way of explaining the expected return which is supposed to underlie investment spending. The model is anomalous in that it explains one element of growth, namely capital formation, by ignoring the key ingredient of modern growth, namely technical change.[8]

THE DETERMINANTS OF INVESTMENT UNDER TECHNOLOGICAL COMPETITION

Micro-level studies show that technical change takes place in a variety of settings and through diverse mechanisms. That is, the locus of innovation, the motivation behind it, and the way it diffuses, varies between sectors (Nelson and Winter 1977). This variation appears to be at least in part due to differences in market structure. For example, if firms are unlikely to expand their shares, they have little incentive to engage in R & D and tend not to generate new products and processes. Such producers have no objection to sharing technical knowledge. The classic example of this type of market is agriculture, a sector that is dependent on outside sources for new technology. Innovation comes from suppliers and cooperative or government-funded research institutions (Nelson 1981, pp. 1050–51). By contrast, firms locked into competition for market share tend to invest in research and development as part of the competitive struggle.[9]

Empirical studies indicate that R & D is a necessity for firm survival in a number of industries. In these industries effective entry requires some technical advance, and technical improvements constitute entry barriers. For example in pharmaceuticals profit is largely dependent on a firm's innovative success (Kamien and Schwartz 1982, pp. 70–74). The first firm to introduce a successful innovation gains a significant advantage over existing and potential rivals. The advantage may be due to patents, development of expertise, realization of extraordinary profits that are available for R & D and/or the acquisition of brand reputation and consumer loyalty. The discussion presented below is concerned with industries where innovation is the dominant mode of competition and the users of the new technology do the research themselves.

In dealing with technological competition, the best the decision makers can do is to assess a limited set of alternatives. The possibilities of research available and known to all firms in an industry are limited by existing managerial and technical skills in the industry. The set of possibilities is 'local' in this sense (Nelson and Winter 1982a). Given a limited list of projects available to firms in an industry, what leads to an expectation of success rather than loss? A firm may choose not to invest in research, and lose market share if other firms do engage in successful research. If the firm does invest in the research, it faces the dangers of first, losing the resources because the effort fails on technical grounds or the result is not commercially viable, given (future) input prices and other variables; and second, not being able to appropriate the result of successful research, so that others exploit the commercial potential of the new technology. Appropriability is partly a function of patent laws and the cost of enforcing them. Partly it is due to the specific features of the technology, and the possibility of keeping the knowledge secret (Levin *et al.* 1987). Appropriability is a crucial variable determining the extent and composition of private research efforts. However, it is beyond the scope of this chapter, and the discussion below is confined to other technical and market considerations.

Without knowing all or even most possibilities of new knowledge, or the exact probabilities of finding solutions and successfully exploiting them, managers do have an idea that a particular direction of research is more likely to be successful than others. They also realize that the danger of being superseded is greater in certain situations than in others. If wrong decisions are made, if investment opportunities are ignored or unsuccessful investments undertaken, the firm's long-term existence is endangered. (A large literature directed at business executives claims to teach them how to manage the product cycle and the making of these decisions, for example Foster 1986; Drucker 1985.) What factors shape perceptions of potential success and failure?

The unit of analysis here is the industry, defined by a 'product', rather than the individual firm. The perception of technological opportunities is, of course, not equally distributed among the firms that are in (or may enter) the market. Differences between firms in a sector may be substantial (Nelson and Winter 1982a), but in order to keep the discussion within manageable limits these differences will not be considered here.

Many products follow an s-shaped growth path (Kuznets 1929). On the one hand this path is seen as tracing the exploitation of (diminishing) technological possibilities. In his supply side interpretation, Kuznets considered market growth simply to follow the rate of improvement in product and process. On the demand side, Schmookler (1966) found that technological improvements are themselves induced by market growth, and come to an end when demand is satiated. Schmookler concludes:

> ... the S-shaped long-run growth curve for individual industries, in which output tends to grow at a declining rate, usually reflects demand, not supply, conditions. The concomitant retardation in each industry's rate of technical progress is to be explained by the retardation in the rate of growth, not vice versa, although there is, of course, some feedback. (Schmookler 1966, p. 196)

These demand and supply effects are best seen as interactive complements, rather than substitutes (Kamien and Schwarz 1982).

There is an important qualification to the Schmookler hypothesis that market growth induces technical change. Rosenberg (1982) has pointed out that market demand depends on the existence of a more or less well defined product with commonly known characteristics. The initial appearance of the product cannot be attributed to the strength of the demand for it. In fact, Schmookler demonstrated the positive relationship between industry growth rate and invention only in long established sectors, such as railroads and construction.[10] He showed that within a spectrum of already established products, those with a faster growing market attract more research and innovation than the slow growth products. I will accept the proposition that market growth induces investments that lead to process innovation, but this does not explain product innovation. When it happens, product innovation opens up new potential for productivity growth, that is, a radical change in the product or a brand new product starts a new cycle of investment and innovation.

On this basis, we can express the Schmookler hypothesis as:

$$R_t = f(g_t) \text{ for } g_t > g_1 \tag{10.3}$$

R_t is research spending for period t, g_t the corresponding output growth rate of the product under consideration, and g_1 the minimum market growth rate necessary for research activities to take place. Since the 'industry' is defined by its product, a product innovation creates a new industry. This simplifying assumption rules out changes in the product along the product cycle. The elasticity of research spending with respect to market growth is:

$$E_R = \frac{dR/R}{dg/g} \tag{10.4}$$

We will now consider the variables that determine the market growth rate dg/g through time, in the presence of ongoing process innovation.

The latent technological opportunities in a potential research area can be measured (Nelson 1988) by the expected elasticity:

$$E_y = \frac{dy/y}{dR/R} \tag{10.5}$$

where y is a measure of productivity and R the total research spending on the product.[11]

The question of productivity measurement is complicated. Most of the existing literature considers total factor productivity to be the correct measure of technical change. There are several objections to this measure. First, the view of growth that underlies growth accounting and the calculation of total factor productivity, namely independent and separable contributions by factor inputs and technology, excludes the interactive mechanism described here (Abramovitz 1989). Second, micro-level studies of technical change show that the distinction between movement along a production function and a shift of the function is in practice unoperative, since a change in the capital–labour ratio means a change in the technology (Dosi 1988a). It is this distinction that makes it possible to define total factor productivity growth as technical change. Third, the marginal productivity explanation of income distribution, which is used to justify income shares as weights in the measurement of total factor productivity, is flawed on capital theoretic grounds (Garegnani 1970). For the purpose of the argument here, y is taken as simple labour productivity, that is, output per worker hour.

There is a documented positive relationship between R & D spending and productivity growth, that is, E_y is positive (Griliches 1987). We will hypothesize that the expected response of productivity to research is higher in some industries than in others at any one time. Specifically, it is high at the beginning of a product's life cycle. It diminishes as research and production proceed and the possibilities are realized. E_y measures the technical factors that determine the outcome of the investment.[12] The technical potential has to be considered in conjunction with future market possibilities. The rate of growth of the market depends on the changes in the price of the product. Over the secular time path of the product's development, the price moves inversely with productivity:

$$E_p = \frac{dp/p}{dy/y} < 0 \tag{10.6}$$

Given an expected increase in productivity, the higher the response in demand, the greater the potential for gaining an edge over competitors. The responsiveness of the market (output) growth rate to price changes is:

$$E_g = \frac{dg/g}{dp/p} \tag{10.7}$$

The price elasticity concept used here is somewhat different from the standard one. Textbook price elasticity describes a movement along the demand curve; that is, it measures the sensitivity of demand to price *given* preferences, consumer incomes, prices of related products, and so on. By contrast, we are here concerned with the secular development of a market over time. Therefore all else is *not* equal as the price of the product changes. Preferences, in particular, change over the product cycle. The demand response to the secular decline of the price shows the integration of the product into the lifestyles of cumulatively larger segments of the population. The demand elasticity (E_g) thus measures the evolution of consumer tastes, rather than static income and substitution effects.[13]

The higher the expected gains in productivity and the demand elasticity, the greater the probability of a high return on the investment. Furthermore, the higher these elasticities, the higher the expected loss due to not undertaking the investment, since the firms that do invest will reap large gains in productivity and market growth. The perception of these opportunities acts as both carrot and stick to the firm, opening up the possibility of accelerated growth, as well as the threat that others may utilize innovations to its detriment. What can we say about the elasticities? We can now investigate the interaction between product price, productivity, market growth and investment spending.

INVESTMENT IN RESEARCH AND DEVELOPMENT ALONG THE PRODUCT CYCLE

The latent technological possibilities represented by the productivity response (E_y), and the price and market growth elasticities (E_p, E_g) motivate research spending and capital formation. The investments thus motivated exploit the technical potential. Once the initial bugs are ironed out, the most obvious and easiest changes in the production process take place. These result in large productivity gains during the early phase of the product cycle. Subsequent improvements are more difficult and expensive. Hence there are diminishing returns to research spending on the particular product.

Figure 10.1 shows a likely scenario. The variables y, p, g, R (productivity, price, output growth rate, research spending) are graphed in logarithmic form so that the slopes of the functions are equivalent to the various elasticities. The time subscripts on the graphs indicate that the functions are irreversible. Figure 10.1 traces out the industry's expansion, and the relationships do not follow the same path in reverse when the industry is contracting. Cyclical ups and downs have been averaged out.[14]

The evolution of the elasticity of productivity (E_y) as the product matures is shown in Figure 10.1, Quadrant II. The function yy' traces the impact of research spending on productivity. During the early part of the product's development the yy' function is steep (E_y is low) because research in uncharted terrain yields only slow improvement in productivity. Productivity growth takes off as the full technological potential of the product is realized (the function flattens out as E_y increases). As the limits of the body of applied science that is relevant for the product are approached, research runs into diminishing returns; falling elasticity of productivity translates to a steeper yy'.

The relationship between labour productivity and the per unit price of the product is shown in Quadrant III of Figure 10.1. The function pp' is

Figure 10.1   Productivity growth and market expansion

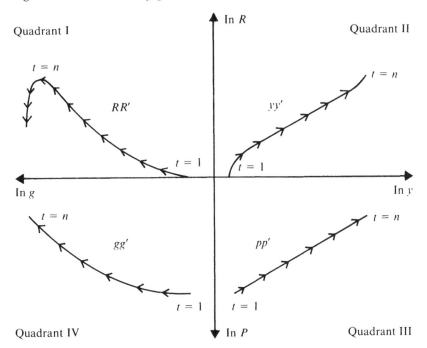

drawn on the assumption that there is a linear relationship between price and productivity, that is, E_p is constant. Price is a function of per unit cost, and falls as productivity increases. This process continues until productivity growth tapers off at time $t = n$. At that point, the price becomes constant.

Quadrant IV depicts the dynamic inverse relationship between the growth of demand and price. Initially the product is a novelty and a fall in its price makes it available to a larger fraction of the population. Therefore E_g is high and the function gg' is flat. Later in the process the use of the product is already widespread, so reductions in price have smaller impact. At the end of the expansion phase ($t = n$) market growth becomes price inelastic.

Quadrant I shows Schmookler's demand-side mechanism determining the level of research activity for a given product (equation 10.4). The total funds devoted to research in the industry by all firms increases with the growth of sales and output. Research by businesses starts after a minimum rate of growth (g_1) is reached at time $t = 1$.

These relationships initially result in a virtuous circle of investment and growth. Research spending leads to higher productivity (Quadrant II). The latter, through lower prices (Quadrant III), yields higher rates of market growth (Quadrant IV), which encourage more research spending (Quadrant I). The story can also be told with a Schmooklerian emphasis, by starting from Quadrant I: market growth leads to research, to productivity growth, and a lower price, coming full circle back to more market growth.

The virtuous circle comes to an end for two reasons. One, the technological potential of the product is exhausted. Productivity growth slows down, so that less is achievable for every dollar spent on research (E_y falls). Two, output growth slows down as the market for the product reaches its limits (E_g falls). The two limits need not occur simultaneously, of course, but this does not alter the basic pattern. The supply side potential is exhausted and demand becomes less elastic: every increment to productivity is more costly to achieve and gives rise to fewer additional sales for the industry. Individual firms may grow faster at the expense of others, and those who continue to invest in research may increase their market share at the expense of the firms that stop investing as the return on research declines. But overall research on the product declines as firms perceive that opportunities in the area are dwindling. Figure 10.1 does not show what goes on after the expansion phase.[15]

Figure 10.2, Quadrant I represents the transition from the expansion phase of the product life cycle to the maturity phase. The price and the level of labour productivity remain constant at the values achieved at time *n*. At time *x*, the growth rate has fallen to g_x, and no research is done on

Figure 10.2   Capital formation along the product cycle

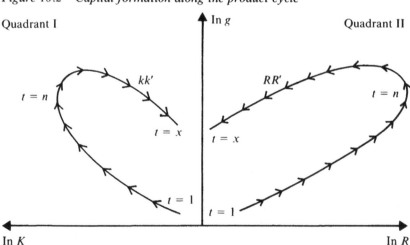

the product (Figure 10.2, Quadrant II). The growth rate experienced by the industry from time x on, g_x, depends on population and income growth, and the income elasticity of the now established product. Productivity and prices are constant, and growth depends on macro-level forces rather than innovation in the industry. A new product brings a new set of technological and market opportunities, thus starting off another life cycle. The product innovation may or may not come from the firms that were operating in $t = 1 \ldots n \ldots x$.

INVESTMENT IN PLANT AND EQUIPMENT

The framework presented so far does not address the issue of how investment in plant and equipment relates to investment in R & D. There is some empirical evidence that *lagged* R & D expenditure and recent innovation by a firm have a positive influence on its spending on new plant and equipment (Nelson and Winter 1977, p. 65). But it is not clear that this micro-level finding generalizes to an industry level relationship. The finding may be about the allocation of aggregate investment between firms, not its total magnitude. Firms with higher research expenditures can be expected to grow at the expense of others. Again at the micro-level, there appears to be a negative correlation between current R & D and investment. One empirical study indicates that R & D is a substitute for investment in plant and equipment, rather than an encouragement to it (Johnson 1966, p. 172). All in all, it seems that spending on research translates to industry level capital formation with a lag.

The degree of embodiment of new knowledge varies. According to Abramovitz:

> How much the exploitation of new knowledge depends upon the installation of newly designed equipment is not known. Some progress certainly takes the form of improvement in managerial routines, in the flow of work, and in the motivation of workers. Some requires but minor modifications in existing equipment. But the experience of most observers suggests that much progess is embodied in new capital. (Abramovitz 1989, p. 23)

Gross investment in plant and equipment takes place to:

a. replace worn-out capacity with similar plant and capacity
b. build up additional capacity with existing technology to meet the growth of demand
c. replace technologically obsolete capacity with new types of plant and equipment
d. create a new industry.

These categories involve different types of motivation.[16] Replacement of existing capacity with the same technology (a) is a function of the rate of depreciation of plant and equipment, while exogenous growth of the market (b) depends on macro factors like the growth of national income and business cycles. Investment due to new technology (c and d) depends on the factors described in the previous section above.

For a given industry there is a pattern to the *mix* between technologically motivated investment (c and d) and that due to exogenous market growth (b). During the virtuous circle of accelerating research and growth, investments of type (c) predominate. During the transition to slower growth the motivation behind investment shifts to replacement of worn-out capacity and demand satisfaction. The maturity phase of the industry brings the dominance of (a) and (b) type investment, with market growth determined by macro-level forces, including monetary and fiscal policies. A change in the product brings about another growth cycle of research and capital formation to embody new technology.

As capital formation shifts to types (a) and (b), away from (c), it tends to slow down. Market growth is faster during the expansion phase because it is driven by the secular decline in price (as well as by incremental improvements in product quality that are ignored here). Initially investment in plant and equipment accelerates as past research brings improvements in productivity that are then embodied in physical capital. This leads to reductions in price that encourage market growth, further fueling capital formation. The capital formation function KK' in Quadrant I of Figure 10.2 has an upward slope between $t = 1$ and $t = n$. At time n the potential for productivity growth for the given product is exhausted, and the price stabilizes. At time x, market growth slows down to g_x, a magnitude that depends on depreciation and exogenous growth of demand.

SOME MACRO IMPLICATIONS

When a sufficient number of industries are accelerating and slowing down simultaneously, the process traced out in Figure 10.1 for a single product applies to aggregate magnitudes. Research takes place in different industries to exploit the potential of the original innovations. New applications give rise to investment in physical capital and to overall productivity growth. The rise in national income brings about an increase in aggregate consumption, while the demand for new products increases at a higher

Figure 10.3   Macrogrowth process based on inter-linked product cycles

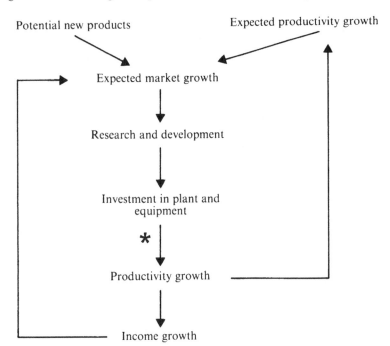

rate than aggregate demand. This channels research into these industries, where the potential for productivity growth is also greater. Thus the virtuous product cycle generalizes to the macroeconomy.

A macro-level growth process based on inter-linked product cycles is depicted in Figure 10.3. Investments in research and physical capital turn the possibilities of the new technological regime to actual gains in productivity and income. The process is a closed loop, with realized productivity and market growth feeding the expectations that underly investment decisions. Firms that do not invest are left behind by the tide; competitive pressure drives investment.

As the technological potential is exhausted (that is, as link * in Figure 10.3 weakens), productivity gains become more difficult and hence costlier. The cluster of new industries mature, and the composition of aggregate investment shifts to replacement of existing capacity and satisfaction of additional demand for established products. The neoclassical investment model may be more relevant in understanding investment at such times, when the changes described here may be justifiably ignored.

The links of the closed loop, as discussed earlier for a single product, are relatively clear. The least-known aspect of the process is how it begins. What initially fuels the perceptions that lead to research, innovation and capital formation in certain areas? This was what made the entrepreneur a central figure for the young Schumpeter, and this was the role that later in his career he assigned to oligopolistic corporations. In the late twentieth century various kinds of agents contribute to the process by which research decisions are made. Depending on the industry and on the stage of industrialization of the country in question, the agent may be entrepreneur, corporate research department, or public official.[17] Very little is known about the factors underlying the perceptions of these agents about technical and market potential in different industries.

An advanced industrial economy consists of industries at different stages of the product life cycle, some just starting off, others growing fast, others stagnating. In itself the s-shaped pattern of industry and product development says nothing about the overall rate of investment and technical change. However, it is possible that at a given time a particular phase of product development dominates a sufficient number of sectors to affect the entire economy. Various scenarios of secular growth have suggested that clusters of industries go through expansion and maturity simultaneously, driving the economy up during the former and pulling it down during the latter (cf. Schumpeter 1950). For example, a recent technological shift involving almost all industries is thought to centre around microchips and computers, bringing new methods of production such as computer-aided design and manufacturing, new products, and revolution in some existing products. Yet, if there really was such a basic shift, this has not yet been reflected in the aggregate investment rate and productivity growth in the United States, which remain at a low level compared to the 1950s and 1960s (Baily and Chakrabarti 1988).

The macro effect of a radical innovation on aggregate investment spending depends not only on the industries that directly use it, but also on the linkages these have to other industries. The steam engine, for example, was a 'major' innovation precisely because it was used in two key sectors, railroads and shipping, which provided transportation services to all other industries. Thus in addition to the industries using it directly, the steam engine had economy-wide forward linkages through the new modes of transportation. It also had extensive backward linkages through the demand it created for iron and coal. In retrospect it is obvious that just about every part of the economy was affected by the steam engine, whether as direct user, as purchaser of products from users of steam power, or as supplier of inputs to users. But it is not clear what general proposition follows from this historical picture. There is no clear criterion that can be applied to a recent innovation to determine whether it has potential linkages of sufficient magnitude to accelerate macro capital formation.

The crucial issue in assessing the aggregate impact of a new technology, namely how extensive its impact will be on other industries, is complicated by the institutional adjustments it requires. A systemic innovation is embodied in a set of complementary capital goods and requires particular organizational forms. Macro investment can be seen as a function of the inter-related product cycles that belong to a technological regime, the exploitation of which requires institutional overhauls.[18] As Freeman puts it:

> The potential leap to much higher levels of productivity from a radical inno-vation may only become a reality when it is complemented by a whole set of other innovations, including especially organizational, managerial and social innovations. (Freeman 1989, p. 11)

The changes include restructuring the national education system to provide the relevant skills, and other public policies such as the allocation of funds for research, as well as changes in business management prac-tices. Since they are likely to be slow, the aggregate impact may not follow the availability of the technology. Freeman (1989) and David (1989)[19] argue that this is the reason computers currently have not led to an acceleration of investment and productivity growth.

The propositions put forth in this chapter are a step toward understand-ing the complicated process behind capital formation and growth. The interaction between investment, technology, price, and market growth, as described here, has to be further elucidated and documented if we are to understand the process. If it can be empirically supported, then an inter-esting policy implication follows. Governments now rely on monetary policy and tax incentives to encourage investment spending. If the vari-ables described here underlie capital formation, then public support of R & D should be considered at least as important a policy tool. Nelson (1989) argues that the slow growth of the US economy during the last two decades is due to the reduction of federal research expenditures. Rosen-berg and Mowery (1989), in a similar vein, suggest that the commercial spill-overs from military R & D (the largest single component of federal research) have petered out. The framework developed here fits these interpretations. But the elasticities have to be empirically specified and estimated before policy implications can be drawn.

NOTES

1. Investment in inventory is probably subject to different considerations, and is not treated here.
2. In a more detailed model the rental cost also includes depreciation allowance and may be adjusted for tax credits. See Dornbusch and Fischer (1984, pp. 205–18).
3. As Haavelmo (1960) pointed out. See Lund (1971, p. 17).
4. An early version of this critique was put forth by Joan Robinson and Nicholas Kaldor. Dosi (1988a) makes the same point on the basis of empirical studies of technical change.
5. As Maddison (1982, p. 57) puts it, 'The progress of technology is influenced to an important degree by the amount of investment that is carried out, because this involves improvement engineering and learning by doing, which are always necessary in the practical implementation of new techniques.'
6. The other interdependency discussed by Nelson and Abramovitz, that between technical change and the quality of labour input, lies outside the scope of this chapter.
7. The pathbreaking historical studies of the evolution of the modern firm are by Alfred Chandler (1969). Oliver Williamson (1981, 1985) has a theoretical approach that parallels Chandler's historical one. David Teece (1982) applies Williamson's analysis of transaction cost specifically to research and development by the firm. Nelson and Winter (1982a) have proposed a framework incorporating technical change and this type of firm behaviour.
8. The post-Keynesian growth models of the 1950s and 1960s were intended to integrate capital formation and technical change. For an evaluation of these models, see Kurdas (1991). For a review of Kaldor's cumulative causation hypothesis, see Ricoy (1987).
9. It would seem that the point Schumpeter was making in his oft-cited chapter 'Creative Destruction' concerns the difference between real world approximations of perfect competition such as farming and oligopolistic corporations fighting for market share. The interpretation by some researchers in industrial organization (Kamien and Schwarz 1982) of the chapter as an argument that monopoly favors technical change is unwarranted.
10. A number of writers argue that the rate of growth of demand plays a significant role for existing products (Freeman 1986a, p. 211).
11. The concept of technological potential is discussed by Abramovitz (1989).
12. It should be noted that in many cases the perception of technological opportunities has lagged behind what in retrospect appears to be the actual potential, even after the innovation was made (Rosenberg 1982). Such lags are ignored here, for the sake of simplicity.
13. Income elasticity is also relevant in the evaluation of various risks. A product with high income elasticity can be produced in larger volumes in the future, and the commercial success of an innovation may depend on the volume of production. This concept is not used in the text because it would complicate but not change the basic scheme.
14. Obviously, the product cycle concept is not related to the business cycle.
15. Needless to say, the same firms may conduct research in other areas. Indeed, their continued existence depends on their doing so.
16. This distinction of technically-induced versus demand-related investment is not the same as net versus gross investment. Some part of aggregate net investment is expansion due to the expected growth of demand.
17. Amsden (1989) makes this point for South Korea, and sees it as a general characteristic of late industrializers like Japan and Korea.
18. Nelson and Winter describe technological trajectories; Dosi (1988a) writes of technological paradigms; Freeman (1989) uses the expression technological regime.
19. David (1989) shows that the full macro impact of the electric motor lagged behind the innovation by several decades.

REFERENCES

Abernathy, W.J., Clark, K.B. and Kantrow, A.M. (1983) *Industrial Renaissance. Producing a Competitive Future for America*, New York: Basic Books.

Abramovitz, M. (1989) *Thinking About Growth. And Other Essays on Economic Growth & Welfare*, Cambridge: Cambridge University Press.

Amsden, A.H. (1989) *Asia's Next Giant: South Korea and Late Industrialization*, Oxford: Oxford University Press.

Arrow, K. (1962) 'The Economic Implications of Learning by Doing' *Review of Economic Studies.*

Arrow, K. (1989) 'Joan Robinson and Modern Economic Theory' in Feiwel, G. (1989) *Joan Robinson and Modern Economic Theory*, New York: New York University Press.

Baily, M.N. and Chakrabarti, A.K. (1988) *Innovation and the Productivity Crisis*, Washington, DC: Brookings Institution.

Boskin, M.J. (1988) 'Tax Policy and Economic Growth: Lessons From the 1980s', *Journal of Economic Perspectives.*

Chandler, A.D. (1969) *Strategy and Structure: Chapters in the History of the American Industrial Enterprise*, Cambridge, MA: MIT Press.

Chandler, A.D. (1977) *The Visible Hand. The Managerial Revolution in American Business*, Cambridge, MA: Belknap Press.

Clark, K.P. (1979) 'Investment in the 1970s: Theory, Performance, and Prediction', *Brookings Papers on Economic Activity,* 1.

Coen, R.M. and Eisner, R. (1987) 'Investment' in J. Eatwell, M. Milgate and P. Newman (eds), *The New Palgrave: A Dictionary of Economics*, New York: The Stockton Press.

David, P. (1975) *Technical Choice. Innovation and Economic Growth*, Cambridge: Cambridge University Press.

David, P. (1989) 'Computer and Dynamo: The Modern Productivity Paradox in a Not-Too-Distant Mirror': paper presented at the conference on The Process of Technological Change. New York: New School for Social Research.

Denison, E.F. (1962) *The Sources of Economic Growth in the United States*, New York: Committee for Economic Development.

Denison, E.F. (1985) *Trends in American Economic Growth. 1929–1982*, Washington, DC: The Brookings Institution.

Dornbusch, R. and Fischer, S. (1984) *Macroeconomics* (3rd ed.), New York: McGraw-Hill.

Dosi, G. (1982) 'Technological Paradigms and Technological Trajectories. A Suggested Interpretation of the Determinants and Directions of Technical Change', *Research Policy.*

Dosi, G. (1986) Technology and Conditions of Macroeconomic Development' in C. Freeman (ed.), *Design, Innovation and Long Cycles in Economic Development*, London: Francis Pinter.

Dosi, G. (1988a) 'Sources, Procedures, and Microeconomic Effects of Innovation', *Journal of Economic Literature*, Sept.

Dosi, G. (1988b) 'Institutions and Markets in a Dynamic World', *The Manchester School*, June.

Drucker, P.E. (1985) *Innovation and Entrepreneurship. Practice and Principles*, New York: Harper & Row.

Eatwell, J. and Milgate, M. (eds) (1983) *Keynes' Economics and the Theory of Value and Distribution*, New York: Oxford University Press.

Fischer, S. (1988) 'Symposium on the Slowdown in Productivity Growth', *Journal of Economic Perspectives*, Fall.

Foster, R.N. (1986) *Innovation. The Attacker's Advantage*, New York: Summit Books.

Fransman, M. (1985) 'Conceptualizing Technical Change in the Third World in the 1980s: An Interpretive Survey', *Journal of Development Studies*.

Freeman, C. (1986) *The Economics of Industrial Innovation* (2nd edn), Cambridge, MA: MIT Press.

Freeman, C. (1989) 'The Nature of Innovation and the Evolution of the Productive System', *OECD* International Seminar on Science, Technology, and Economic Growth.

Freeman, C. and Perez, C. (1988) 'Structural Crises of Adjustment, Business Cycles and Investment Behaviour', in Dosi, G. *et al.* (eds) *Technical Change and Economic Theory*, London: Pinter Publishers.

Garegnani, P. (1970) 'Heterogeneous Capital, the Production Function and the Theory of Distribution', *Review of Economic Studies*.

Garegnani, P. (1987a) 'Capital and Effective Demand', in A. Barriere (ed.), *Keynes Today*, London: Macmillan.

Garegnani, P. (1987b) 'Two Views of Effective Demand', unpublished manuscript.

Griliches, Z. (1987) (ed.) *R & D Patents, and Productivity*, Chicago: University of Chicago Press.

Griliches, Z. (1988) 'Productivity Puzzles and R&D: Another Nonexplanation', *Journal of Economic Perspectives*.

Haavelmo, T. (1960) *A Study in the Theory of Investment*, Chicago: University of Chicago Press.

Hayes, R.H. and Wheelwright, S. (1979) 'The Dynamics of Process-Product Life Cycles', *Harvard Business Review*.

Hollander, S. (1965) *The Sources of Increased Efficiency: A Study of Du Pont Rayon Plants*, Cambridge: MIT Press.

Johnston, R.E. (1966) 'Technical Progress and Innovation', *Oxford Economic Papers*.

Jorgenson, D. (1988) 'Productivity and Postwar U.S. Economic Growth', *Journal of Economic Perspectives*.

Kaldor, N. (1957) 'A Model of Economic Growth', *Economic Journal*.

Kaldor, N. (1967) *Strategic Factors in Economic Development*, Ithaca, NY: Cornell University Press.

Kaldor, N. (1985) *Economics Without Equilibrium*, Armonk, NY: M.E. Sharpe.

Kamien, M.I. and Schwartz, N.L. (1982) *Market Structure and Innovation*, (Cambridge: Cambridge University Press.

Knight, F.H. (1971) *Risk. Uncertainty, and Profit*, Chicago: University of Chicago Press.

Kurdas, C. (1991) 'Robinson's Dark Room: Investment in Post-Keynesian Growth Theory', in I. Rima (ed.), *The Joan Robinson Legacy*, Armonk, NY: M.E. Sharpe.

Kuznets, S. (1929) 'Retardation of Industrial Growth', *Journal of Economic and Business History*.

Levin, R. and Klevorick, A., Nelson, R. and Winter, S. (1987) 'Appropriating the Returns from Industrial Research and Development', *Brookings Papers on Economic Activity*, **3**.

Lund, P.J. (1971) *Investment. The Study of an Economic Aggregate*, Amsterdam: North-Holland.

Maddison, A. (1982) *Phases of Capitalist Development*, Oxford: Oxford University Press.

Maddison, A. (1987) 'Growth and Slowdown in Advanced Capitalist Economies', *Journal of Economic Literature*, June.

Mansfield, E. (1968) *The Economics of Technological Change*, New York: Norton.

Nell, E.J. (1987a) 'Accumulation of Capital', in J. Eatwell, M. Milgate and P. Newman (eds), *The New Palgrave: A Dictionary of Economics*, New York: The Stockton Press.

Nell, E.J. (1987b) 'Transformational Growth and Stagnation', in R. Cherry *et al.* (eds), *The Imperiled Economy*, New York: URPE.

Nell, E.J. (1988) *Prosperity and Public Spending. Transformational Growth and the Role of Government*, Winchester, MA: Allen & Unwin.

Nell, E.J. (1989) 'Accumulation and Capital Theory', in G. Feiwel (1989) (ed.), *Joan Robinson and Modern Economic Theory*, New York: New York University Press.

Nelson, R. (1973) 'Recent Exercises in Growth Accounting: New Understanding or Dead End?', *American Economic Review*.

Nelson, R. (1981) 'Research on Productivity Growth and Productivity Differences: Dead Ends and New Departures', *Journal of Economic Literature*.

Nelson, R. (1988) 'Modelling the Connections in the Cross Section Between Technical Progress and R&D Intensity', *Rand Journal of Economics*.

Nelson, R. (1989) 'U.S. Technological Leadership: Where Did it Come From and Where Did it Go?', Columbia University.

Nelson, R. and Winter, S. (1973) 'Toward an Evolutionary Theory of Economic Capabilities', *American Economic Review*, May.

Nelson, R. and Winter, S. (1977) 'In Search of a Useful Theory of Innovation', *Research Policy*.

Nelson, R. and Winter, S. (1978) 'Forces Generating and Limiting Competition Under Schumpeterian Conditions', *Bell Journal of Economics*.

Nelson, R. and Winter, S. (1982a) *An Evolutionary Theory of Economic Change*, Cambridge, MA: Harvard University Press.

Nelson, R. and Winter, S. (1982b) 'The Schumpeterian Trade-Off Revisited', *American Economic Review*.

Pasinetti, L.L. (1981) *Structural Change and Economic Growth. A Theoretical Essay on the Dynamics of the Wealth of Nations*, Cambridge: Cambridge University Press.

Pavitt, K. (1986) 'Chips and Trajectories: How Does the Semiconductor Influence the Sources and Directions of Technical Change?', in R.M. Macleod (ed.), *Technology and the Human Prospect. Essays in Honor of Christopher Freeman*, London: Francis Pinter.

Ricoy, C. (1987) 'Cumulative Causation', in J. Eatwell, M. Milgate and P. Newman (eds), *The New Palgrave: A Dictionary of Economics*, New York: The Stockton Press.

Robinson, J. (1965) *The Accumulation of Capital*, New York: St. Martin's Press.

Rosenberg, N. (1972) *Technology and American Economic Growth*, Armonk, N.Y: M.E. Sharpe.

Rosenberg, N. (1976) *Perspectives on Technology*, Armonk, NY: M.E. Sharpe.

Rosenberg, N. (1982) *Inside the Black Box. Technology and Economics*, Cambridge: Cambridge University Press.

Rosenberg, N. and Frischtak, C. (1984) 'Technological Innovation and Long Waves', *Cambridge Journal of Economics*.

Rosenberg, N. and Mowery, D. (1989) *Technology and the Pursuit of Economic Growth*, Cambridge: Cambridge University Press.

Salter, W.E.G. (1960) *Productivity and Technical Change*, Cambridge: Cambridge University Press.

Schmookler, J. (1966) *Invention and Economic Growth*, Cambridge, MA: Harvard University Press.

Schumpeter, J.A. (1950) *Capitalism, Socialism and Democracy*, New York: Harper and Row.

Schumpeter, J.A. (1955) *The Theory of Economic Development. An Inquiry into Profits, Capital, Credit, Interest, and the Business Cycle*, Cambridge, MA: Harvard University Press.

Sen, A. (ed.) (1970) *Growth Economics*, Harmondsworth: Penguin.

Simon, H.A. (1959) 'Theories of Decision Making in Economics', *American Economic Review*, June.

Solow, R.M. (1970) *Growth Theory*, Oxford: Oxford University Press.

Sylos-Labini, P. (1969) *Oligopoly and Technical Progress*, Cambridge, MA: Harvard University Press.

Sylos-Labini, P. (1984) *The Forces of Economic Growth and Decline*, Cambridge, MA: MIT Press.

Teece, D. (1982) 'Towards an Economic Theory of the Multiproduct Firm', *Journal of Economic Behavior and Organization*.

Teece, D. (1986) 'Profiting from Technological Innovation: Implications for Integration, Collaboration, Licencing, and Public Policy', *Research Policy*.

Thomson, R. (1986) 'Technological Change as New Product Development', *Social Concept*.

Thomson, R. (1987) 'Learning by Selling and Invention: The Case of the Sewing Machine', *Journal of Economic History*.

Waterson, M. (1984) *Economic Theory of the Industry*, Cambridge: Cambridge University Press.

Williamson, O.E. (1981) 'The Economics of Organization: The Transaction Cost Approach', *American Journal of Sociology*.

Williamson, O.E. (1985) *Economic Institutions of Capitalism*, New York: Free Press.

Winter, S. (1971) 'Satisficing, Selection and the Innovating Remnant', *Quarterly Journal of Economics*.

11. Critical Notes on Kalecki's Theory of Investment

Fabio Petri

I

I have elsewhere (Petri 1989) investigated the question of whether the traditional thesis of a negative elasticity of investment with respect to the rate of interest has solid theoretical foundations in marginalist/neoclassical economic theory. My conclusion was negative, and a brief summary of how it was reached is given below. The present chapter poses the same question for Kalecki's theory of investment based on the 'principle of increasing risk', and again answers in the negative. But the reasoning through which this result is reached also throws doubt on some central features of Kalecki's theory of investment. But while the present chapter is mainly critical, constructive implications emerge from the criticisms.

It will be argued that two sharply differing views of the determinants of investment can be found in Kalecki's writings.[1] In the first, a direct determining role is given to the own capital of firms and to the rate of profits, because the desired capital stock of firms is determined by the own capital of firms and by their desired leverage (or gearing) ratio. This depends on the ratio of the (essentially given) rate of interest to the rate of profits: demand is only able to affect investment by affecting the rate of profits via changes in the degree of utilization of capacity. In the second view, demand has a direct effect on investment, the own capital of firms and the leverage ratio losing nearly all importance. It will be argued that the second view is the more satisfactory one, but that, when consistently developed (Kalecki fails to do this), it implies abandoning the distinguishing Kaleckian features and adopting the theory that gross investment depends on (expected) demand because it has the purpose of adapting capacity to demand (the old acceleration principle).

It is convenient to start with a brief summary of Petri (1989), because it provides the background to the argument of the present chapter. Garegnani (1978–9) has argued that the derivation of the traditional aggregate investment schedule, a decreasing function of the rate of interest, is impossible unless one accepts as valid the traditional marginalist conception of 'capital' as a single, homogeneous factor of production, capable of changing 'form' (that is, composition) without changing in quantity, and the demand for which is a decreasing function of the rate of interest. This traditional conception of capital was the basis for the derivation of an investment schedule reflecting the demand for 'free capital': it was more or less explicitly admitted that at each moment the greater part of capital is embodied in concrete capital goods and therefore can only change form gradually, through the reinvestment of depreciation allowances into the purchase of capital goods different from the depreciating ones. Other factors, it was admitted, cannot usually be combined in varying proportions with the existing capital of given form (a variation of the capital–labour proportion adopted in an industry was admitted generally to require the use of *different* capital goods). What the rate of interest can act upon is therefore only the proportion in which free capital (gross savings) is combined with the proportion of other factors freed, or released, by the closure of old plants. The investment schedule is then simply the demand curve for free capital, indicating – to put it simply rather than rigorously – the marginal product of the flow of free capital when combined with the flow of other free factors,[2] and being therefore, in essence, a reduced-scale copy of the demand-for-capital schedule. Short-period phenomena such as variations in the state of confidence, or irregular replacement needs, or anticipated closure of plants due to the variation of the rate of interest, can only cause temporary divergences from this basic correspondence between the investment schedule and the demand curve for capital, divergences which disappear or tend to compensate one another in the long run.

After thus reconstructing the traditional derivation of a decreasing investment schedule, Garegnani notices that it is undermined by the recent advances in capital theory, which have shown that the 'demand curve' for capital can have shapes which make it impossible to interpret it as in fact a demand curve: it may not be single valued, it may present increasing segments ('reverse capital deepening') and even when not increasing it may be highly inelastic (see also Garegnani 1970, Appendix). Thus the presumption that – at least in the absence of monetary complications – the rate of interest can act as the price bringing investment into equality with full-employment savings is shown to be without foundations.

After a presentation of this argument, in Petri (1989) I pose the question whether Garegnani's criticism can be extended to the recent reformulations of neoclassical investment theory, where the derivation of the investment function is different, and sometimes no explicit role is given to the traditional marginalist conception of capital. The answer is yes, because the other attempts to justify a negative dependence of investment on the interest rate (Lerner's increasing supply price of capital goods argument; adjustment cost theories; Jorgenson's so-called 'neoclassical' approach; Tobin's q-theory) can all be shown to be indefensible, both for reasons specific to each, and for a common reason which is important because it also crops up in discussing Kalecki's theory of investment: expected returns are illegitimately treated as independent of the rate of interest.[3] Investment decisions are long-period decisions, and in the long run the rate of interest and the rate of return on investment cannot be independent of each other. An autonomous decrease in the rate of interest, for instance, means that investors can be content with a lower rate of return, and competition can be expected to cause a decrease in prices relative to money wages, which will in fact bring about such a lower rate of return. Such a result would usually be conceded for single industries in which for example, because of government subsidies, the cost of borrowing decreased; but it must also be conceded for the whole economy if one accepts that competition means a readiness to undercut competitors and enlarge market shares by lowering prices. Therefore, if the real rate of interest is given, the rate of profits will tend to be such as to permit paying that rate of interest, plus the normal differential necessary to persuade capital to be invested into risky undertakings rather than in safe bonds.[4] (This appears to be what Sraffa (1960, p. 33) was aiming at when he suggested that the rate of profits appears 'susceptible of being determined from outside the system of production, in particular by the level of the money rates of interest.') The conclusion is that one basic pillar of the marginalist/neoclassical theory of value, distribution and employment, namely the tendency toward full employment, is deprived of theoretical justification because the mechanism which in that theory should ensure the transformation of full-employment savings into investment lacks plausibility.

II

But a different foundation for the thesis that a permanent[5] decrease of the rate of interest will stimulate investment might be provided by Kalecki's 'principle of increasing risk'. In his early writings, preceding his reading of Keynes's *General Theory*, Kalecki considered investment to depend on the rate of interest, and on the ratio P/K of gross profits to capital (Kalecki also calls it 'rate of profits'), but the rate of interest is then left aside, on the basis that it moves in the same direction as the P/K ratio, although to a lesser extent. The reasons for the dependence of investment on P/K and on the rate of interest are not explicitly discussed; there appears only a sentence on 'the stimulating effect of the increase in $[P/K]$ upon investment' (Kalecki 1933, p. 14) which must 'outweigh the restraining influence of the rise in the rate of interest' if investment is to increase; no microfoundations are provided for these views.

Explicit microfoundations are provided (for what remains fundamentally the same theory of aggregate investment) only by the 'principle of increasing risk', for which the basic reference is Kalecki (1937b). There Kalecki argues that the Marginal Efficiency of Capital, MEC, (the rate of return earned on an additional unit of capital) for a single firm should be taken to be *constant*, not decreasing, in competitive conditions. The competitive firm treats prices (of inputs as well as of outputs) as given; decreasing returns to scale are seen by Kalecki as an implausible assumption because replication of plant (including hired managers) is always possible. Therefore in a competitive firm, even if one investment project only had an MEC greater than the rate of interest, the firm would plan to replicate it indefinitely, that is, it would plan an infinite amount of investment. Why does this not happen?[6] Kalecki's reply introduces his own theory of investment: because, he argues, the size of firms is limited by the fact that risk is an increasing function of the indebtedness ratio. In order to invest more, the owners of a firm must increase the ratio of debt to own capital (given that a part of investment normally comes from internal funds, so not all assets are matched by a corresponding debt), thus increasing both their risk of losing their own wealth, and the danger of 'illiquidity'. Because of this, and in order to induce the owners to invest, a greater differential between the constant MEC and the rate of interest is required, the greater the ratio of debt to own capital; and also, owing to increasing risk for the lender, a rising marginal addition to the basic 'safe' rate of interest must be offered to lenders. Let us call σ the sum of the two marginal risk differentials. The amount of investment, Kalecki says, is determined by the equality between the rate of return r (which for the single firm is independent of the amount of investment) and the rising marginal cost of borrowing, resulting from the addition of σ to the given basic 'safe' rate of interest i.

Thus, investment decisions are viewed as determined by the desire of firms to reach the optimal capital stock k_o determined by:

1. the own capital of the firm, which we may indicate with the symbol C
2. the given and constant MEC (which is indistinguishable from the expected rate of profit)
3. the 'safe' or basic interest rate i, and

Figure 11.1   Investment decisions, as viewed by Kalecki

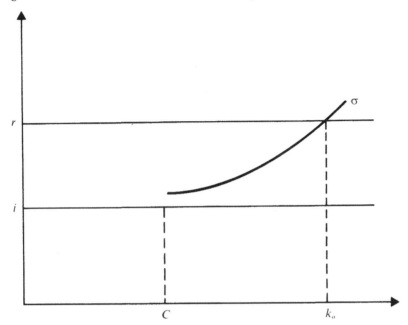

4.   the 'increasing risk' function.

The latter gives the marginal risk rate σ to be added to i in order to get the minimum rate of return necessary to make the holding of the last unit of capital profitable: σ is assumed to be an increasing function of the indebtedness ratio $\delta = (k - C)/C$. If the basic interest rate and the MEC are given, the optimal capital stock of the firm, k_0, is in a fixed ratio, $1 + \delta^*$, to the own capital of the firm: $k_0 = (1 + \delta^*)C$, see Figure 11.1. Essentially the same theory is repeated in Kalecki (1939), where it is explicitly applied to the economy as a whole, rather than to a single firm.

Kalecki himself notices (1937b, p. 444) that his argument implies that a decrease in the basic rate of interest will induce firms to adopt a higher δ, that is, to borrow more and invest more. Another implication of the theory is that one should not necessarily prefer fiscal over monetary policy as a way to increase employment, so long as the monetary authorities are able to influence the real interest rate.[7]

The same conclusion might be derived from the essentially Kaleckian theory of investment adopted by Minsky (1975, pp. 109–16). Similar theories are reviewed in Ackley (1978, Ch. 19), and in Nickell (1978, Ch. 8), where on p. 198 the seminal role of Kalecki (1937b) is recognized.

Figure 11.2   Investment decisions, showing rate of return on own capital

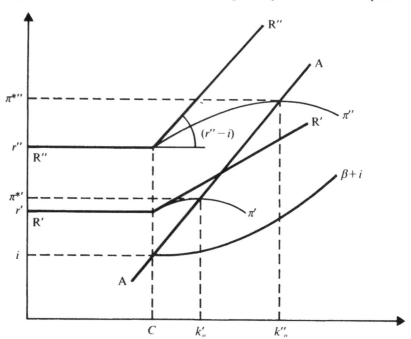

III

Kalecki's approach shares with other approaches to investment (see **I** above) the questionable treatment of the expected rate of return on investment (the expected rate of profits, in effect) as given independently of the cost of borrowing. If, on the contrary, it is accepted that autonomous variations in the real interest rate will result in variations in the same direction of the rate of profits via variations of the price level relative to money wages, then a decrease in the interest rate will *not* increase the differential between interest rate and profit rate and therefore will not create any incentive to investment, even when the other elements of Kalecki's analysis are accepted.

It is convenient at this point to re-draw Figure 11.1 as Figure 11.2, which explicitly shows the rate of return on the own capital (C) of firms, as well as its maximization, and which allows one readily to see that, if the rate of return moves in step with the rate of interest, no change occurs in the optimal capital stock k_0. The owners of C may be assumed to maximize their earnings, which is the same thing – C being given – as maximizing the rate of return on C. Let r be the rate of profits on the total (own and borrowed) invested capital k. If the firm had to pay $i(k-C)$ on the borrowed capital, its earnings would be given by $rC+(r-i)(k-C)$. The rate of return on C would therefore be given by $r+(r-i)(k-C)/C$. Graphically this is the RR line in Figure 11.2, a horizontal line of height r up to C, at which point it becomes an upward-sloping straight line of slope $r-i$. From this, in order to obtain the net-of-leverage-risk rate of return π, one must subtract β, the *average* risk differential to be added to i, an increasing function of $(k-C)/k$, which we assume, following Kalecki, to have positive second derivative: the connection with Kalecki's σ is that $d\beta/dk = \sigma$. To the right of C, one obtains a concave π curve, at first increasing, then decreasing. The maximum π, let us call it π^*, is obtained where $r-i = d\beta/dk$. If $i < r$ (as required for k to be positive: if $i \geqslant r$, all savings would go to safe bonds only), and $\beta(k-C)$ is only positive for $k > C$, then $\pi^* > r$.

Let us indicate with τ the differential between rate of return on industrial capital π^* and rate of interest on safe bonds i, necessary to recompense the 'risk and trouble' of entrepreneurship. Then competition will cause π^* to tend to $i + \tau$. The effect of the possibility of borrowing capital at a rate of interest less than the rate of profit r is to make the rate of profit inferior to the required rate of return on own capital $\pi^* = i + \tau$.

The desired optimal capital stock k_0, given C and i, can be determined as follows. Let us hypothetically vary r. For each level of r, one can draw the corresponding RR line: as r is increased, the slope $r - i$ of the RR line to the right of C increases, so the level of k for which $r - i = d\beta/dk$ increases too. Let us call AA the upward-sloping locus of π^* points corresponding to increasing values of r. It suffices to find the point on this locus of height $i + \tau$ to find k_0 (and the level of r yielding $\pi^* = i + \tau$).

Let us now assume that i varies. If r varies by the same amount, and if the slope of the β function remains unaltered, then the value of k for which π is maximized, that is, for which $r - i = d\beta/dk$, remains unchanged. This means that the AA locus simply shifts up or down by the same amount as the rate of interest. Thus, if the differential τ is also unchanged, and if competition ensures that $\pi^* = i + \tau$, then changes of i only change r by the same amount, while the optimal capital stock k_0 is not affected. If τ is an increasing function of i, then if i decreases k_0 decreases as well: the opposite of Kalecki's result.

Do we have the right to distinguish a 'risk and trouble' differential τ from a 'leverage' differential β? The answer is that we do. The former differential refers to what is necessary to make it attractive to invest one's capital into ownership of a firm, even with no external borrowing. External borrowing adds a further risk element, which requires the further addition of the second differential (which, let us remember, includes both a borrower's and a lender's risk: the latter, if positive, implies that the actual rate of interest paid by the firm on its debt is higher than i). The rate π is already net of this second differential, and this is why it can be compared directly with $i + \tau$. If $\pi > i + \tau$, then there is an incentive for some financial capital to become industrial capital: unless competition among already existing firms ensures the decrease of prices and hence of π until $\pi = i + \tau$, some financiers will utilize their capital to set up new firms. This actual or potential entry can be presumed to be a powerful element of competition, pushing the rate of return net of leverage risk toward equality with $i + \tau$.

This reasoning allows one to conclude that it is not legitimate to derive from Kalecki's principle of increasing risk that a lower rate of interest will induce firms to increase their capital stock. But it has implications which go beyond this result, and impinge on Kalecki's own views on the determinants of investment. It implies, in fact, that *one has no right to assume that the total own capital of the aggregate of firms is given*. Thus the conclusion, reached above, that k_0 (in fact, the optimal leverage) is not affected by changes of the rate of interest, does *not* mean that firms in the aggregate never alter their total own capital except as a consequence of the reinvestment of (part of) their profits. They may increase it by issuing equity; or new firms may be born, with new own capital;[8] or the flow of capital into the purchase of existing equity may raise equity values, thus increasing C. As will be seen next, this means that, even accepting the principle of increasing risk, demand may have a direct influence on the desired total stock of capital because the own capital of firms adapts itself to the desired total stock of capital.

Before discussing Kalecki's own acceptance of this point, it will be useful to discuss one conceivable objection to the thesis that the rate of return moves in step with the rate of interest. It might be argued that if the leverage risk differential β were given, then it would be correct that the rate of return must decrease with the rate of interest; but there is another possibility – that as investment increases, the indebtedness of firms, and β with it, increases also – there is then an increase in the level of investment which makes a constant rate of return compatible with a lower rate of interest.

Two counter-replies can be advanced. The first, based on the distinction between determining the optimal capital stock and determining the investment flow (on which see **V** below), is that given the own capital C of firms, the differential β is for Kalecki a function of the stock of capital, not of the flow of investment. This means that if the interest rate goes down, even if net investment were stimulated, the indebtedness ratio of firms can be altered only gradually (at least at the economy-wide level, since investment cannot be infinite). So even if investment were to vary, this would only alter β slowly through time, as indebtedness increased. Meanwhile, each firm would have the time to try and steal customers from its competitors by lowering prices. (This process of price undercutting is perhaps implausible if the economy is working near or at very full capacity, so that no firm is afraid of losing custom; but one cannot assume that capital is fully utilized all the time, otherwise there would never be cycles.) The second reply is that, as argued above, it is not legitimate to take the total own capital of firms as given; the possibility of previously non-industrial capital becoming entrepreneurial capital will ensure that leverage will not vary.

IV

Kalecki himself admitted in later writings the possibility of a *direct* influence of expected demand on investment. In Kalecki's first trade cycle models in which the principle of increasing risk is the foundation of the theory of investment (Kalecki 1937a, 1939), demand does exercise an influence on investment, but only indirectly, by influencing total profits P, hence the rate of profits P/K, hence (the basic rate of interest and the own capital of firms being given) the desired degree of leverage. Even the influence of demand on the general mood of confidence, and thus on the expected rate of profits and on the estimation of risk (Dibenedetto 1990, pp. 82–6; Kalecki 1937a, p. 87), operates through its influence on P/K. Over time, the own capital of firms changes owing to the reinvestment of profits: in these writings Kalecki assumes the complete re-investment of savings into the firms' own capital (Dibenedetto 1990, pp. 61–4; Kalecki 1949, p. 61, note 1, and 1971, pp. 116–17); savings are assumed to be a fixed proportion of profits, and only the capitalists–entrepreneurs save.

In later writings Kalecki (1944b, 1971) abandons the assumptions that the owners of firms alone save, and that all savings are reinvested. In the revised version of the corresponding chapter of Kalecki (1944b), contained in Kalecki's (1954) *Theory of Economic Dynamics* (and reprinted in Kalecki 1971), it is recognized that only a fraction *a* of savings may be reinvested. It is in the discussion of the determinants of *a*, that a direct influence of expected demand on investment orders is admitted: Kalecki considers *a* to depend on the size of 'the market for the firm's products' and more generally on the desirability of investment:

> The reinvestment of savings on a *ceteris paribus* basis, that is, with constant aggregate profits, may encounter difficulties because the market for the firm's products is limited, and expansion into new spheres of activity involves considerable risk. On the other hand, an increment in 'internal' savings enables the firm to absorb outside funds at a higher rate if investment *is* considered desirable. This factor tends to increase investment decisions by more than the

increment in 'internal' savings. These conflicting factors leave us still uncertain about whether *a* will be greater or less than 1. (Kalecki 1971, p. 120)

These considerations amount to admitting that the increase of the own capital of firms is determined by shareholders on the basis of their idea of what the capital stock *should* be – an idea influenced by their expectations of sales, that is, of demand and by the associated productive capacity requirements. It does not seem to have been widely noticed[9] that in this way Kalecki totally reverses the line of causation of his previous writings. In Kalecki (1937a and 1939) he had made the reinvestment of profits (savings) determine the own capital of firms, hence the optimal stock of capital, and hence investment and output; expected demand played no role. In his later writings variations in the own capital of the firm no longer determine the variations in the desired total capital, rather the latter – determined by demand expectations – determine the desired own capital of the firm, and hence the amount of reinvested savings. Unfortunately, Kalecki does not integrate this insight into his theory of the cycle: the percentage *a* of savings which is reinvested remains a fixed number[10] as in 1944. He should, on the contrary, have treated such a coefficient as endogenously determined by expected demand, and therefore varying over the cycle.[11] This chain of causation is perfectly compatible with the rate of profits moving in step with the rate of interest.[12] It also avoids some little-noticed difficulties with the previous chain of causation, difficulties which will now be illustrated.

V

A first difficulty relates to a stock-flow problem in the determination of investment. Kalecki (1937b) says that his theory determines 'the amount invested k_0' (p. 443) or 'the size of investment planned' by a firm (p. 444) but in fact what his argument determines is the *optimal capital stock k_0* of the firm. The determination of the (rate of) investment, a flow, therefore gives rise to problems if the optimal capital stock changes discontinuously, unless a theory is provided determining the speed with which the actual capital stock is adjusted to the new optimal one. In the penultimate section of the article, Kalecki discusses the effects of a discontinuous variation of the rate of interest, and, in the last section, the effects of a discontinuous variation of the rate of return on capital, and he simply assumes that the rate of investment will be such as to bring, within the given period, the stock of capital to the new optimal amount k_0'. As is now well known, this amounts to leaving the rate of investment undetermined, because it is dependent on whether the period taken by the stock of capital to pass from k_0 to k_0' is arbitrarily assumed to be a year or a month or a week, etc. In his theory of the trade cycle, Kalecki is able unequivocally to derive the rate of investment (or rather, of investment orders) from this analysis only because he assumes that the rate of interest is given and constant and that C and MEC are continuous functions of time; then k_0 too is a continuous function of time, and its derivative with respect to time gives the rate of (net) investment orders. But this analysis cannot claim general validity. The constancy of the rate of interest is obviously untenable if the rate of interest is considered a policy variable: in that case one must admit the possibility that the rate of interest may be discontinuously changed. That C can only change continuously, at the level of individual firms or in the aggregate, is a plausible assumption *only if* it is assumed that its variations come only from the re-investment of profits of firms, a flow; but it becomes implausible the moment the possibility is admitted of lump-sum transfers of money capital (for example, previously accumulated savings held until then in the form of Treasury bonds) into an industry or firm, corresponding to an event such as the creation of a new firm, or the issue of new shares. That the rate of profits can only change continuously is also implausible. Kalecki obtains this result from the fact that the rate of profits is determined as the ratio of total profits to stock of capital, P/K, where profits are a *constant* share of income and the stock of capital is the integral of past new investment; thus, as income and the stock of capital only change gradually, so does P/K. But the assumption that the share of profits in national income is constant (or changes only gradually) appears hardly acceptable – empirical observation shows occasional sharp jumps of real wages, sometimes by more than 30 per cent in a single season of contract renewals (as in the Italian 'Hot Autumn' of 1969).

Therefore Kalecki's theory cannot do without a theory of the speed of adjustment to the optimal capital stock, but he does not provide such a theory. He does not accept the 'rising supply price of capital goods' argument of Keynes, Lerner, Witte and so on. His admission in Kalecki (1937a, p. 87) that a rise in investment may raise the price of investment goods is immediately qualified by noticing that the supply curve of investment goods 'is only slightly increasing', and in 1949 he writes of Keynes's theory of investment, 'The most important objection against this theory is that it presupposes a rising supply curve in production of investment goods which is unrealistic, at least for a considerable range of output' (Kalecki 1949, p. 61). Now, reverse L-shaped cost curves, Kalecki's characteristic assumption within his theory of investment appear to imply what might be called a bang-bang behaviour: when the economy's productive capacity is less than desired capacity, the investment goods industries should be observed to work at full capacity; when capacity exceeds desired capacity, gross investment should be zero. This conclusion throws doubt on such an approach to the explanation of investment, since empirical observation does not seem to support such behaviour – the generality of investment goods industries is often observed to work at less, even considerably less, than full capacity, even when net investment is positive. A more natural candidate to explain this observation is a direct dependence of desired capacity on demand. The latter, at least at the aggregate level, does change only gradually; therefore desired capacity also changes gradually, and investment is a finite flow.

VI

Some further implausible consequences of Kalecki's theory can be traced to his leaving out of consideration the existence of a direct tendency of productive capacity to adapt to production. To point them out, let us first briefly remember the way Kalecki connects the principle of increasing risk with the explanation of fluctuations in his writings on the cycle of the period 1937–39. The rate of interest is given,[13] and so are prices. The own capital of each firm C is given by the integral of past reinvested savings of the firm's owner(s). Kalecki assumes that firms try, at time t, to reach the desired total capital stock $k_0(t)$ by issuing investment orders for the necessary amount. Therefore, if the own capital of firms C changes over time in a continuous manner, and if the rate of profit and hence the debt to own capital ratio δ are given, net investment orders D_t are equal to $dk_0/dt = (1 + \delta)dC/dt$. Kalecki assumes that net savings S (which are assumed to come entirely from the capitalists–entrepreneurs) are all reinvested, that is, they go entirely to increase C; hence, $dC/dt = S_t$. If the rate of return remained constant, net investment decisions and orders at time t, D_t, would therefore be given by $D_t = (1 + \delta)S_t$, or, since savings equal investment, $D_t = (1 + \delta)I_t$; assuming, as Kalecki does, a lag of length $\frac{1}{2}\theta$ between investment orders and investment (production of investment goods),[14] that is $I_t = D_{t - \frac{1}{2}\theta}$, one would obtain $D_t = (1 + \delta)D_{t - \frac{1}{2}\theta}$, which implies

$$I_t = (1 + \delta)I_{t - \frac{1}{2}\theta} \qquad (11.1)$$

(It is not very convincing that investors should persistently ignore the construction lag θ, should have static expectations in the face of a reality which persistently contradicts them, and should not try to extrapolate economic conditions so as to reach time $t + \theta$ with the stock of capital, or productive capacity, which is expected to be optimal then, rather than with the one that would have been optimal at time t. But for our purposes, this deficiency is relatively unimportant and will not be further discussed.)

This extremely simple relationship[15] is not what Kalecki obtains, simply because he makes the average rate of profit depend on the aggregate capital–output ratio. Kalecki takes the *share* of profits in national income P/Y as given and derives the variations in the *rate* of profits P/K from the variations in national income, where K is treated as unaffected by changes in Y (or P). Variations of investment cause proportional variations of income (because of the multiplier, which is assumed to be instantaneous), hence proportional variations of P/K, hence (assuming the rate of interest to be given or to vary less than the rate of profits) variations of the optimal leverage ratio, hence of investment decisions. Thus, the accumulation of reinvested profits and the realized rate of profits determine the optimal amount of capital, which firms proceed to try and reach, without any role being given to the long-period tendency to minimize costs of production by adapting productive capacity to production. Thus, for instance, Kalecki's theory (which, as noticed above, never incorporates into its formalization the sensible observations of 1954 on demand directly influencing investment) would have us believe that, given a situation of optimal utilization of capacity and a decrease in demand, the average utilization of capacity becomes less than optimal, yet firms may still decide on net investment if the effect on the desired capital stock k_0 (as determined by the principle of increasing risk), of the increase in own capital out of current profits outweighs the depressing effect of the lower average rate of return P/K. But why, in this case, should firms invest rather than be content with their plants, or disinvest by waiting until wear and tear has brought capacity back into line with demand?

Another way of making the same point is by reflecting on the implications of Kalecki's theory for the degree of utilization of capacity in steady growth. The conditions for steady growth imply, within Kalecki's theory, that the degree of capacity utilization is endogenously determined, and therefore there is no room for its determination on the basis of cost minimization. This can be shown very easily, if the assumption is made that all savings are reinvested (the case of a different from 1 would not alter the conclusions so long as a is given, but the formulae would be more cumbersome). Let us simplify the notation by choosing the time unit so that the average period of production $\theta = 2$, and hence $\frac{1}{2}\theta = 1$. Then equation 11.1, which must be valid in steady growth, becomes:

$$I_t = (1 + \delta)I_{t-1} \qquad (11.2)$$

where, given the rate of interest, the optimal degree of leverage δ is a function of the rate of profits $r = P/K$: $\delta = \delta(r)$. Equation 10.2 shows that, with our choice of the time unit, since $I_t = I_0 e^{gt}$, it is also true that $1 + \delta = e^g$. It is well known that, in steady growth, for an economy where income is divided between wages and profits, and where savings are a given percentage s_P of profits only, the formula $g = s_P r$ holds where $r = P/K$ is the rate of profits. Thus we get

$$1 + \delta(r) = e^{s_P r} \tag{11.3}$$

one equation in one unknown variable, r. Kalecki takes as given, not r, but the share of profits in national income P/Y. If we call $v = K/Y$ the capital–output ratio, or degree of utilization of capacity, we obtain $P/Y = (P/K)\cdot(K/Y) = rv$. Thus, in steady growth, rv being given and r being determined by equation 11.3, v is endogenously determined. Yet firms are not dissatisfied with it. There is no room for v being determined by the tendency to long-run cost minimization, that is, by the tendency to adopt the optimal degree of utilization of capacity. Thus Kalecki's theory denies the existence of a force which is definitely at work in capitalist economies. What seems to have escaped Kalecki is that investors would be irrational to plan having a degree of utilization on new plants equal to the one on existing plants (when the latter degree of utilization is not optimal), rather than plan investment so that new plants are (expected to be) optimally utilized (Vianello 1989, p. 180).

VII

This last observation appears to throw doubt on one further aspect of Kalecki's theory. As pointed out by Vianello (1989) and others, what has just been said implies that the expected rate of profits on new plants is going to be the one connected with a normal (optimal) degree of utilization of capacity; therefore, it is not going to be altered by changes in the degree of utilization of capacity of already existing plants. This is the 'normal' rate of profits, which governs capital mobility across industries, and therefore enters 'normal' long-period prices, and determines the value of existing plants.[16] Therefore, a decrease of the degree of capacity utilization of a firm, if expected to be lasting, will cause a decrease of the value of the firm's fixed capital, which will become roughly equal to the value of the fixed capital of a firm producing the same volume of production from fixed plants of the same expected economic life but of optimal size for that volume of production. Accordingly, the meaning of a given own capital of firms becomes unclear in the face of changes in the degree of utilization of capacity.

VIII

The preceding arguments imply that Kalecki's *theoretical* reasons for stressing the accumulation of own capital by firms and the differential between rate of profits and rate of interest as the main determinants of aggregate investment are unconvincing. If we leave technical progress aside, aggregate investment would appear to depend on expected demand. If and only if a durable increase in demand is expected, investors will expect to sell an increased amount of product at prices not below normal (and thus affording at least the ruling 'normal' rate of profits on the new investment); otherwise they will not effect net investments, whatever the rate of profits and the market form.[17]

On the other hand, at least the present writer – admittedly not a specialist on this last topic – is not aware of convincing *empirical* evidence in support of Kalecki's theory.[18] If I may be allowed some tentative remarks, I find it difficult to imagine bankers refusing credit to efficient firms, for investments clearly corresponding to expansions of demand; as to entrepreneurs, they are seldom going to miss opportunities for sales increases and they can raise capital in a variety of ways, including the emission of new equity; or there will be creation of new firms. The normal situation of capitalist economies (except when the monetary authorities impose forms of credit rationing) would appear to be one of chronic excess of investible funds relative to investment outlets.

NOTES

1. In reconstructing the historical evolution of Kalecki's views on investment I make no claim to originality: my discussion is based on Chilosi (1979) and even more on the detailed study by Dibenedetto (1990).
2. As for example Wicksell realized, when capital is measured as an amount of value the rate of interest is not equal to the 'marginal product' of capital; see Garegnani (1970), Wicksell (1934, p. 268).
3. The same criticism applies to one derivation of a decreasing investment schedule which is sometimes claimed to make no reference to capital–labour substitution, the 'array of opportunities' approach where a list of investment projects is assumed to be available, with the stream of expected net returns given, and independent of the rate of interest.
4. See Garegnani (1979), Panico (1985), Vianello (1985), Schefold (1985), Pivetti (1985). Pivetti is perhaps the most explicit on the broader implications of such a view; also see Pivetti (1988), where he convincingly responds to some critical comments by Nell and Wray. The notion of competition implicit in this theory is not the neoclassical one of price-taking but the classical one of price undercutting if one can afford to; see Petri (1989).
5. The study of the effects of variations in the rate of interest which are believed to be temporary would require a different analysis, taking into account the peculiarities of each situation; this was not attempted in Petri (1989) nor will it be in the present chapter.

6. Kalecki's criticism of Keynes's argument for a decreasing MEC schedule had been based, in his review of the *General Theory*, on the argument that 'it says nothing about the investment *decisions* of entrepreneurs, who make their calculations in disequilibrium on the basis of the *existing* prices of investment goods ... Keynes's theory only determines the *ex post* level of investment and says nothing about *ex ante* investment' (Kalecki 1936, our trans. from the Italian trans., p. 213). But it is not clear why Keynes ought not to have proceeded as he did: entrepreneurs will be quick to revise their investment plans if their attempts to implement them change the data motivating those plans, in particular, prices: it is rather Kalecki's theory which can be accused of neglecting this latter fact. The same counter-objection can be raised against the criticism of the Keynesian rationale for a decreasing MEC in Kalecki (1937b). Kalecki essentially identifies investment *ex ante* and *ex post* (his own positive theory determines *ex ante* investment decisions, but in his cycle theory it is implicitly taken to determine *ex post* investment as well: in other words, Kalecki implicitly assumes that investment orders are never cancelled owing to a modification of economic conditions due to the investment orders themselves). But such an identification is only legitimate if investment plans *can* be realized. An infinite investment plan is not realizable, and would only result in an increase in input prices which would quickly cause firms to revise their plans. Therefore the fact that firms may plan an infinite *ex ante* investment does not appear to be a decisive weakness of the theory Kalecki criticizes: it suffices to assume, as Keynes implicitly does, that the investment decisions adjust with sufficient speed to their own effects on prices. On the contrary, one advantage of Keynes's approach over Kalecki's is the ability of the former, but not of the latter, to take into account the formation of new firms. In support of the need for a different theory of investment, Kalecki also argues that the size of *individual* firms, and, in particular, the fact that 'in a given industry at the same time large and small enterprises are started', is not explained by Keynesian arguments, nor by recourse to imperfect competition (Kalecki 1937b, p. 442). But the possibility of starting new firms may itself cause an indeterminacy in passing from the decisions of individual firms to aggregate investment, an indeterminacy which does not arise in Keynes's case.

7. Kalecki (1944a) again openly admits that a decrease of the rate of interest will increase investment; he then adds that such a decrease should not be relied upon as a means of reaching and maintaining full employment, because the long-term rate of interest changes only very slowly, and its decrease encounters a lower limit in the fact that it must always be somewhat higher than the short-term rate of interest, which cannot be negative. Thus the theoretical principle is admitted, although its practical relevance is belittled. But Kalecki does not deny that if a gradual decrease only of the rate of interest were needed, and if the lower limit were not very close to the actual level of the rate of interest, then a decrease of the rate of interest might be a feasible way to increase employment.

8. These observations are not new. Buchanan and Calkins (1938) objected to Kalecki that the principle of increasing risk would not operate if the new capital were raised by issuing ordinary shares rather than by borrowing. Kalecki (1938) replied that the issue of ordinary shares will encounter a limit in the fact that the controlling shareholders do not want to dilute their control; later he added two further 'restraining factors': 'There is a risk that the investment financed by an issue of shares may not increase company profits proportionately as much as the issue increased the share and reserve capital'; 'Share issues are restrained by the limited market for shares of a given company' (Kalecki, 1971, pp. 107–8). None of the three obstacles appears convincing. Of the first, Kalecki himself (1971, p. 107) observes that it can be overcome by the controlling group building up holding companies. The second can only arise if the issue of new shares is excessive relative to the prospective profits. As to the third, the market for the shares of a given company depends on the latter's prospective profitability – thus the prospect of profitable investments due to demand expansion enlarges that market. The objection that investment may come from the creation of new firms is in Ackley (1978, p. 651). If

one tried to answer it by arguing that the creation of new firms would require an increase in the proportion of shares and/or of loans to firms in the portfolios of financial investors, and thus an increase in the rates of return on shares or on loans to firms relative to the basic interest rate (so that portfolio-choice considerations replace the leverage ratio of firms as the reason for an upward-sloping aggregate supply schedule for credit), then one would have first to demonstrate the dubious proposition that the supply schedule for credit actually is upward sloping. But even then, the argument would hold that the rate of profits will tend to move in step with the interest rate.

9. Neither Chilosi (1979), nor Sawyer (1985), nor Laski (1987) notice it.

10. See Kalecki (1971), the coefficient *a* in equation 10.2, p. 113.

11. No thorough examination will be offered here of Kalecki's last attempt at a theory of investment (Kalecki 1968), both because it is often unclear (for example, the foundations of the crucial statement, on p. 169, that 'the higher, *ceteris paribus*, the level of investment, the lower the rate of profit it "fetches" ' remain obscure), and because a thorough discussion would have required an analysis of the influence of technical progress on investment, a topic falling outside our present concerns. Anyway, in that article the observations of 1954 on the potential direct effect of demand on investment are not taken up.

12. It may be noticed that admitting, as Kalecki does, that the percentage of savings reinvested into firms may be *greater* than 100 per cent comes very close to admitting that the rate of profits will move in step with the rate of interest. It means, in fact, that firm owners may own savings invested elsewhere, for example, in securities (Kalecki 1971, p. 106), and that they may at a certain point decide to invest them into their own firm. It is then only a short step from this to admitting a general mobility of financial capital into or out of ownership of firms depending on the relative convenience of doing so – a mobility which must result in an equalization of the net-of-risk rates of return (cf. Panico 1985).

13. In 1933 Kalecki had assumed that 'the rate of interest increases sufficiently slowly in relation to the gross profitability P/K for $[I/K]$ to be an increasing function [of P/K]' (Kalecki 1933–[1971], p. 7), but this has the same consequences as assuming that the basic rate of interest does not change, which is what he assumes in later works.

14. The reason for the lag is well summarized by Chilosi, 'Investment consists of the total production of investment goods, which . . . does not coincide with the creation of new productive capacity, because it includes the production, in its various stages, of the yet-to-be-completed investment goods. But, given the implicit hypothesis that the construction of investment goods proceeds at a uniform pace, investment is equal, in each unit of time, to the total value of the yet-to-be-completed orders divided by the production period and, approximately, to the amount of investment orders issued at the moment which precedes the actual one by half the production period [i.e. by half of θ − F. P.]' (Chilosi 1979, p. 31, our transl.).

15. The only difference in the formal analysis of Kalecki (1971) is that only a fixed percentage *a* of savings is reinvested, so that equation 10.1 becomes $I_t = (1 + \delta)aI_{t - \frac{1}{2}\theta}$.

16. The 'normal' rate of profits, and not P/K as defined by Kalecki, is what is determined by the rate of interest according to the considerations of section I above. But up to this point in our discussion, the distinction was not relevant. In particular, in an equilibrium steady growth P/K ought to coincide with the 'normal' rate of profits. In fact, P/K would always coincide with the 'normal' rate of profits, if the value K of the existing stock of capital were determined by capitalizing the future stream of net returns (and therefore varied with the degree of utilization, as noticed in the remainder of the section), rather than being a constant as Kalecki assumes.

17. Cf. Garegnani (1962, p. 91, note 1).

18. The view that investment depends on demand does not exclude an influence, in certain cases, of the wealth of the owners of a firm on the amount of credit they can obtain. But if certain firms cannot grow as big as they would like, this does not meant that other

firms – perhaps new entrants – will not make up for it. Nor is it excluded that evidence might be collected, showing investment to be positively related to internal liquidity (e.g. Fazzari and Mott 1986–7); not only will internal liquidity be greater when sales are greater, but also investment will presumably be higher in the industries where the rate of profits is higher, because of capital's search for the highest return. Therefore, firms or industries which invest more should be expected to be more profitable, hence to have more retained earnings and liquidity. Thus the evidence may simply reflect on one side, the influence of demand, and on the other, the forces determining the *composition* of investment, rather than its aggregate amount.

REFERENCES

Ackley, G., (1978) *Macroeconomics: Theory and Policy*, New York: Collier Macmillan.

Buchanan, N.S., and Calkins, R.D. (1938) 'A Comment on Mr. Kalecki's Principle of Increasing Risk', *Economica*, **15**, 455–8.

Chilosi, A. (ed.) (1979) *Kalecki: Antologia di scritti di teoria economica*, Bologna: Il Mulino.

Dibenedetto, G. (1990) *La teoria degli investimenti di Michal Kalecki*, unpublished MA dissertation, Facoltà di Scienze Economiche e Bancarie, University of Siena.

Fazzari, S.M. and Mott, T. (1986–7) 'The Investment Theories of Kalecki and Keynes: An Empirical Study of Firm Data, 1970–82', *Journal of Post Keynesian Economics*, **9** (2), Winter.

Garegnani, P. (1962) *Il problema della domanda effettiva nello sviluppo economico italiano*, Roma: SVIMEZ.

Garegnani, P. (1970) 'Heterogeneous Capital, the Production Function and the Theory of Distribution', *Review of Economic Studies*, **37**, 407–36.

Garegnani, P. (1978–9) 'Notes on Consumption, Investment and Effective Demand – Parts I and II', *Cambridge Journal of Economics*, **2** and **3**, 335–53, 63–82.

Garegnani, P. (1979) 'Notes on Consumption, Investment and Effective Demand: A Reply to Joan Robinson', *Cambridge Journal of Economics*, **3**, June.

Kalecki, M. (1933) 'Outline of a Theory of the Business Cycle' (English Trans. of 'Pròba teorii koniunktury', Warsaw, 1933), in Kalecki (1971).

Kalecki, M. (1936) 'Alcune considerazioni sulla teoria di Keynes' (Ital. trans. of 'Pare uwag o teorii Keynesa', *Ekonomista*), in Chilosi (1979).

Kalecki, M. (1937a) 'A Theory of the Business Cycle', *Review of Economic Studies*, **4**, 77–97.

Kalecki, M. (1937b) 'The Principle of Increasing Risk', *Economica*, **4**, 440–47.

Kalecki, M. (1938) 'A Reply to "A Comment on Mr. Kalecki's Principle of Increasing Risk" ', *Economica*, **5**, 459–60.

Kalecki, M. (1939) *Essays in the Theory of Economic Fluctuations*, London: Allen and Unwin.

Kalecki, M. (1944a) 'Three Ways to Full Employment', in Oxford University Institute of Statistics, *The Economics of Full Employment*, Oxford: Blackwell.

Kalecki, M. (1944b) *Studies in Economic Dynamics*, New York: Farrar and Rinehart.

Kalecki, M. (1949) 'A New Approach to the Theory of Business Cycles', *Review of Economic Studies*, **16**, 57–64.

Kalecki, M. (1968) 'Trend and the Business Cycle', *Economic Journal*; repr. in Kalecki (1971).

Kalecki, M. (1971) *Selected Essays on the Dynamics of the Capitalist Economy*, Cambridge: Cambridge University Press.

Laski, K. (1987) 'Kalecki, Michal', in J. Eatwell, M. Milgate, P. Newman, eds, *The New Palgrave – Dictionary of Economics*, London: Macmillan.

Minsky, H. (1975) *John Maynard Keynes*, New York: Columbia University Press.

Nell, E. (1988) 'Does the Rate of Interest Determine the Rate of Profit?', *Political Economy: Studies in the Surplus Approach*, **4**, 263–7.

Nickell, S. (1978) *The Investment Decisions of Firms*, Cambridge: Cambridge University Press.

Panico, C. (1985) 'Market Forces and the Relation between the Rates of Interest and of Profits', *Contributions to Political Economy*, **4**, 37–60.

Petri, F. (1989) 'Notes on Investment as a Decreasing Function of the Interest Rate', unpublished paper, read at the 1989 Trieste Summer School of Economics.

Pivetti, M. (1985) 'On the Monetary Explanation of Distribution', *Political Economy: Studies in the Surplus Approach*, **1** (2), 73–103.

Pivetti, M. (1988) 'On the Monetary Explanation of Distribution: A Rejoinder to Nell and Wray', *Political Economy: Studies in the Surplus Approach*, **4** (2), 275–83.

Sawyer, M.C. (1985) *The Economics of Michal Kalecki*, London: Macmillan.

Schefold, B. (1985) 'Cambridge Price Theory: Special Model or General Theory of Value?', *American Economic Review*, **75**, 140–45.

Sraffa, P. (1960) *Production of Commodities by Means of Commodities*, Cambridge: Cambridge University Press.

Vianello, F. (1985) 'The Pace of Accumulation', *Political Economy: Studies in the Surplus Approach*, **1** (1), 69–87.

Vianello, F. (1989) 'Effective Demand and the Rate of Profits: Some Thoughts on Marx, Kalecki and Sraffa', in M. Sebastiani (ed.), *Kalecki's Relevance Today*, London: Macmillan.

Wicksell, K. (1934) *Lectures on Political Economy*, vol. I, London: Routledge and Kegan Paul.

Wray, L.R. (1988) 'The Monetary Explanation of Distribution: A Critique of Pivetti', *Political Economy: Studies in the Surplus Approach*, **4** (2), 269–73.

12. Class Conflict and Accumulation

Peter Skott[1]

The process of accumulation has been analysed from many different perspectives, with neoclassical, neo-Marxian and post-Keynesian theories being perhaps the most influential. In this chapter I shall disregard neoclassical theories, which assume full employment at all times, and focus instead on the neo-Marxian and post-Keynesian approaches. These two approaches emphasize different aspects of the economy. Post-Keynesians primarily consider the product market and the equilibrium between desired saving and desired investment. Neo-Marxians, in contrast, often play down 'realization problems' in order to analyse the conflict between capitalists and workers over the intensity of work and the distribution of income. Thus, the two approaches may appear to be complementary, and the main purpose of this chapter is to discuss the possibility of integrating neo-Marxian and post-Keynesian insights within a common framework. A large and growing literature has been devoted to this problem and much of what I have to say may sound familiar. But although there are similarities between my analysis and other recent contributions[2] there are also, I believe, important differences.

In order to focus more strongly on some key issues I shall follow most of the existing literature and consider neither technical progress nor the choice of technique; there will be no discussion of open-economy issues, sectoral disaggregation or the public sector, and financial and monetary problems will also be ignored. The analysis will be conducted within a simple one-sector economy with two types of agent, households and firms, and a fixed-coefficient production function.

Needless to say, these simplifications cannot be justified by the unimportance of the issues which have been excluded. Technical progress and the spatial unevenness of the growth process arguably constitute the two most important questions in long-term growth. The questions analysed here would also, however, have to be faced in a more complete analysis of the growth process.

The chapter is in three sections. First, some simple neo-Marxian and post-Keynesian models are described. A synthesis of the two theories is presented, and this is followed by a few concluding remarks on the consistency of the synthesis with the stylized facts. Numerical simulations are given in the Appendix.

NEO-MARXIAN AND POST-KEYNESIAN THEORIES

The dynamic interactions between distribution and accumulation are central to neo-Marxian theory. The distribution of income, in this approach, is determined by the relative strength of the two major classes, workers and capitalists. In some simple specifications, relative strength is taken as an exogenous variable, and the share of labour (or the real wage rate) then may also be treated as exogenous. Marglin (1984b), for instance, assumes that there is a given 'conventional wage' and a given conventional share of wage in income:

$$\omega = \omega_o \qquad (12.1a)$$

where ω is the wage share.

The conventional wage reflects 'community standards' which depend, in part, on 'class power'. It may not be satisfactory, however, to treat wages as exogenous, and the relative strength of the classes is often related to the size of the reserve army of labour, workers being strong when the reserve army is small (when the unemployment rate is low).[3] Algebraically, this leads to the specification:

$$\omega = f(1 - e); f' < 0 \qquad (12.1b)$$

where e is the rate of employment.

Alternatively, one might argue that high employment leads to *increasing* real wages. This assumption yields the Goodwin specification,[4]

$$\hat{\omega} = \varphi(1 - e); \varphi' < 0. \qquad (12.1c)$$

Equations 12.1a–12.1c represent three different neo-Marxian specifications of the distribution of income, and the dynamic behaviour of the economy clearly depends on the chosen specification as well as on the determination of saving and investment. With respect to this latter question there is near-unanimity among neo-Marxian writers. Standard assumptions imply that the rate of accumulation is positively related to the rate of profits and by assumption, both the capital–ouput and the capital–labour ratios are constant. It follows that the rate of accumulation is equal to the rate of growth of employment and that both are inversely related to the share of wages in income,

$$\hat{K} = \hat{L} = g(\omega); \, g' < 0. \tag{12.2}$$

The combination of equations 12.1a and 12.2 implies steady growth at the rate $g(\omega_0)$. An increase in the exogenous wage share ω_0 thus reduces the growth rate. If equation 12.1b is used instead of 12.1a we get a simple differential equation. The rate of employment grows at the rate $\hat{L} - n$, where n is the growth rate of the labour force, and it follows that:

$$\hat{e} = g(f(1 - e)) - n = \psi(e); \, \psi' < 0 \tag{12.3b}$$

Assuming that there is an equilibrium solution $g(f(1 - e^*)) = n$ with $0 < e^* < 1$, it follows from equation 12.3b that the economy converges to this equilibrium, and in equilibrium the rate of growth is equal to the natural growth rate n. Hence an increase in workers' strength – an upward shift in the wage function f – will have no permanent effects on the growth rate but merely increase the rate of unemployment.

A similar conclusion applies to the model described by equations 12.1c–12.2. This two-dimensional system of differential equations represents a slightly generalized version of Goodwin's classic formulation of Marx's 'general law of accumulation' (Goodwin 1967), and in contrast to the specification 12.1b–12.2. we get conservative fluctuations in employment and income shares. But an upward shift in the φ-function leads to a rise in the equilibrium rate of unemployment.

The equilibrium condition for the product market is the starting point for post-Keynesian growth theory. A general specification assumes that both I/K and S/K are functions of the utilization rate u and the profit share π,

$$I/K = i(u,\pi) \, ; \, i_u > 0 \, , \, i_\pi > 0 \tag{12.4}$$

$$S/K = s(u,\pi) \, ; \, s_u > 0 \, , \, s_\pi > 0 \tag{12.5}$$

and the equilibrium condition becomes:

$$i(u,\pi) = s(u,\pi). \tag{12.6}$$

Equation 12.6 does not suffice to determine both u and π (and thereby $\hat{K}$), and there are several ways of closing the model.[5] Kaldor's solution in his work on growth and distribution was to impose full employment,

$$\hat{L} = n. \tag{12.7a}$$

With a fixed coefficient production function the change in utilization is then given by:

$$\hat{u} = \hat{L} - \hat{K} = n - i(u.\pi) + \delta \tag{12.8a}$$

where δ is the rate of depreciation. Assuming that equation 12.6 defines π as a function of u,

$$\pi = \theta(u), \tag{12.9}$$

the evolution of u is determined by a simple differential equation:

$$\hat{u} = n - i(u,\theta(u)) + \delta = \xi(u). \tag{12.10a}$$

This equation has a stable equilibrium solution for $\xi' < 0$.[6]

Marglin (1984a) uses a different closure. He implicitly assumes that the utilization rate is at a given, constant level:

$$u = \bar{u}. \tag{12.7b}$$

Using equations 12.7b and 12.9 the equilibrium growth rate is fully determined in this version of post-Keynesian theory.[7] A Kaleckian mark-up specification, finally, has been used by Rowthorn (1981); Dutt (1984), and Taylor (1985). Ignoring raw materials and intermediate inputs and assuming a fixed coefficient production function, a constant mark-up on variable cost is equivalent to a constant profit share:

$$\pi = \bar{\pi}. \tag{12.7c}$$

With π given by firms' pricing behaviour, the equilibrium condition for the product market now determines the utilization rate of capital.[8]

These post-Keynesian models can be used to analyse the effects of changes in 'animal spirits' and other factors influencing the equilibrium condition for the product market. But the absence of a labour market is an important limitation and much richer results can be obtained by combining the post-Keynesian and neo-Marxian frameworks.

A SYNTHESIS

The integration of Marxian and Keynesian theories can be accomplished in a variety of ways. One approach – described more fully in Skott (1989b,

1989c) – is to relate firms' production and employment decisions explicitly to both the state of demand in the product market and the relative strength of workers in the labour market.

The existence of a production lag implies that output and employment are predetermined at any moment in time. But – in the tradition of Keynes's analysis in the *Treatise on Money* – it may be assumed that product prices and profit margins adjust so as to bring the demand for output into equality with supply. Realized profit margins thus reflect the state of demand: the profit margin is high when production is below the level that firms would have chosen had they been able to fully anticipate the level of demand. Firms react to discrepancies between actual production and desired production, and changes in employment and production should therefore be positively related to the realized profit margin.

The profit margin – or the profit share, there is a one-to-one correspondence – are not the only influence on output growth: the labour market and the relative strength of labour must also be taken into account. A low rate of unemployment makes it more difficult for firms to attract additional workers with suitable qualifications and furthermore, it shifts the balance of power in favour of workers. A strong working class can be expected to dampen firms' expansion plans so these effects point in the same direction. They suggest that changes in production and employment will be inversely related to the employment rate.

Algebraically, the analysis can be summarized by a relation linking changes in production to both the profit share and the employment rate:

$$\hat{Y} = h(\pi, e) \; ; \; h_\pi > 0, \, h_e < 0. \tag{12.11}$$

By assumption, the output–labour ratio is constant and the labour force grows at the rate n. Equation 12.11 – the *output expansion function* – can therefore be rewritten in terms of employment changes:

$$\hat{e} = \hat{Y} - n = h(\pi, e) - n. \tag{12.12}$$

Equation 12.12 is now combined with the Keynesian saving and investment functions, equations 12.4–12.5. The equilibrium condition 12.6 defines π as a function of u – cf. Equation 12.9 – and if it is assumed that $i_u > s_u$ and $i_\pi < s_\pi$ then π is increasing in u. Substituting this equilibrium condition into equation 12.12 we get:

$$\hat{e} = h(\theta(u), e) - n \; ; \; \frac{\partial h}{\partial u} = h_\theta \theta' > 0, \, h_e < 0. \tag{12.13}$$

The time-path of u is also fully described. We have

$$\hat{u} = \hat{Y} - \hat{K} = h(\theta(u),e) - i(u,\theta(u)) + \delta. \qquad (12.14)$$

and equations 12.13–12.14 define an autonomous, two-dimensional system of differential equations. Using the Poincaré–Bendixson theorem it can be shown that under reasonable assumptions (*i*) the system has a unique equilibrium, (*ii*) the equilibrium is locally asymptotically unstable but (*iii*) a limit cycle exists and the economy will exhibit perpetual fluctuations around the equilibrium solution (see Skott 1989b, 1989c).

Essentially, the local instability of the equilibrium is caused by the interaction of Keynesian multiplier and accelerator mechanisms: the output expansion function describes the (fast) multiplier adjustment of output towards a (moving) short run equilibrium level, while the investment function includes the accelerator influence of utilization rates on accumulation. One would expect the interaction of these forces to generate a trade cycle with a periodicity of four to six years and this is not the kind of cycle often discussed by Marxists: the Goodwin model, it has been argued, yields cycles of approximately 20–25 years.[9]

Can the existence of long cycles be explained within the present framework? And what kind of interaction exists between the different cyclical mechanisms and the cycles they produce? The balance of power between the classes varies with the employment rate but in addition to these short-term fluctuations over the trade cycle there may be long-term forces at work.

A deep depression with mass unemployment is likely to have lasting effects on workers' attitudes while, conversely, prolonged periods with high average rates of employment slowly undermine discipline in the labour market. Thus, if one wants to understand the surge in labour militancy in the late 1960s 'it is hardly irrelevant that by the late sixties only a minor part of the active population had had personal experience of the huge unemployment of the pre-war depression' (Gelting 1981, p. 4).

Slow and cumulative changes in workers' militancy can be captured by including a separate variable x in the output expansion function and the investment function, this variable expressing the effects of underlying working class militancy on firms' production and investment decisions. The system then becomes:

$$\hat{e} = h(\theta(u,x),e,x) - n \; ; \; h_x < 0 \qquad (12.15)$$

$$\hat{u} = h(\theta(u,x),e,x) - i(u,\theta(u,x),x) + \delta \; ; \; i_x < 0 \qquad (12.16)$$

and a new equation describing the time-path of x must be added. The assumed dependency of x on past movements in employment can be formalized in different ways, the simplest specification being:

$$\hat{x} = f(e) \; ; f' < 0. \tag{12.17}$$

This new three-dimensional system – equations 12.15–12.17 – incorporates the original two-dimensional system as a special case but, more interestingly, it also generalizes the simple Goodwin structure in a straightforward manner.

Goodwin – along with most Marxists – disregarded Keynesian problems and the associated short-term fluctuations in the utilization of capital, and if we impose the condition $u = \bar{u}$ instead of equation 12.16 we get a Goodwin-type system. The growth rate of employment (the rate of accumulation) becomes inversely dependent on workers' strength and militancy, and militancy, in turn, increases when employment is high. The negative feedback from the level of employment to changes in employment will, however, alter the dynamic picture: the original Goodwin system is – as is well known – structurally unstable, and the negative feedback in the present model implies damped rather than conservative fluctuations. The simple Lotka–Volterra system with conservative fluctuations emerges as a limiting case for $h_e \to 0$.

More interesting dynamics can be generated if equation 12.17 is replaced by a slightly more complicated feedback system. Animal spirits and business confidence, rather than worker militancy, are the proximate influences on firms' production and investment decisions. High worker militancy undermines business confidence and reduces animal spirits but it may be useful to distinguish between militancy itself and its cumulative effects on animal spirits. If $-x$ and z express animal spirits and worker militancy, respectively, then equations 12.15–12.16 remain unchanged but equation 12.17 is replaced by the following new relations:

$$\dot{x} = k(z) \; ; k' > 0. \tag{12.17a}$$

$$\dot{z} = l(e) \; ; l' > 0. \tag{12.17b}$$

Equation 12.17a describes the effect of militancy on animal spirits and 12.17b relates changes in militancy to employment.

It is readily seen that if the reaction speeds in equations 12.17a–12.17b are slow relative to the fast trade cycle movements in equations 12.15–12.16 – and this is what one would expect – then the complete system, equations 12.15–12.16 and 12.17a–12.17b, will almost decouple. The fast system – equations 12.15–12.16 – generates fluctuations in e around an average $\bar{e} = \bar{e}(x)$ determined by the slow-moving variable x, and fast trade cycle fluctuations will almost cancel out in their effect on militancy.

A good approximation to the movement of the system can therefore be obtained by using the average value $\bar{e}$ instead of e in equation 12.17b,

$$\dot{z} = 1(\bar{e}(x)) \, ; \frac{d\dot{z}}{dx} = 1'\bar{e}' < 0 \qquad (12.17b')$$

and equations 12.17a and 12.17b′ describe a self-contained Lotka–Volterra system.

This analysis suggests that the formalization in equations 12.15–12.16 and 12.17a–12.17b of a Marxian–Keynesian synthesis may produce two distinct cycles: the Marxian interaction between militancy, business confidence and employment may generate a long cycle while a Keynesian multiplier–accelerator mechanism (augmented by labour market effects on production decisions) may generate fast trade-cycle movements around these long swings.[10] The alternative system 12.15–12.17 includes a stabilizing negative feedback. With a slow speed of convergence – and a cycle length of about 25 years – it may not however, be empirically relevant whether in fact the cycles are damped or conservative.

Complete analytical solutions of the systems cannot be obtained and numerical methods are needed to check these conjectures. Simulation experiments have therefore been carried out and some of the results for a typical run of the model are presented in the Appendix. The intuitive expectations have been confirmed for a range of parameter values, but the simulations have also shown that the outcome can be sensitive to the precise specification of the functional relationships.

It should be noted that in this model there is a connection between the severity of the trade cycle and the phase of the long Marxian cycle: trade cycle fluctuations are pronounced during depressed periods while periods of prosperity and high average employment reduce the amplitude of the trade cycle (or eliminate the trade cycle altogether). There is a straightforward explanation for this result. The negative feedback from $\hat{e}$ to e in equation 12.15 tends to stabilize the system, and output growth is more sensitive to marginal variations in the rate of employment when employment is high than when there is a large reserve army of labour. Firms' production plans – the value of $\hat{Y}$ – is unlikely to depend critically on whether the reserve army is 20 per cent or 21 per cent of the labour force; a reserve army of 1 per cent, on the other hand, is very different from a reserve army of 2 per cent. The model therefore predicts milder fluctuations during phases of prosperity than during depressions.

THE STYLIZED FACTS – SOME CONCLUDING REMARKS

The models analysed in this chapter are simple, and it can be dangerously misleading to apply highly abstract models directly to empirical observations. Nevertheless, it may be interesting briefly to consider the stylized facts on employment, capital utilization, profitability and worker militancy.

With respect to the long swings in militancy and employment, the formal model predicts that the employment rate should lead militancy by approximately a quarter of a cycle and that militancy should be rising (falling) when the employment rate is at its peak (through). Militancy is difficult to measure but arguably strike activity can be used as a reasonable indicator, and for the post-war period we have strike data for most OECD countries. Figure A12.1 presents some of this evidence and the observed pattern does not contradict the theoretical prediction. High strike activity in the late 1940s is followed by high unemployment in the 1950s. Strike activity reaches a trough in the late 1950s and early 1960s, and after a lag of 5–10 years unemployment falls to its lowest level. Strike activity then increases rapidly in the late 1960s and the rise in unemployment follows with a 5–10 year lag. This lag, finally, is maintained when strike activity and unemployment reach new peaks in the mid 1970s and early 1980s, respectively.[11]

Turning to the stylized pattern of short-term trade cycles, it is well established that profitability and capital utilization tend to move together over the cycle and that these two variables lead movements in the employment rate (see for example, Hahnel and Sherman 1982, and Zarnowitz 1985). This is precisely the pattern predicted by the short-term interactions in equations 12.15–12.16 (see Skott 1989b).

The model, in conclusion, is highly simplified but it does seem to be consistent with the stylized pattern of both long- and short-term fluctuations in the advanced capitalist economies.

NOTES

1. I wish to thank Arne Vajhøj and, especially, Erland H. Nielsen for initiating me into the art of computer simulation and for sorting out the errors in some of the first simulations. This chapter has also benefited from discussion at the conference on *Alternative Traditions in Macroeconomics* and from detailed comments by Fabio Petri and an anonymous referee.
2. For example Rowthorn (1977); Marglin (1984a, 1984b); Dutt (1984); Taylor (1985); Gordon *et al.* (1983); Marglin and Bhaduri (1990); Bowles and Boyer (1988), and Sawyer (1986).

3. The efficiency wage literature offers a possible formalization of the influence of the reserve army on distribution (see for example, Bowles 1985, and Green 1988).
4. This specification may reflect a 'dynamic efficiency wage framework'. The position of the labour extraction function depends on workers' wage aspirations (and on worker attitudes in general) and it is plausible to assume that wage aspirations are determined partly by historical and conventional standards which change gradually in response to current labour market conditions; see Green (1988); Skott (1991, 1992).
5. Some special cases of equations 12.4–12.6 determine the growth rate without additional assumptions. If, for instance, I/K and S/K depend exclusively on the profit rate (that is, on the product $u\pi$) then the equilibrium condition

$$i(u\pi) = s(u\pi) \qquad (12.6')$$

    may determine both $(u\pi)$ and $\hat{K}$. This kind of specification is used in Robinson (1962).
6. Kaldor's introduction of the technical progress function complicates matters but does not alter the qualitative analysis. See Skott (1989a) for further discussion. The stability question in Kaldor's (1957) model is analysed in Champernowne (1971), but see also Skott (1989a, Chapter 9).
7. See Skott (1989c, Chapter 8) for further discussion.
8. See Auerbach and Skott (1988) for a critical discussion of Kaleckian theories of monopoly capitalism.
9. See Atkinson (1969), and Desai (1984); Glombowski and Krüger (1988), however, question the robustness of this conclusion.
    Fluctuations of Kondratieff-length have been analysed by Bowles *et al.* (1986) as well as by Boyer (1987, 1988) and other members of the French 'Regulation School' but the empirical evidence in favour of Kondratieff cycles appears questionable. Solomou (1988) finds strong evidence in favour of Kuznets-swings with a periodicity of 15–25 years but Kondratieff-cycles, he argues, cannot be detected in the data.
10. This description exaggerates the separation between Keynesian factors (dominating the short-run) and Marxian factors (determining long-run movements). The Marxian militancy variable enters the short cycle and affects the shape of the cycle (cf. below), and the short cycle conversely, influences the long cycle and makes it less regular.
11. The pattern of wage inflation has many similarities with the conflict series, and the present approach – drawing on both Marxian and Keynesian theory – may help to explain the shifting NAIRUs and the inflationary experience in the post-war period (see Skott 1992).

REFERENCES

Atkinson, A. (1969) 'The Timescale of Economic Models: How Long is the Long Run', *Review of Economic Studies*, **36**, 137–52.

Auerbach, P. and Skott, P. (1988) 'Concentration, Competition and Distribution', *International Review of Applied Economics*, **2**, 42–61.

Bowles, S. (1985) 'The Production Process in a Competitive Economy: Walrasian, Neo-Hobbesian, Marxian Models', *American Economic Review*, **75**, 16–36.

Bowles, S. and Boyer, R. (1988) 'Labour Discipline and Aggregate Demand', *American Economic Review Papers and Proceedings*, **78**, 395–400.

Bowles, S., Gordon, D.M. and Weisskopf, T.E. (1986) 'Power and Profits: The Social Structure of Accumulation and the Profitability of the Postwar U.S. Economy', *Review of Radical Political Economics*, 132–67.

Boyer, R. (1987) 'Formalizing Growth Regimes within a Regulation Approach', CEPREMAP Discussion Paper 8715.

Boyer, R. (ed.) (1988) *The Search for Labour Market Flexibility*, Oxford: Oxford University Press.

Champernowne, D.G. (1971) 'The stability of Kaldor's 1957 Model', *Review of Economic Studies*, **38**, 47–62.

Desai, M. (1984) 'An Econometric Model of the Share of Wages in National Income: UK 1855–1965', in R.M. Goodwin, M. Krüger and A. Vercelli (eds), *Non-linear Models of Fluctuating Growth*, Berlin: Springer.

Dutt, A.K. (1984) 'Stagnation, Income Distribution and Monopoly Power', *Cambridge Journal of Economics*, **8**, 25–41.

Gelting, J.H. (1981) 'The End of the Full-Employment Interlude and its Reflexion in Economic Theory', mimeo, University of Aarhus.

Glombowski, J. and Krüger, M. (1988) 'A Short Period Growth Cycle Model', *Recherches Economiques de Louvain*, 423–38.

Goodwin, R.M. (1967) 'A Growth Cycle', in C.H. Feinstein (ed.), *Socialism, Capitalism and Growth*, Cambridge: Cambridge University Press.

Gordon, D.M., Weisskopf, T.E. and Bowles, S. (1983) 'Long Swings and the Nonreproductive Cycle', *American Economic Review Papers and Proceedings*, **73**, 152–7.

Green, F. (1988) 'Neoclassical and Marxian Conceptions of Production', *Cambridge Journal of Economics*, **12**, 299–312.

Hahnel, R. and Sherman, H. (1982) 'The Rate of Profit over the Business Cycle', *Cambridge Journal of Economics*, **6**, 185–94.

Kaldor, N. (1957) 'A Model of Economic Growth', *Economic Journal*, **67**, 591–124.

Keynes, J.M. (1930) *A Treatise on Money*, London and Basingstoke: Macmillan.

Marglin, S.A. (1984a) *Growth Distribution and Prices*, Cambridge, MA: Harvard University Press.

Marglin, S.A. (1984b) 'Growth, Distribution, and Inflation: a Centennial Synthesis', *Cambridge Journal of Economics*, **8**, 115–44.

Marglin, S. and Bhaduri, A. (1990) 'Distribution, Capacity Utilization, and Growth', in S. Marglin and J. Schor (eds), *The Golden Age of Capitalism*, Oxford: Oxford University Press.

Paldam, M. and Pedersen, P. (1984) 'The Large Pattern of Industrial Conflict', *International Journal of Social Economics*, 3–28.

Robinson, J. (1962) *Essays in the Theory of Economic Growth*, London and Basingstoke: Macmillan.

Rowthorn, R. (1977) 'Conflict Inflation and Money', *Cambridge Journal of Economics*, **1**, 215–39.

Rowthorn, R. (1980) *Capitalism, Conflict and Inflation*, London: Lawrence and Wishart.

Rowthorn, R. (1981) 'Demand, real wages and economic growth', *Thames Papers in Political Economy*, Autumn.

Sawyer, M. (1986) 'Conflict over Aggregate Demand in Post Keynesian Economics, the Problem of Overdeterminacy', mimeo.

Skott, P. (1989a) *Kaldor's Theory of Growth and Distribution*, Frankfurt am Main: Verlag Peter Lang.

Skott, P. (1989b) 'Effective Demand, Class Struggle and Cyclical Growth', *International Economic Review*, **30**, 231–47.

Skott, P. (1989c) *Conflict and Effective Demand in Economic Growth*, Cambridge: Cambridge University Press.

Skott, P. (1991) 'Efficiency Wages, Mark-up Pricing and Effective Demand', in J. Michie (ed.), *The Economics of Restructuring and Intervention*, Aldershot: Edward Elgar.

Skott, P. (1992) 'Inflation, Unemployment and the Distribution of Income', forthcoming in B. Amoroso and J. Jespersen (eds), *Macroeconomic Theories and Policies for the 1990's*, London and Basingstoke: Macmillan.

Solomou, S. (1988) *Phases of Economic Growth*, Cambridge: Cambridge University Press.

Taylor, L. (1985) 'A Stagnationist Model of Economic Growth', *Cambridge Journal of Economics*, **9**, 383–403.

Zarnowitz, V. (1985) 'Recent Work on Business Cycles in Historical Perspective: A Review of Theories and Evidence', *Journal of Economic Literature*, **23**, 523–80.

APPENDIX

The simulations assume that

I/K is linear in u

S/K is proportional to the profit rate

$\hat{Y}$ is an s-shaped function of $v = (\pi - \beta_1/(1-e) - \beta_2 x)$ (cf. Skott 1989b, 1989c).

$\dot{x}$ and $\dot{z}$ are linear in z and e, respectively.

Whenever possible the parameter values have been chosen in accordance with observable stylized facts. Additional information about the simulation experiments and details of the functional forms and parameters are available on request.

Figure A12.1   Unemployment and strike activity in the OECD, 1948–1987

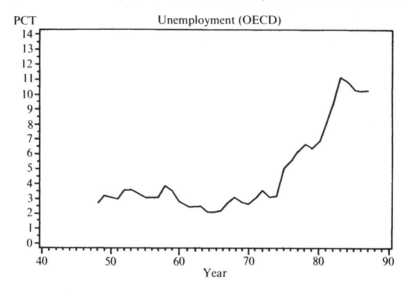

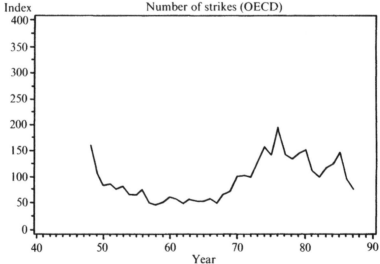

Notes
1. Strike activity is measured as the number of strikes (rather than the number of days lost).
    According to Paldam and Pedersen (1984), this series represents the best indicator of the
    'climate' in the labour market (the extent of discontent in the labour market).
2. Strike data are not available in a comparable form for Germany and Austria, and the
    Belgian series was discontinued in 1980. The data reported in the figure are unweighted
    averages for the remaining OECD countries. The figure has been prepared by Flemming
    Nielsen using the databank of my colleague Martin Paldam.

Figure A12.2   Typical simulation paths

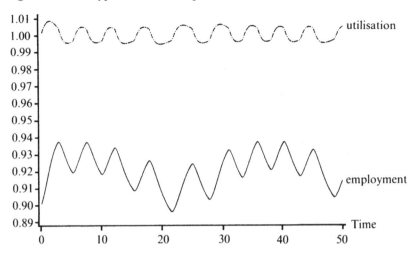

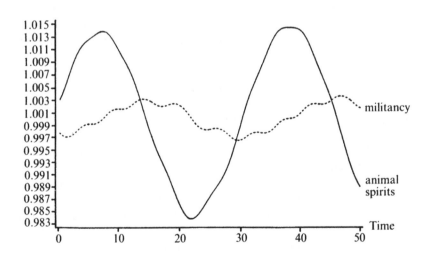

13. Does Joan Robinson's Critique of Equilibrium Entail Theoretical Nihilism?

Avi J. Cohen

INTRODUCTION

Joan Robinson was well known for her relentless critique of equilibrium as a 'self-contradictory' concept. She argued that since the outcomes of a closed deterministic equilibrium model are not the end of an actual economic process, they are of minimal relevance to the analysis of the actual history of an economy. Her critique, if accepted, seems to destroy the legitimacy of the standard model-building technique of the theorist, leading many, including Robinson herself at the end of her life, to draw nihilist conclusions about economic theory.

I argue, however, that Robinson's critique of equilibrium does not entail theoretical nihilism. The essence of theorizing is abstraction – isolating the most important causal forces while excluding all else. Robinson retains equilibrium as a useful abstraction for isolating actual causal forces. Her critique is directed only at the *outcomes* of the associated deterministic equilibrium models, which she discards as useless because they are not the end of an actual economic process. The equilibrium abstractions of actual causal forces cannot be embedded in a closed deterministic model if one is legitimately to move to actual outcomes. The forces must instead be embedded in an open historical model that allows for a causal explanation of an actual economic process.

THE CRITIQUE OF EQUILIBRIUM AND APPARENT THEORETICAL NIHILISM

Changing Views on Method

Joan Robinson's critique of equilibrium stands in sharp contrast to her earliest published views on method. In *Economics is a Serious Subject,*

Robinson (1932) thinks so highly of the equilibrium model-building technique that she claims that 'the subject matter of economics is neither more nor less than its own technique'. She goes on to say that economists have

> a body of technique – imperfect, primitive, incomplete, only capable of giving unreal answers to unreal questions – but a body of technique which we need none of us be ashamed. The time has come when the economists must stake their faith on their technique. (Robinson 1932, pp. 4–5)

Robinson accepts the unreality of the assumptions as a necessary trade-off for analytical manageability. She offers the traditional defence to the charge of unrealistic assumptions; that with time, we will be able to build even more complicated models with less restrictive assumptions that more closely resemble reality.[1]

But Robinson's defence of equilibrium model-building eventually gave way to her familiar critique of equilibrium. In commenting on her 1932 paper, she said,

> I never had the pamphlet reprinted because I soon ceased to believe in its main argument – that if economists could avoid certain bad habits and arrive at a consistent set of assumptions, however abstract, they could approach reality step by step by making more complicated models. (Robinson 1980c, p. 110)[2]

Instead of being proud of the equilibrium technique as the essence of economics as a serious subject, she came to believe that 'To construct models that cannot be applied is merely an idle amusement' (1980b, pp. 223–4). To transform economics into a serious subject she claimed that it is now necessary to 'throw out concepts and theories that are logically self-contradictory, such as the general equilibrium of supply and demand . . .' (1980b, p. 227). In the empty space left behind, 'It is only by interpreting history . . . that economics can aspire to be a serious subject' (1980b, p. 224).

Why did Robinson switch her allegiance from equilibrium to history, and come to believe that equilibrium models 'cannot be applied' and are 'logically self-contradictory'? The explanation lies in her distinction between closed deterministic models which operate in logical time and open models which operate in historical time.

Logical and Historical Time
In a closed deterministic model operating in logical time, equilibrium is the solution to 'a closed circle of simultaneous equations. The value of each element is entailed by the values of the rest. At any moment in logical time, the past is determined just as much as the future' (Robinson 1962b, p. 26). A logical time model is closed in that outside influences are closed

off through *ceteris paribus* assumptions. This closure is intended to produce a determinate (one-to-one) correspondence between initial conditions and outcomes, just like the controlled conditions of a laboratory experiment.[3] An increase in supply will, *ceteris paribus*, invariably correspond with a decrease in price. As the phrase 'simultaneous equations' implies, closed deterministic models describe correspondences, associations, but *not* processes over time. With simultaneous determination, there is no sequence of events over real or historical time, and hence no causation.

In order to use such models to analyse events occurring in historical time, one must add something about process. The traditional addition is the belief that equilibrium is a useful reference point of the actual expected outcome of the system – 'the end of an economic process' (Robinson 1974, p. 49), a stable outcome of a disequilibrium process. Such a belief is usually justified with a stability story. In the supply and demand example, price is said to fall if it is above the equilibrium price, and rise if it is below the equilibrium price. There may be temporary over- or under-shooting of the equilibrium, but the equilibrium point 'is said to be like the vertical position of a pendulum. The pendulum may be said to be *tending* towards the vertical even at those moments when it is moving away from it' (Robinson 1962b, pp. 22–3). Any perturbation away from equilibrium will be self-correcting, just like the pendulum returning to the vertical position.

This stability story makes some sense if agents' actions do not affect the equilibrium position. But that is generally not the case. For example, a higher than usual price, instead of falling, may lead agents to revise upwards their expectation of the level of the 'usual' price. A lower than usual price, instead of rising, may lead firms to introduce technological innovations that make production profitable at what is perceived as a now lower 'usual' price. Once the system is out of equilibrium, a chain of events can be set in motion which changes the equilibrium position. Agents, rather than acting to restore the original equilibrium, revise the parameters on which the original equilibrium is based. These are the possible movements that lead Robinson to say that

> It is only in a metaphorical sense that price, rate of output, [etc.] can move in the plane depicted in a price–quantity diagram. Any movement must take place through time, and the position at any moment of time depends on what it has been in the past. . . . *The point is that the very process of moving has an effect upon the destination of the movement, so that there is no such thing as a position of long-run equilibrium which exists independently of the course which the economy is following at a particular date.* (Robinson 1953, p. 234, emphasis added)

This is an early and clear statement of the idea of the path dependence of equilibrium. The stability story of price adjustment can only be a 'metaphor' because it takes place off the diagram; it describes a course of out-of-equilibrium positions that is not represented in the simultaneous equations of a closed deterministic model. The closed model describes only a set of associations existing in logical time, *ceteris paribus*. Once we are out of equilibrium, *ceteris* may not be *paribus* and a process over historical time is set in motion – a causal sequence of events.

Robinson's views are validated by the modern stability literature, much of which is limited to stories or metaphors because there are no strong technical demonstrations of stability in general equilibrium models.[4] Scarf (1960) was the first to show that perfectly well-behaved general equilibrium systems, each with a unique equilibrium, will none the less be characterized by the global instability of competitive equilibrium. His results showed that a general stability theorem was impossible. Without a demonstration of the stability of equilibrium, Hahn (1984, p. 53) is forced to admit that 'the Arrow–Debreu construction . . . must relinquish the claim of providing necessary descriptions of terminal states of economic processes.' Fisher (1989, p. 317), in stressing how crucial the stability issue is, echoes Robinson's critique of equilibrium: 'If it is not true that one can embed competitive equilibrium in a disequilibrium story that is stable, there is no point in discussing competitive equilibrium.' He goes on to say that

> there is a tendency to confuse the view that if one is not at an equilibrium, one will not stay where one is, with the view that one must approach equilibrium – and that is quite a different and much harder proposition. . . . [T]here is a big gaping hole in the center of what economists know, namely, the question of what happens out of equilibrium and whether we ever get close to equilibrium, and so forth. It is an important gaping hole because most of what we do depends on assuming that it is not a problem. And we really have very little basis for that. (Fisher 1989, p. 320)

The significance of equilibrium results is called into serious question because of the lack of stability results.[5]

Equilibrium positions or paths are not useful reference points, according to Robinson, because they do not represent the actual outcome of a process of getting into equilibrium. This critique also applies to comparisons of equilibrium positions. Economists traditionally use comparative statics or comparative dynamics to explain changes over time. In comparing two equilibrium positions, it is assumed that the economy 'moves' from an original to a new position in response to some exogenous change in parameters. But the new equilibrium position is the position that would obtain if the economy had always been adjusted to the new parameters. It is not the outcome of an economic process beginning with the parameter change. A parameter change, just like an out-of-equilibrium position, induces a chain of events (economic process) whose outcome may have no relation to the new position of the equilibrium model.[6]

For Robinson, the analysis of out-of-equilibrium economic processes must use open models operating in historical time. While a detailed discussion of such models appears later in this Chapter, a simple definition for contrast with closed deterministic models is appropriate here. An open model is open to outside influences – *ceteris* need not be *paribus*. There is no intention of establishing a determinate (one-to-one) correspondence between initial conditions and outcomes, because other influences or forces are allowed to operate. The model is not closed off like a controlled laboratory experiment. An increase in supply may be followed by a decrease in price or, if income increases dramatically, it may be followed by an increase in price. Instead of determinate outcomes, open models describe tendencies, possible sequences of events that are contingent on historical context, and processes over historical time. While a closed, deterministic equilibrium model of simultaneous equations has no causation, in 'an historical model, causal relations have to be specified' (Robinson 1962b, p. 23). An open historical model describes the causal sequence of historical events which happens 'off the page' in the actual economy.

These distinctions between logical and historical time are at the root of Robinson's critique of equilibrium. Her characterization of equilibrium as a 'logically self-contradictory' concept is, on the face of it, misleading. Equilibrium is a logical and consistent concept within the context of a closed deterministic model operating in logical time. Her real complaint is that the equilibrium concept is inconsistent with the phenomenon it is intended to explain – a sequence of events occurring in historical time (cf. Robinson 1974, pp. 49–50). Her claim that equilibrium models 'cannot be applied' is based on a similar criticism. Equilibrium models do not describe resting points of the forces operating within an actual economic system. They cannot be usefully applied in the explanation of historical events because they do not describe the outcome of an actual economic process. Unlike the pendulum always returning to the vertical position, the outcome of an economic process in historical time will not generally be described by an equilibrium position.

> Once we admit that an economy exists in time, that history goes one way from the irrevocable past into the unknown future, the conception of equilibrium based on the mechanical analogy of a pendulum swinging to and fro in space becomes untenable. The whole of traditional economics needs to be thought out afresh. (Robinson 1972, p. 172)

The inconsistency between the equilibrium concept and the analysis of events in historical time is the impetus for Robinson's switch of allegiance from equilibrium to history.

Theoretical Nihilism?

Robinson's critique of equilibrium obviously has destructive implications for the traditional methodology of neoclassical theory. But Robinson was also, at times, pessimistic about the development of alternative theories that could avoid her critique, creating an overall sense of apparent theoretical nihilism. As many commentators close to Robinson have noted, '[b]y the end of her life . . . she was almost nihilistic about economic theory, method and their potential development' (Harcourt 1990, p. 411).[7]

Three of the most important passages that are often cited as evidence of her tendency towards theoretical nihilism are reproduced below. The first, aimed specifically at neoclassical theory, is the conclusion from 'History versus Equilibrium':

> The lack of a comprehensible treatment of historical time, and failure to specify the rules of the game in the type of economy under discussion, make the theoretical [equilibrium] apparatus offered in neo-neoclassical text-books useless for the analysis of contemporary problems, both in the micro and macro spheres. (Robinson 1974, p. 58)

The second passage is from a paper informally referred to as 'Spring Cleaning':

> It seems to me that the whole complex of theories and models in the text-books is in need of a thorough spring cleaning. We should throw out all self-contradictory propositions, unmeasurable quantities and indefinable concepts and reconstruct a logical basis for analysis with what, if anything, remains. (Robinson 1985, p. 160)

Both passages, while obviously critical of neoclassical, equilibrium-based theories, at least implicitly leave the door open for the development of alternative theories. The third passage – in 'Thinking About Thinking' – seems to shut that remaining door:

> It is often said that one theory can be driven out only by another; the neoclassicals have a complete theory (though I maintain that it is nothing but a circular argument) and we need a better theory to supplant them. I do not agree. I think any other 'complete theory' would be only another box of tricks. What we need is a different habit of mind – to eschew fudging, to respect facts and to admit ignorance of what we do not know. (Robinson, 1980c, p. 119)

All of these passages are pessimistic, but are not, I would argue, nihilistic. Robinson's familiar criticisms are there – the inadequate treatment of historical time, equilibrium as a self-contradictory concept – but so is the implicit possibility of a theory that would avoid those criticisms. In the first passage, although Robinson dismisses the text-book theories as useless, she implies that if we can adequately treat historical time and specify the 'rules of the game' – the institutional and social framework including 'the rules and motives governing human behaviour' (Robinson 1962b, p. 34) – then theory could be useful. The second passage, while advocating that we throw out most of what is in the text-books, also suggests that we 'reconstruct a logical basis for analysis'. Even in the third passage, Robinson does not rule out all alternative approaches, only an alternative 'complete theory'. By 'complete theory', I understand her to mean an alternative, closed deterministic model which moves only in logical time and which uses assumptions to get a determinate correspondence between initial conditions and outcomes within a closed set of simultaneous equations.[8]

Robinson still positively advocates an alternative approach in the form of 'a different habit of mind' which eschews fudging, respects the facts, and admits our ignorance. The fudging that must be eschewed refers to confusions of logical and historical time. She refers to her own early equilibrium-based work in *The Economics of Imperfect Competition* as 'a shameless fudge'; meaning that '[t]he whole analysis, which in reality consists of comparisons of static equilibrium positions, is dressed up to appear to represent a process going on through time' (1969b, p. vi). The facts that must be respected and incorporated are social conventions and institutional arrangements. And admitting our ignorance means we must incorporate uncertainty into the analysis rather than assume it away.

In order to argue that Robinson's critique of equilibrium does not entail theoretical nihilism, this rough conception of a 'different habit of mind' must be transformed into a more precise conception of an open historical model. What form would a theory take that incorporates Robinson's concern for history without simultaneously relinquishing the abstraction that is the essence of theorizing? And what role, if any, should equilibrium play within that theory?

WHY ROBINSON IS NOT A THEORETICAL NIHILIST

The best way to understand an open historical model is to compare its three-stage theoretical process with the traditional two-stage theoretical process of a closed deterministic model. To make that comparison, it is necessary to define more precisely the concepts of equilibrium, abstraction and assumption.

Equilibrium, Abstractions and Assumptions

Bliss (1975, p. 27) makes a useful distinction between two conceptions of equilibrium. One is of equilibrium as an actual outcome 'which would be expected to be realized, because the dynamic forces which operate ... bring the economy to an equilibrium.' The other is of equilibrium as 'no more than an analytical stepping stone, as a necessary simplification to render possible some progress in an otherwise hopelessly difficult analytical endeavour.' Robinson clearly rejects the conception of equilibrium as an actual outcome of dynamic forces operating in the economy. However, we shall see that she accepts the usefulness of equilibrium as an analytical stepping-stone, a simplification which identifies real dynamic forces without associating those forces in a determinate way with specific outcomes.

The theoretical connections between causal forces and outcomes involve the concepts of abstraction and assumption. Abstraction is the process of excluding from consideration all but the most important explanatory or causal forces. Most equilibrium models focus on the causal forces of self-interest and competition in explaining economic outcomes, and exclude, for example, the role of kinship relations. The role of abstraction in simply selecting the most important among all of the real forces operating in the actual economy is consistent with the conception of equilibrium as 'an analytical stepping-stone', a 'necessary simplification'.

The abstractions are combined with assumptions to create a closed, deterministic equilibrium model. Assumptions, rather than selecting among *real* forces (as do abstractions), are explicitly *unreal*, fictional or ideal. Assumptions are simplifications, but they are simplifications 'usually designed to achieve mathematical tractability, system closure or some such thing, rather than an understanding of the real causal mechanisms at work' (Lawson 1989, p. 72). Assumptions about an infinity of agents or the continuity or convexity of a mathematical function are clearly fictional and are made in an attempt to get a model to yield a determinate outcome. Assumptions are crucial in forging the connections between the causal forces of the abstractions and the outcomes of an equilibrium model.

These concepts of equilibrium, abstraction and assumption allow a better understanding of the differences between the processes of building a closed deterministic model and an open historical model. All theorizing starts with some phenomenon to be explained. Once there is a theoretical focus, it becomes possible to distinguish between a two-stage and a three-stage theoretical process.

Two-Stage Theoretical Process: Closed Deterministic Models
The traditional theoretical process in economics consists of two stages:

1.   building a closed, deterministic equilibrium model, and
2.   subjecting it to empirical test.

Model-building begins with abstractions to isolate key causal forces, and uses equilibrium as an analytical stepping-stone. The abstractions are then buttressed with fictional assumptions so that the associated equilibrium model will (hopefully) yield clear determinate outcomes.

Since the equilibrium outcomes of the model are directly subjected to empirical test, there is an implicit if not explicit belief that they will be detected in the real world. This is now the stronger conception of equilibrium as an actual outcome of real dynamic forces. There is a belief that the equilibrium outcomes capture the effect of the most important forces actually operating in the economic system. This belief presupposes the stability of equilibrium outcomes, but no adequate demonstrations have ever been provided of the disequilibrium dynamics that ensure stable outcomes. Believers must, therefore, resort either to 'faith' that the disequilibrium dynamics results will someday arrive or to an 'as if' methodological justification.

Bliss nicely characterizes the resort of 'faith':

> In the face of all the [disequilibrium dynamics] problems it may seem more sensible to *simply assume* that equilibrium will prevail . . . [W]e could attempt to justify this procedure as a useful starting point to what one might *eventually hope* to see realized in a complete account of the behaviour of the economy, including a full specification of its disequilibrium dynamics. This approach . . . may seem to be more attractive, if only because more tractable, than the Herculean programme of constructing a *complete theory* of the behaviour of the economy out of equilibrium. (Bliss 1975, p. 28, emphasis added)

While I will later want to connect Bliss's hope for 'a complete theory' with Robinson's dismissal of 'any other "complete theory"' as just 'another box of tricks', the point here is the sidestepping of the stability problems by declaring faith in their eventual solution through future research.

The 'as if' methodological justification – associated most closely with Friedman (1953) – makes no claims that the outcomes of an equilibrium model actually occur. The model simply predicts empirical outcomes that are the same 'as if' they were the result of an equilibrating process. Whether or not the model's equilibrium outcomes are the end of an *actual* economic process is deemed irrelevant. All that matters in the predictive accuracy of the model.

Whether 'faith' or an 'as if' methodology is used as justification, a distinguishing characteristic of the two-stage theoretical process is the direct testing of the equilibrium outcomes of a model with empirical evidence.

For the two-stage process, theoretical progress occurs through the continual reworking of the stage (1) model. That reworking consists of 'relaxing the assumptions' or 'removing the scaffolding' in an attempt to build less restrictive, more general, more realistic models. Examples would be moving from a partial to a general equilibrium model, or from a closed to an open economy model. This is the idea of theoretical progress which the young, optimistic Joan Robinson believed in; that economists could 'approach reality step by step by making more complicated models'.

The phrase 'relaxing the assumptions' is quite misleading as a characterization of the reworking process. The goal of the process is, in fact, making *fewer abstractions* or simplifications, allowing more of the real causal forces operating in the actual economy to be included in ever more complex models. But more general or complex models still must strive to yield determinate equilibrium outcomes since there is only one model-building stage before testing. A more general model including more causal forces, if it is to maintain determinacy, actually requires ever *more assumptions*, not fewer. Since fewer causal forces are excluded from the model, there are more possible combinations of the effects of these forces, where some forces have reinforcing effects and others have offsetting effects. With these additional complexities, more assumptions are needed in order to approach determinate outcomes. For example, the progressive move from partial to general equilibrium analysis has been accompanied by *more assumptions* about mathematical properties of functions, not fewer.[9] Since determinacy must come entirely within the closed equilibrium model of stage (1), it is crucial that abstractions be buttressed with enough assumptions to yield determinate outcomes.

Even allowing for this form of theoretical progress, Robinson's critique of equilibrium is not answered. Increasingly general or complex models are still models of equilibrium outcomes, and hence go no further than simple models in demonstrating equilibrium as the end of an economic process. More general models may incorporate more causal forces, but only within the context of a closed deterministic model. From Robinson's perspective, the crucial causal force or mechanism (of equilibrium as the actual outcome of a disequilibrium process) is still missing. So when Robinson's critique of equilibrium is applied to the two-stage theoretical process, it is easy to see why theoretical nihilism results. Not only are the existing models inadequate, so are all possible improved future models within the associated conception of theoretical progress.

All that remains as a justification for considering equilibrium positions as outcomes of actual economic processes is either 'faith' or an 'as if' methodological story. Robinson has no such faith, and she dismisses the 'as if' method as inadequate for explaining causal sequences of events –

processes in historical time. Her critique of equilibrium precludes her from directly testing equilibrium outcomes with empirical evidence. If 'an hypothesis is framed in terms of the position of equilibrium . . . there is no point in testing it; we know in advance that it will not prove correct' (Robinson 1962a, p. 71). But her lack of faith and dismissal of the 'as-if' method does not lead to theoretical nihilism. Instead, it leads to a belief in the necessity of adding another stage to the theoretical process.

Three-Stage Theoretical Process: Open Historical Models

Robinson describes her alternative three-stage theoretical process most clearly in *The Accumulation of Capital*:

> The method of analysis which has been developed in economic theory is to set up a highly simplified *model* of an economy, which is intended to bring into an orderly scheme of ideas the main movements that may be expected to occur in reality, while ruling out innumerable detailed complications. By thinking about the behaviour of such a simplified model we hope to be able to disentangle the broad movements and so gain insight into the behaviour of the actual complicated economy. (It is important to remember, however, what complications have to be reinserted before conclusions drawn from a model can be confronted with evidence from reality.) (Robinson 1969a, pp. 63–4)

There are three stages in this process:

1. building a closed, deterministic equilibrium model,
2. embedding it in an historical context to create an open historical model, and
3. confronting the open historical model with empirical data.

Stage (1) is similar to stage (1) of the traditional two-stage approach. The abstractions of Robinson's equilibrium model select the important causal forces, or 'the main movements that may be expected to occur in reality'. In the face of Robinson's tireless critique of equilibrium, it is worth emphasizing that she considered equilibrium to be a very useful concept in stage (1).[10] Equilibrium is a useful abstraction or simplification for 'get[ting] the logic clear in a tightly specified model' (Robinson 1980a, p. vii). Its most important function is as an abstraction isolating causal forces operating in historical time in the actual economy. But another function of equilibrium within a closed deterministic model ('tightly specified') is to check the logic of an argument by seeing if one can get the model to yield a clear outcome (not to be equated with a real world outcome). This function of an equilibrium model requires the use of fictional assumptions, since they are necessary for clear determinate outcomes. Robinson emphasizes both of these functions in describing an equilibrium model as 'useful for eliminating contradictions and pointing towards causal relations that will have to be taken into account in interpreting history' (1980b, p. 223).

Despite the similarities between Robinson's equilibrium model and that of the two-stage theoretical process, there is a crucial difference. While both models isolate real causal forces, Robinson stresses that the outcomes of her model cannot be interpreted as real outcomes of those forces. Her equilibrium outcomes have no empirical significance, while the equilibrium model outcomes of the two-stage theoretical process are conceived of as the end of an actual economic process. As she says in *The Accumulation of Capital*, we must remember 'what complications have to be reinserted before [the outcomes of] a model can be confronted with evidence from reality.'

To obtain explanations of actual outcomes, the causal forces of the stage (1) model must be embedded in a specific historical and institutional context to see how the forces work themselves out. These historical and institutional facts are the complications that have to be reinserted before the outcomes of the now open historical model can be confronted with data.

> A model applicable to actual history has to be capable of getting out of equilibrium; indeed, it must normally not be in it. To construct such a model we specify the technical conditions obtaining in an economy and the behaviour reactions of its inhabitants, and then, so to say, dump it down in a particular situation at a particular date in historic time and work out what will happen next. (Robinson 1962b, p. 25)

The equilibrium model must be loosened up and combined with specific factual information to create a stage (2) open historical model that will be useful for the analysis of actual outcomes (cf. Robinson 1980a, p. vii). 'Loosening up' the model has two meanings. One is relaxing the *assumptions* of the closed equilibrium model that were necessary for a determinate outcome. The other is allowing for differing combinations of causal forces (identified by abstraction), both in and beyond the stage (1) model, to see the net effect in a particular context.

This loosening up seems totally nihilistic from the two-stage process perspective, since the determinacy of the closed equilibrium model crumbles without the supporting assumptions and restricted abstractions. But from Robinson's perspective, the real abstractions from the equilibrium model are buttressed with factual information – the rules of the game, behavioural responses, institutional description, historical parameters – so that the now open historical model will still provide explanations of (actual) outcomes to 'be confronted with evidence from reality'.

Abandoning the unjustifiable 'faith' that equilibrium is the outcome of an actual economic process need not lead to theoretical nihilism but can instead lead to a focus on other institutional sources of determinacy and explanation. The determinacy of outcomes provided by the assumptions in a closed equilibrium model can be provided instead by the stability of the institutional structure. Lawson makes a similar argument in defending Keynes's fundamental uncertainty against the charge of theoretical nihilism. A knowledge of social practices (like Robinson's 'rules of the game') can provide the stability of outcomes that uncertainty precludes in closed deterministic models. 'Such stability, far from being analytically innocuous or destructive may therefore facilitate methods of "empirical modelling" based on such historical regularities as can be detected' (Lawson 1985, p. 921).

Robinson's willingness to forgo the laboratory-like determinacy of a closed model for the looser explanation of an open historical model buttressed by institutional information is consistent with her Marshallian upbringing.[11] She characterized Marshall's world as one

> inhabited by businessmen, housewives, workers, trade union leaders, bankers and traders . . . [Marshall] was studying a recognizable economy in a particular phase of its historical development, in which recognizable classes of the community interact with each other in a particular framework of law and accepted conventions. [In contrast, equilibrium analysis, at the hands of] Pigou emptied history out of Marshall and reduced the analysis to a two-dimensional scheme. (Robinson 1974, pp. 53–4)

Robinson's approach, like Marshall's, yields historically contingent explanations of outcomes of actual economic processes by replacing the fictional assumptions in closed equilibrium models with factual institutional information. She describes the two-stage process as a search for general laws in the form of closed, deterministic equilibrium models while her three-stage process is a looser attempt to discover how things happen. She advocates 'that we give up the search for grand general laws and [be] content to try and enquire how things happen' (Robinson 1980b, p. 228).

CONCLUSIONS

Robinson's critique of equilibrium outcomes does entail theoretical nihilism in the context of the two-stage process of building and testing closed, deterministic equilibrium models. Regardless of any future theoretical progress in building more general models, they will still (strive to) be closed and deterministic and therefore will still not incorporate the crucial causal demonstration of equilibrium as the end of an actual economic process. All theoretical progress is in the world of logical time, while what is needed is progress in explaining the world of historical time. Hence, Bliss's hope 'of constructing a complete theory of the behaviour of the economy out of equilibrium' is misguided, because all such 'complete theories' exist only in logical time. In the theoretical world of logical time, Robinson's critique of equilibrium outcomes is tantamount to nihilism.

Robinson's rejection of 'any other "complete theory" [as] only another box of tricks' seems to imply theoretical nihilism for alternative, non-neoclassical theories such as neo-Ricardian theory. To the extent that neo-Ricardian theory takes the form only of closed deterministic models, Robinson's critique applies not only to Walrasian theory but also to 'the system of Sraffa or von Neumann' (Robinson 1974, p. 52). She objects to the conception of long-period positions as 'centres of gravitation' for the same reason that she objects to the conception of equilibrium as the end of an actual economic process – there is no adequate specification of the disequilibrium dynamics which push (in historical time) the economy to those positions or outcomes. This leads Garegnani to appraise Robinson as a theoretical nihilist:

> [Robinson's] methodological stance . . . if strictly applied, would severely limit the possibilities of economic theory, and hinder the necessary work of theoretical reconstruction. It would prevent the use and development of the firm basis for such work provided by the approach to distribution and accumulation of the classical economists. (Garegnani 1989, p. 360)

All of this apparent theoretical nihilism disappears, however, in moving out of the traditional two-stage theoretical process of closed deterministic model-building to Robinson's alternative three-stage theoretical process of building open historical models.

This three-stage theoretical process is a more precise description of Robinson's desired 'different habit of mind' which avoids confusions of logical and historical time and which incorporates the facts of economic life. Although limited, there is a clear and useful role for equilibrium within this process. There is also room for alternative theories. Following her criticism of the closed deterministic aspects of Sraffa's work, Robinson (1985, p. 164) says 'that does not mean that we cannot make use of it in reconstructing analysis after the spring cleaning has been completed'. In reconstructing the analysis in the form of a three-stage theoretical process, there is no longer any theoretical nihilism. Equilibrium provides the abstraction or simplification that is the essence of theorizing. Institutional, behavioural and factual information must be incorporated to provide common sense stories of sequence of events, and the causal story of the open historical model can be confronted with empirical data.[12]

The adoption of Robinson's approach is difficult, as much judgement and intuition is involved in deciding which causal forces and which factual information to include. This is responsible, in part, for Robinson's pessimism – not nihilism – about the future of economic theory. But the task is no more difficult, I would argue, than providing the stability analysis that is necessary to justify the *explanatory* (rather than just predictive) use of closed deterministic models. Such models appear more straightforward and simpler to use, but those apparent advantages are illusory and based only on 'faith' in the eventual provision of disequilibrium dynamics.

If economic theory is to move forward and provide adequate explanations of the real causal forces which drive the economy through historical time, we must give up pretensions to a 'complete theory' and face squarely the difficult problems involved in enquiring 'how things happen'.[13] Robinson's open historical models and the three-stage theoretical process provide more positive guidance in this quest than unjustified resorts to 'faith' or 'as-if' methodologies.

NOTES

1. 'I know very well that the world to which my technique applies is not the real world, but I am one of the optimistic economists, and when I have got well used to using my two-dimensional technique I will try to evolve a three-dimensional or an *n*-dimensional technique which will be capable of solving the problems which arise on [more realistic] assumptions' (Robinson 1932, p. 7).
2. For articles which appear in Robinson's *Collected Economic Papers*, the reference uses the date of the original article, but page numbers refer only to the *CEP*.
3. Phrases like 'clear determinate outcomes' should be interpreted as the desired goal of model builders. That goal is not altered by the fact that problems often arise regarding the uniqueness of an equilibrium solution, and that stochastic models may yield a probability distribution of outcomes rather than a determinate outcome.
4. Arrow (1989) offers a 'we are not alone' defence of verbal stability stories after acknowledging the lack of neoclassical stability results – 'In general, a Walrasian (intertemporal) system will not converge to a steady state. . . . This can be regarded as a damaging result. But it is equally true of any other system I know of. I do not see that neo-Ricardian economics has spelled out its dynamics. It has the same kind of verbal dynamics that we all use: say demand exceeds supply, price rises, this attracts more resources; something shifts, this shifts, that shifts, etc. . . . That kind of verbal story is the same kind of story that is told in a neo-Ricardian setting with different topics. So all systems have the same difficulty of showing stability in a multi-market context. There is nothing peculiar to the difficulties encountered in the neoclassical setting.' (pp. 148, 150)
5. In a comprehensive survey of the significance of poor stability results for the general equilibrium research programme, Ingrao and Israel (1985, pp. 101–2) draw the following conclusions: 'the analysis of the global stability of a perfectly competitive market does not produce satisfactory results, and the general . . . tendency has been to play down the importance of these negative results. . . . [But] if we accept that one essential aspect of the notion of general equilibrium is the idea that "a social system moved by independent actions in pursuit of different values is consistent with a final coherent state

of balance" ([Arrow and Hahn 1971], p. 1), it would be very odd indeed to accept the validity of any model which, while demonstrating the existence of a "final coherent state of balance", did not admit the system's capacity to place itself in that state by a price adjustment process. It would be a model in which the market forces are unable to lead the market to equilibrium, or in which Adam Smith's "invisible hand" is waving, Sisyphus-like, around the equilibrium without managing to "push" the system into it.'

6. Robinson (1980a, p. vii) 'frequently had occasion to complain of the inability of neo-classical writers to distinguish between a *difference* in the parameters of an equilibrium model and the effects of a *change* taking place at a moment of time.'

7. Harvey Gram (1989b, p. 879) noted 'At the end of her life, Joan was distressed by the course of developments in economic theory, including those in the classical tradition she had helped to revive. She regarded equilibrium as a deadening influence seeping back into every revolutionary break with neoclassical theory. The last time I saw her she was asking what had gone wrong.'

   Ruth Cohen (1983, p. 2) said this about Robinson at a memorial service: 'In the last few years of her life she became very depressed at the state of economics. She spent a lot of the time then reassessing the course of economic doctrine, struggling towards a theory that could create models that could grapple with history, with ecological balances in individual communities, and particularly with technological change. She was trying to evolve a different technique of thought.'

8. Gram (1989a, p. 287) offers a similar interpretation of the third passage: 'Robinson meant by *complete* any argument which specifies, independently of *historical* and *institutional* context, short-period reactions to unanticipated events.'

9. Kaldor (1972, p. 1239) makes this observation about general equilibrium theory: 'The process of removing the "scaffolding", as the saying goes – in other words of *relaxing* the unreal basic assumptions – has not yet started. Indeed, the scaffolding gets thicker and more impenetrable with every successive reformulation of the theory, with a growing uncertainty as to whether there is a solid building underneath.'

10. 'There is much to be learned from *a priori* comparisons of equilibrium positions, but they must be kept in their logical place' (Robinson 1962b, p. 25).

11. '[L]ong chains of deductive reasoning are directly applicable only to the occurrences of the laboratory. By themselves they are seldom a sufficient guide for dealing with the heterogeneous materials and the complex and uncertain combinations of forces of the real world. For that purpose they need to be supplemented by specific experience, and applied in harmony with, and often in subordination to, a ceaseless study of new facts, a ceaseless search for new inductions' (Marshall 1920, Appendix C, p. 771).

12. Keynes (1973b, p. 296) makes similar statements about the theoretical process. 'The object of a model is to segregate the semi-permanent or relatively constant factors from those which are transitory or fluctuating so as to develop a logical way of thinking about the latter, and of understanding the time sequences to which they give rise in particular cases.' Elsewhere Keynes (1973a, p. 297) writes, 'The object of our analysis is, not to provide ourselves with a machine or method of blind manipulation which will furnish an infallible answer, but to provide ourselves with an organised and orderly method of thinking out particular problems; and, after we have reached a provisional conclusion by isolating the complicating factors one by one, we then have to go back on ourselves and allow, as well as we can, for the probable interactions of the factors amongst themselves. This is the nature of economic thinking.' (See also Marshall 1920, pp. 366, 368.)

13. Solow (1985, p. 23) has implicitly endorsed Robinson's approach in writing, 'There is enough for us to do without pretending to a degree of completeness and precision which we cannot deliver. To my way of thinking, the true functions of analytical economics are best described informally: to organize our necessarily incomplete perceptions about the economy, to see connections that the untutored eye would miss, to tell plausible – sometimes even convincing – *causal stories* with the help of a few central principles, and to make rough quantitative judgements about the consequences of economic policy and other exogenous events. In this scheme of things, the end-product of economic analysis

is likely to be a collection of models *contingent on society's circumstances – on the historical context*, you might say – and not a single monolithic model for all seasons' (emphasis added).

REFERENCES

Arrow, K. (1989) 'Joan Robinson and Modern Economic Theory: An Interview', in G. Feiwel (ed.), (1989), 147–85.

Arrow, K. and Hahn, F. (1971) *General Competitive Analysis*, San Francisco: Holden-Day.

Bliss, C. (1975) *Capital Theory and the Distribution of Income*, Amsterdam: North-Holland.

Cohen, R. (1983) 'Address at the Memorial Service in Kings College Chapel for Joan Robinson', mimeo, Marshall Library (29 October), 1–3.

Feiwel, G. (ed.), (1989) *Joan Robinson and Modern Economic Theory*, London: Macmillan.

Fisher, F.M. (1989) 'Stability Analysis in Micro and Macro Theory: An Interview', in G. Feiwel (ed.), (1989), 311–22.

Friedman, M. (1953) 'The Methodology of Positive Economics', in *Essays in Positive Economics*, Chicago: University of Chicago Press, 3–43.

Garegnani, P. (1989) 'Some Notes on Capital, Expectations and the Analysis of Changes', in G. Feiwel (ed.), (1989), 344–67.

Gram, H. (1989a) 'Ideology and Time: Criticisms of General Equilibrium', in G. Feiwel (ed.), (1989), 285–302.

Gram, H. (1989b) 'Memories of Joan Robinson', in G. Feiwel (ed.), (1989), 877–80.

Hahn, F. (1984) *Equilibrium and Macroeconomics*, Cambridge, MA: MIT Press.

Harcourt, G. (1990) 'Joan Robinson's Early Views on Method', *History of Political Economy*, **22**, Fall, 411–27.

Ingrao, B. and Israel, G. (1985) 'General Economic Equilibrium Theory. A History of Ineffectual Paradigmatic Shifts', *Fundamenta Scientiae*, **6** (1–2), 1–45, 89–125.

Kaldor, N. (1972) 'The Irrelevance of Equilibrium Economics', *Economic Journal*, **82**, Dec., 1237–55.

Keynes, J.M. (1973a) *Collected Writings*, vol. III, London: Macmillan.

Keynes, J.M. (1973b) *Collected Writings* vol. XIV, London: Macmillan.

Lawson, T. (1985) 'Uncertainty and Economic Analysis', *Economic Journal*, **95**, Dec., 909–27.

Lawson, T. (1989) 'Abstraction, Tendencies and Stylised Facts: A Realist Approach to Economic Analysis', *Cambridge Journal of Economics*, **13**, March, 59–78.

Marshall, A. (1920) *Principles of Economics*, 8th edition, London: Macmillan.

Robinson, J. (1932) *Economics is a Serious Subject*, Cambridge: W. Heffer & Sons Ltd.

Robinson, J. (1953) ' "Imperfect Competition" Revisited', in J. Robinson (1960), *Collected Economic Papers*, vol. 2, Oxford: Basil Blackwell, 222–38.

Robinson, J. (1962a) *Economic Philosophy*, London: C.A. Watts & Co.

Robinson, J. (1962b) *Essays in the Theory of Economic Growth*, London: Macmillan.

Robinson, J. (1969a) *The Accumulation of Capital*, 3rd edition, London: Macmillan.

Robinson, J. (1969b) *The Economics of Imperfect Competition*, 2nd edition, London: Macmillan.

Robinson, J. (1972) 'What Has Become of the Keynesian Revolution?' in Robinson (1980a), 168–77.

Robinson, J. (1974) 'History Versus Equilibrium', in Robinson (1980a), 48–58.

Robinson, J. (1980a) *Collected Economic Papers*, vol. 5, Oxford: Basil Blackwell.

Robinson, J. (1980b) 'Time in Economic Theory', *Kyklos*, **33** (2), 219–29.

Robinson, J. (1980c) 'Thinking About Thinking', in Robinson (1980a), 110–19.

Robinson, J. (1985) 'The Theory of Normal Prices and Reconstruction of Economic Theory', in George Feiwel (ed.), (1985), *Issues in Contemporary Macroeconomics and Distribution*, London: Macmillan, 157–65.

Scarf, H. (1960) 'Some Examples of Global Instability of the Competitive Equilibrium', *International Economic Review*, **1**, September, 157–72.

Solow, R.M. (1985) 'Economics: Is Something Missing?' in William N. Parker (ed.), (1985), *Economic History and the Modern Economist*, Oxford: Basil Blackwell, 21–9.

Index

Printed and bound by CPI Group (UK) Ltd, Croydon, CR0 4YY

23/04/2025

14661001-0003